D1335160

AUTO-BIOGRAPHY

COOPER

This page enables you to compile a list of useful data on your car, so that whether you're ordering spares or just checking the tyre pressures, all the key information - the information that is "personal" to your car - is easily within reach.

Registration number ....

Model ....

Body colour ....

Paint code number ....

Date of first registration ....

Date of manufacture (if different) ....

Chassis or 'VIN' number ....

Engine number ....

Transmission number ....

Axle casing number ....

Tyre size: front ....

Tyre size: rear ....

Tyre pressures (normally laden):

Tyre pressures (fully laden):

Front: .... Rear: ....

Front: .... Rear: ....

Ignition key no. ....

Door lock key/keys no. ....

Fuel locking cap key no. (if fitted) ....

Alarm remote code (if fitted) ....

Alarm remote battery type ....

Radio Security Code No. (if fitted) ....

Insurance: Name, address and telephone number of insurer

....

....

Modifications: information that might be useful when you need to purchase parts

....

....

....

Suppliers: Address and telephone number of your garage and parts supplier

....

....

....

Step-by-Step Service Guide to the Mini & Mini Cooper

A PORTER PUBLISHING Book

First Published 1994 by Porter Publishing Ltd

Published and Produced by
Porter Publishing Ltd
The Storehouse
Little Hereford Street
Bromyard
Hereford
England HR7 4DE

British Library Cataloguing in Publication Data
A catalogue record for this book is available from the British Library
ISBN 1-899238-01-8

Series Editor: Lindsay Porter
Technical Editor: John Mead
Design: Lindsay Porter and John Rose, TypeStyle
Printed in England by The Trinity Press, Worcester

Other Titles in this Series
MGB (including MGC, MGB GT V8 and MG RV8) Service Guide
Land Rover Series I, II, III Service Guide
VW Beetle (all models to 1980) Service Guide
With more titles in production

Every care has been taken to ensure that the material contained in this Service Guide is correct. However, no liability can be accepted by the authors or publishers for damage, loss, accidents, or injury resulting from any omissions or errors in the information given.

CONTENTS

	Auto-biography	1
	Introduction and Acknowledgements	6
	Using This Book	7
CHAPTER 1:	*Safety First!*	8
CHAPTER 2:	*Buying Spares*	12
CHAPTER 3:	*Service Intervals, Step-by-Step*	
	Using the Service Schedules	15
	500 miles, or Weekly	18
	1,500 miles, or Every Month	25
	3,000 miles, or Every Three Months	27
	6,000 miles, or Every Six Months	41
	12,000 miles, or Every Twelve Months	56
	Spark Plug Conditions	65
	24,000 miles, or Every Twenty Four Months	68
	36,000 miles, or Every Thirty Six Months	74
	Longer Term Servicing	75
CHAPTER 4:	*Repairing Bodywork Blemishes*	77
CHAPTER 5:	*Rustproofing*	81
CHAPTER 6:	*Fault Finding*	85
CHAPTER 7:	*Getting Through the MOT*	89
CHAPTER 8:	*Facts and Figures*	99
CHAPTER 9:	*Tools and Equipment*	105
APPENDIX 1:	*Lubrication Chart*	108
APPENDIX 2:	*American and British Terms*	109
APPENDIX 3:	*Specialists and Suppliers*	110
APPENDIX 4:	*Service History*	111

Keep a record of every service you carry out on your car.

INTRODUCTION AND ACKNOWLEDGEMENTS

BY JIM PATTEN

Introduction

I cut my teeth on Minis. In those days at college I just managed to figure out where the oil and water went. When things eventually let go in a big way, I had no option but to take the bus and add another subject to my already heavy curriculum - car repairs. The sad thing is, had I known a little more about preventative maintenance, I could have spent a little more time in bed in the morning and a little less time in a freezing bus shelter. Once I buried myself in the subject though, I couldn't let go and soon launched into a succession of Minis from the tired to the tarty. Since then there has been a whole barrow-load of cars, switching quite early on to my passion, Jaguars. But I never lost my respect for the Mini, small it may be but never humble. That first lesson was hard won. Whatever car I now own, be it a hack of a runabout or a pristine 'E' type Jaguar, they will all spend a few hours in the garage every so often for a regular check up. I need to know that my transport will be safe, reliable and ready to perform what is required of it.

Porter Publishing Service Guides are the first books to give you all the service information you might need, with step-by-step instructions, along with a complete Service History section for you to complete and fill in as you carry out regular maintenance on your car over the months ahead. Using the information contained in this book, you will be able to:

• see for yourself how to carry out every Service Interval, from weekly and monthly checks, right up to longer-term maintenance items.

• carry out regular body maintenance and rustproofing, saving a fortune in body repairs over the years to come.

• enhance the value of your car by completing a full Service History of every maintenance job you carry out on your car.

Here's to a future of reliable, safe motoring in the knowledge that every job done is a job YOU know is done, with a considerable cash saving as a bonus.

Happy motoring!

Jim Patten

Acknowledgements

I can't possibly accept that this book was a sole effort. The basic template for the series I know caused many a late night and brain turmoil for Porter Publishing's MD Lindsay Porter. In turn he had some great backing from Kim Henson and John Williams. Dave Pollard, another author in the series has also had considerable input. The experience and expertise of ex-Haynes personnel, John Rose (layout and design) and John Mead (Technical Editor) has really paid dividends. To quote Lindsay Porter from the MGB Service Guide, the first in the series, "It's a pleasure to work with such people, professionals all, and thoroughly nice folk, to boot". Finally, I must thank my fiance Karen Marks for her unstinting work in compiling the Facts and Figures chapter. Her knowledge has now grown beyond any of her circle and she has become a real 'wow' at parties. Perhaps her honours degree in Social Studies has been a contributing factor.

You would think that any company specialising in the service and repair of Minis would keep well away from this project. On the contrary. Bob Rollins at the A1 Mini & Metro Centre couldn't have been more helpful. He has an extremely enthusiastic team who all understand the quirks of Minis, and as an MoT station, they know just what is required to keep a Mini (or Metro) up to tip top order. Bob likes to think that his customers take an active interest in their cars. If the client handles the basic maintenance, then he is always there for anything major and to help out from their considerable parts division.

Specialist assistance also came from Dunlop/SP Tyres, from Kamasa tools, who kindly supplied almost all of the great range of tools used here and from David's Isopon who supplied expertise on bodywork repair and body filler that is second to none. And of course, there are our old friends Richard Price and Dawn Adams at Castrol whose advice we are always pleased to receive and whose products we can always unhesitatingly recommend. It was Chris Parkinson of Before'n After Prestige who demonstrated the rustproofing techniques using Waxoyl.

Many thanks to everyone listed here as well as to anyone else whom I might inadvertently have missed.

Footnote: Extra special thanks are due to the Worcester Mintro Centre and to John Mead. Without their "life-saving" assistance this book would never have been finished!

USING THIS BOOK

Everything about this book is designed to help you make your car more reliable and long-lasting through regular servicing. But one requirement that you will see emphasised again and again is the need for safe working. There is a lot of safety information within the practical instructions but you are strongly urged to read and take note of *Chapter 1, Safety First!*.

To get the most from this book, you will rapidly realise that it revolves around two main chapters. *Chapter 3, Service Intervals, Step-by-Step* shows you how to carry out every service job that your car is likely to need throughout its life. Then, the final Section, *Service History*, in the back of this book lists all of the jobs described in Chapter 3 and arranges them together in tick-lists, a separate list for each Service Interval, so that you can create your own Service History as you go along. When you have completed the three years of Service History included in this book, continuation sheets can be purchased from Porter Publishing.

Keeping your car in top condition is one thing; getting it there in the first place may be quite another. At the start of Chapter 3, we advise on carrying out a 'catch-up' service for cars that may not have received the de-luxe treatment suggested here. And then there are four other chapters to help you bring your car up to scratch. *Chapter 4 Repairing Bodywork Blemishes* and *Chapter 5 Rustproofing* show how to make the body beautiful and how to keep it that way - not something that is usually included in servicing information but bodywork servicing can save you even more money than mechanical servicing, since a corroded body often leads to a scrapped car, whereas worn out mechanical components can usually be replaced. *Chapter 6* shows you how to carry out *Fault Finding* when your car won't start and *Chapter 7*, describes *Getting Through the MoT*, an annual worry - unless you follow the approach shown here. With *Chapter 2, Buying Spares* describing how you can save on spares and *Chapter 8, Facts and Figures* giving you all the key facts and figures, we hope that this book will become the first tool you'll pick up when you want to service your car!

This book is produced in association with Castrol (U.K.) Ltd.
"Cars have become more and more sophisticated. But changing the oil and brake fluid, and similar jobs are as simple as they ever were. Castrol are pleased to be associated with this book because it gives us the opportunity to make life simpler for those who wish to service their own cars.
Castrol have succeeded in making oil friendlier and kinder to the environment by removing harmful chlorine from our range of engine lubricants which in turn prolong the life of the catalytic convertor (when fitted), by noticeably maintaining the engine at peak efficiency.
In return, we ask you to be kinder to the environment, too ... by taking your used oil to your Local Authority Amenity Oil Bank. It can then be used as a heating fuel. Please do not poison it with thinners, paint, creosote or brake fluid because these render it useless and costly to dispose of."
Castrol (U.K.) Ltd.

SAFETY FIRST! *(vertical side text)*

CHAPTER 1 - SAFETY FIRST!

It is vitally important that you always take time to ensure that safety is the first consideration in any job you do. A slight lack of concentration, or a rush to finish the job quickly can often result in an accident, as can failure to follow a few simple precautions. Whereas skilled motor mechanics are trained in safe working practices you, the home mechanic, must find them out for yourself and act upon them.

Remember, accidents don't just happen, they are caused, and some of those causes are contained in the following list. Above all, ensure that whenever you work on your car you adopt a safety-minded approach at all times, and remain aware of the dangers that might be encountered.

Be sure to consult the suppliers of any materials and equipment you may use, and to obtain and read carefully any operating and health and safety instructions that may be available on packaging or from manufacturers and suppliers.

IMPORTANT POINTS

ALWAYS ensure that the vehicle is properly supported when raised off the ground. Don't work on, around, or underneath a raised vehicle unless axle stands are positioned under secure, load bearing underbody areas, or the vehicle is driven onto ramps.

DON'T suddenly remove the radiator or expansion tank filler cap when the cooling system is hot, or you may get scalded by escaping coolant. Let the system cool down first and even then, if the engine is not completely cold, cover the cap with a cloth and gradually release the pressure.

NEVER start the engine unless the gearbox is in neutral (or 'Park' in the case of automatic transmission) and the hand brake is fully applied.

NEVER drain oil, coolant or automatic transmission fluid when the engine is hot. Allow time for it to cool sufficiently to avoid scalding you.

TAKE CARE when parking vehicles fitted with catalytic converters. The 'cat' reaches extremely high temperatures and any combustible materials under the car, such as long dry grass, could ignite.

NEVER run catalytic converter equipped vehicles without the exhaust system heat shields in place.

NEVER attempt to loosen or tighten nuts that require a lot of force to turn (e.g. a tight oil drain plug) with the vehicle raised, unless it is properly supported and in a safe condition. Wherever possible, initially slacken tight fastenings before raising the car off the ground.

TAKE CARE to avoid touching any engine or exhaust system component unless it is cool enough so as not to burn you.

ALWAYS keep antifreeze, brake and clutch fluid away from vehicle paintwork. Wash off any spills immediately.

NEVER syphon fuel, antifreeze, brake fluid or other such toxic liquids by mouth, or allow prolonged contact with your skin. There is an increasing awareness that they can damage your health. Best of all, use a suitable hand pump and wear gloves.

ALWAYS work in a well ventilated area and don't inhale dust - it may contain asbestos or other poisonous substances.

WIPE UP any spilt oil, grease or water off the floor immediately, before there is an accident.

MAKE SURE that spanners and all other tools are the right size for the job and are not likely to slip. Never try to 'double-up' spanners to gain more leverage.

SEEK HELP if you need to lift something heavy which may be beyond your capability.

ALWAYS ensure that the safe working load rating of any jacks, hoists or lifting gear used is sufficient for the job, and is used only as recommended by the manufacturer.

NEVER take risky short-cuts or rush to finish a job. Plan ahead and allow plenty of time.

BE meticulous and keep the work area tidy - you'll avoid frustration, work better and loose less.

KEEP children and animals right away from the work area and from unattended vehicles.

ALWAYS wear eye protection when working under the vehicle or using any power tools.

BEFORE undertaking dirty jobs, use a barrier cream on your hands as a protection against infection. Preferably, wear thin gloves, available from DIY outlets.

DON'T lean over, or work on, a running engine unless strictly necessary, and keep long hair and loose clothing well out of the way of moving mechanical parts. Note that it is theoretically possible for fluorescent striplighting to make an engine fan appear to be stationary - check! This is the sort of error that happens when you're dog tired and not thinking straight. So don't work on your car when you're overtired!

REMOVE your wrist watch, rings and all other jewellery before doing any work on the vehicle - especially the electrical system.

ALWAYS tell someone what you're doing and have them regularly check that all is well, especially when working alone on, or under, the vehicle.

ALWAYS seek specialist advice if you're in doubt about any job. The safety of your vehicle affects you, your passengers and other road users.

FIRE

Petrol (gasoline) is a dangerous and highly flammable liquid requiring special precautions. When working on the fuel system, disconnect the vehicle battery earth (ground) terminal whenever possible and always work outside, or in a very well ventilated area. Any form of spark, such as that caused by an electrical fault, by two metal surfaces striking against each other, by a central heating boiler in the garage 'firing up', or even by static electricity built up in your clothing can, in a confined space, ignite petrol vapour causing an explosion. Take great care not to spill petrol on to the engine or exhaust system, never alow any naked flame anywhere near the work area and, above all, don't smoke.

Invest in a workshop-sized fire extinguisher. Choose the carbon dioxide type or preferably, dry powder but never a water type extinguisher for workshop use. Water conducts electricity and can make worse an oil or petrol-based fire, in certain circumstances.

FUMES

In addition to the fire dangers described previously, petrol (gasoline) vapour and the vapour from many solvents, thinners, and adhesives is highly toxic and under certain conditions can lead to unconsciousness or even death, if inhaled. The risks are increased if such fluids are used in a confined space so always ensure adequate ventilation when handling materials of this nature. Treat all such substances with care, always read the instructions and follow them implicitly.

Always ensure that the car is outside the work place in open air if the engine is running. Exhaust fumes contain poisonous carbon monoxide - even if the car is fitted with a catalytic converter, since 'cats' sometimes fail and don't function with the engine cold.

Never have the engine running with the car in the garage or in any enclosed space.

Inspection pits are another source of danger from the build-up of fumes. Never drain petrol (gasoline) or use solvents, thinners adhesives or other toxic substances in an inspection pit as the extremely confined space allows the highly toxic fumes to concentrate. Running the engine with the vehicle over the pit can have the same results. It is also dangerous to park a vehicle for any length of time over an inspection pit. The fumes from even a slight fuel leak can cause an explosion when the engine is started.

MAINS ELECTRICITY

Best of all, use rechargeable tools and a DC inspection lamp, powered from a remote 12V battery - both are much safer! However, if you do use a mains-powered inspection lamp, power tool etc, ensure that the appliance is wired correctly to its plug, that where necessary it is properly earthed (grounded), and that the fuse is of the correct rating for the appliance concerned. Do not use any mains powered equipment in damp conditions or in the vicinity of fuel, fuel vapour or the vehicle battery.

Also, before using any mains powered electrical equipment, take one more simple precaution - use an RCD (Residual Current Device) circuit breaker. Then, if there is a short, the RCD circuit breaker minimises the risk of electrocution by instantly cutting the power supply. Buy one from any electrical store or DIY centre. RCDs fit simply into your electrical socket before plugging in your electrical equipment.

THE IGNITION SYSTEM

Extreme care must be taken when working on the ignition system with the ignition switched on or with the engine cranking or running.

Touching certain parts of the ignition system, such as the HT leads, distributor cap, ignition coil etc, can result in a severe electric shock. This is especially likely where the insulation on any of these components is weak, or if the components are dirty or damp. Note also that voltages produced by electronic ignition systems are much higher than conventional systems and could prove fatal, particularly to persons with cardiac pacemaker implants. Consult your handbook or main dealer if in any doubt. An additional risk of injury can arise while working on running engines, if the operator touches a high voltage lead and pulls his hand away on to a conductive or revolving part.

THE BATTERY

Never cause a spark, smoke, or allow a naked light near the vehicle's battery, even in a well ventilated area. A certain amount of highly explosive hydrogen gas will be given off as part of the normal charging process. Care should be taken to avoid sparking by switching off the power supply before charger leads are connected or disconnected. Battery terminals should be shielded, since a battery contains energy and a spark can be caused by any conductor which touches its terminals or exposed connecting straps.

Before working on the fuel or electrical systems, always disconnect the battery earth (ground) terminal.

When charging the battery from an external source, disconnect both battery leads before connecting the charger. If the battery is not of the 'sealed-for-life' type, loosen the filler plugs or remove the cover before charging. For best results the battery should be given a low rate 'trickle' charge overnight. Do not charge at an excessive rate or the battery may burst.

Always wear gloves and goggles when carrying or when topping up the battery. Even in diluted form (as it is in the battery) the acid electrolyte is extremely corrosive and must not be allowed to contact the eyes, skin or clothes.

BRAKES AND ASBESTOS

Whenever you work on the braking system mechanical components, or remove front or rear brake pads or shoes:

i) wear an efficient particle mask,

ii) wipe off all brake dust from the work area (never blow it off with compressed air),

iii) dispose of brake dust and discarded shoes or pads in a sealed plastic bag,

iv) wash hands thoroughly after you have finished working on the brakes and certainly before you eat or smoke,

v) replace shoes and pads only with asbestos-free shoes or pads. Note that asbestos brake dust can cause cancer if inhaled.

Obviously, a car's brakes are among its most important safety related items. Do not dismantle your car's brakes unless you are fully competent to do so. If you have not been trained in this work, but wish to carry out the jobs described in this book, it is strongly recommend that you have a garage or qualified mechanic check your work before using the car on the road.

BRAKE FLUID

Brake fluid absorbs moisture rapidly from the air and can become dangerous resulting in brake failure. Castrol (U.K.) Ltd. recommend that you should have your brake fluid tested at least once a year by a properly equipped garage with test equipment and you should change the fluid in accordance with your vehicle manufacturer's recommendations or as advised in this book if we recommend a shorter interval than the manufacturers. Always buy no more brake fluid than you need. Never store an opened pack. Dispose of the remainder at your Local Authority Waste Disposal Site, in the designated disposal unit, **not** with general waste or with waste oil.

ENGINE OILS

Take care and observe the following precautions when working with used engine oil. Apart from the obvious risk of scalding when draining the oil from a hot engine, there is the danger from contaminates that are contained in all used oil.

Always wear disposable plastic or rubber gloves when draining the oil from your engine.

i) Note that the drain plug and the oil are often hotter than you expect! Wear gloves if the plug is too hot to touch and keep your hand to one side so that you are not scalded by the spurt of oil as the plug comes away.

ii) There are very real health hazards associated with used engine oil. In the words of one Rover car's handbook, "Prolonged and repeated contact may cause serious skin disorders, including dermatitis and cancer". Use a barrier cream on your hands and try not to get oil on them. Where practicable, wear gloves and wash your hands with hand cleaner soon after carrying out the work. Keep oil out of the reach of children.

iii) NEVER, EVER dispose of old engine oil into the ground or down a drain. In the UK, and in most EC countries, every local authority must provide a safe means of oil disposal. In the UK, try your local Environmental Health Department for advice on waste disposal facilities.

PLASTIC MATERIALS

Work with plastic materials brings additional hazards into workshops. Many of the materials used (polymers, resins, adhesives and materials acting as catalysts and accelerators) readily produce very dangerous situations in the form of poisonous fumes, skin irritants, risk of fire and explosions. Do not allow resin or 2-pack adhesive hardener, or that supplied with filler or 2-pack stopper to come into contact with skin or eyes. Read carefully the safety notes supplied on the tin, tube or packaging.

JACK AND AXLE STANDS

Throughout this book you will see many references to the correct use of jacks, axle stands and similar equipment - and we make no apologies for being repetitive! This is one area where safety cannot be overstressed - your life could be at stake!

Special care must be taken when any type of lifting equipment is used. Jacks are made for lifting the vehicle only, not for supporting it. Never work under the car using only a jack to support the weight. Jacks must be supplemented by adequate additional means of support, such as axle stands, positioned under secure load-bearing parts of the frame or underbody. Axle stands are available from many discount stores, and all auto parts stores. Drive-on ramps are limiting because of their design and size but they are simple to use, reliable and the most stable type of support, by far. We strongly recommend their use.

Full details on jacking and supporting the vehicle will be found in *Raising a Car - Safely!* near the beginning of Chapter 3.

FLUOROELASTOMERS -
MOST IMPORTANT! PLEASE READ THIS SECTION!

If you service your car in the normal way, none of the following may be relevant to you. Unless, for example, you encounter a car which has been on fire (even in a localised area), subject to heat in, say, a crash-damage repairer's shop or vehicle breaker's yard, or if any second-hand parts have been heated in any of these ways.

Many synthetic rubber-like materials used in motor cars contain a substance called fluorine. These materials are known as fluoroelastomers and are commonly used for oil seals, wiring and cabling, bearing surfaces, gaskets, diaphragms, hoses and 'O' rings. If they are subjected to temperatures greater than 315 degrees C, they will decompose and can be potentially hazardous. Fluoroelastomer materials will show physical signs of decomposition under such conditions in the form of charring of black sticky masses. Some decomposition may occur at temperatures above 200 degrees C, and it is obvious that when a car has been in a fire or has been dismantled with the assistance of a cutting torch or blow torch, the fluoroelastomers can decompose in the manner indicated above.

In the presence of any water or humidity, including atmospheric moisture, the by-products caused by the fluoroelastomers being heated can be extremely dangerous. According to the Health and Safety Executive, "Skin contact with this liquid or decomposition residues can cause painful and penetrating burns. Permanent irreversible skin and tissue damage can occur". Damage can also be caused to eyes or by the inhalation of fumes created as fluoroelastomers are burned or heated.

After fires or exposure to high temperatures observe the following precautions:

1. Do not touch blackened or charred seals or equipment.

2. Allow all burnt or decomposed fluoroelastomer materials to cool down before inspection, investigations, tear-down or removal.

3. Preferably, don't handle parts containing decomposed fluoroelastomers, but if you must, wear goggles and PVC (polyvinyl chloride) or neoprene protective gloves whilst doing so. Never handle such parts unless they are completely cool.

4. Contaminated parts, residues, materials and clothing, including protective clothing and gloves, should be disposed of by an approved contractor to landfill or by incineration according to national or local regulations. Oil seals, gaskets and 'O' rings, along with contaminated material, must not be burned locally.

WORKSHOP SAFETY - SUMMARY

1. *Always have a fire extinguisher of the correct type at arm's length when working on the fuel system - under the car, or under the bonnet.*

   If you do have a fire, DON'T PANIC. Use the extinguisher effectively by directing it at the base of the fire.

2. *NEVER use a naked flame near petrol or anywhere in the workplace.*

3. *KEEP your inspection lamp well away from any source of petrol (gasoline) such as when disconnecting a carburettor float bowl or fuel line.*

4. *NEVER use petrol (gasoline) to clean parts. Use paraffin (kerosene) or white (mineral) spirits.*

5. *NO SMOKING! There's a risk of fire or transferring dangerous substances to your mouth and, in any case, ash falling into mechanical components is to be avoided!*

6. *BE METHODICAL in everything you do, use common sense, and think of safety at all times.*

CHAPTER 2 - BUYING SPARES

Reliable though the Mini undoubtedly is, there are, of course, occasions when you need to buy spares in order to service it and keep it running. There are a number of sources of supply of the components necessary when servicing the car, the price and quality varying between suppliers. As with most things in life, cheapest is not necessarily best - as a general rule our advice is to put quality before price - this policy usually works out less expensive in the long run! But how can you identify 'quality'? It's sometimes difficult, so stick with parts from suppliers with a reputation, those recommended to you by others and parts produced by well-established brand names. But don't just pay through the nose! The same parts are often available at wildly different prices so, if you want to save money, invest your time in shopping around.

In any event, when buying spares, take with you details of the date of registration of your car, also its chassis (or VIN) and engine numbers (see illustrations below). These can be helpful where parts changed during production, and can be the key to a more helpful approach by some parts salespeople! You may, by now have entered this key information on the Auto-Biography page at the front of this book, for ease of reference. The illustrations on these pages show you where to find the relevant information on your car.

MAIN DEALERS

Always consider your local main dealership as a source of supply of spares. One benefit is that the spares obtained will be 'genuine' items and it has to be said that the only way to be totally certain of 'as new' quality and reliability is to buy Rover main dealer parts for your car.

In addition, the parts counter staff are likely to be more familiar than most with the vehicles, and are only too pleased to help owners identify the spares required - but you can only expect such help if you go to the trouble of taking with you all the data on your car that will be required. (The best way is by filling in the Auto-Biography page at the start of this book and taking it along with you.) Sometimes parts departments will go to the trouble of contacting other dealers, on your behalf, in search of an elusive part, and this can usually be delivered within a day or so, if located at another dealer within the same group of companies, for example. For older Minis and those with smaller production runs, this is likely to be the least of your problems, however! For very many parts for these cars, your main dealer simply won't be able to obtain them at all and it is at this point that you will have to look to the services of a Mini specialist - see below.

But back at the main dealers: prices are occasionally reduced and on 'special offer' from the usual retail level - watch for special deals which are sometimes listed at the parts counter. Try to avoid Saturday and Sunday mornings when buying - weekends are often very busy for parts counters, and you may find the staff have more time to help you if you visit early on a weekday morning, or in the evening, while on your way to or from work. At these times you are also less likely to have to queue for a long time! However, even with a main dealer, there may be parts that just won't be in stock when you want them. Try to find out how long they are likely to take to arrive - or you could even ring around your local main dealerships, if you have a choice in your area - to find out whether the parts you need are currently held in stock.

PARTS FACTORS/MOTOR ACCESSORY SHOPS

Local parts factors and motor accessory shops can be extremely useful for obtaining servicing parts at short notice - many 'accessory' outlets open late in the evening, and on both days at weekends. Most servicing parts for the Mini are readily available, so, for example, requests for 'routine' items such as brake pads and shoes, spark plugs, contact points, rocker cover gaskets, also oil and air filters, are unlikely to draw a blank look from the sales assistant! Some outlets supply 'original' equipment spares, but in many cases the components are 'pattern' parts. In this case, if there is a choice, opt for well-known, respected names, even if the prices are a little higher than those required for possibly dubious 'cheap import' items. This is especially important when shopping for safety-related items such as brake pads. In this example, experience has shown that cheap pads can be subject to excessive brake fade under enthusiastic driving, and in any case such pads often wear rapidly.

Don't overlook the 'trade' motor factors outlets in the UK. You will find them all over the country, but look for them in Yellow Pages, since they are invariably situated in out-of-town areas, such as on trading estates.

MINI SPECIALISTS

There are a multitude of spares suppliers catering for the needs of Mini owners, and they include among their number many who actually run, race, and restore Minis themselves and generally know them inside out. Such specialist are particularly useful when buying components needed for restorations, but of course they will also be pleased to help you with regard to servicing components. Most of the major suppliers run mail order services, and 'next day' deliveries are usually available. The spares supplied are often original specification items (this is not always the case, though, so enquire when buying), and prices are competitive. The only drawback is that you will have to pay postage and packing charges, on which V.A.T. is also levied, in addition to the cost of the spares unless you are fortunate enough to find one in your immediate area.

Many Mini specialists advertise regularly in magazines such as those published by the clubs and the special interest Mini magazines - see below. There are large numbers of such specialists: so much so that it would also be worthwhile looking in your local Yellow Pages to see whether you have one or more such specialists in your area. In their magazine advertisements, many include lists of the parts they have on offer, and the prices they are asking. Again, watch out for special offers which can save you money. If you plan ahead, often you can buy spares now at a preferable rate, and keep them 'in stock' until needed.

The overwhelming advantage of buying from a Mini dealer or specialist (also, see 'Clubs', below) is that a good retailer will have the best stock of parts and the most useful fund of specialised knowledge to be found anywhere.

CLUBS AND MAGAZINES

There are a number of clubs catering for Mini owners. See Appendix 3: Specialists and Suppliers but there are more smaller clubs each with something distinctive to offer the Mini owner. You will find all of the clubs listed in Mini World and Practical Classics magazines, (although not in every month's issue). Members can usually benefit from general spares information provided by club magazines, while conversations with other club members often provide helpful pointers with regard to spares availability. You will also be able to pick up bargains - or even rare parts that you can't find anywhere else, for older cars - from the advertisements in club magazines and from attending club meetings where parts are often traded by private individuals and 'semi-pro.' traders, who are often the source of some of the best 'finds' of all for older, rarer cars.

The two magazines of most relevance to Mini owners are Mini World and Cars and Car Conversions magazines. The former's relevance is obvious, but 'Triple C', as it is known, also features Minis quite regularly. Needless to say, they both include lots of Mini specialists on their advertisement pages, some of them taking multi-page spread adverts. Several classic car magazines also often include Minis on their feature pages, especially Practical Classics and Your Classic magazines, but a random browse on the newsagents racks can be fruitful to pick out the magazine which seems to be favouring Minis most in any given month. One more source of spares, if not of features, is Exchange & Mart in the UK, which lists both general low-cost parts suppliers, who are bound to stock fast-moving Mini parts, and some of the Mini specialists.

BUYING SECONDHAND

We would strongly advise against buying secondhand brake, suspension, and steering components, unless you know the source of the parts, and really are sure that they are in first class condition. Even then, be sure that you see the vehicle they have been taken from, and avoid any such parts from accident-damaged cars. On the other hand, it might make sense to buy, say, a distributor, or carburettors which you know to be 'low mileage' units, to replace your worn out components. Such moves can help your car run more sweetly but for less expense than buying new! In every case, ensure that the components you are buying are compatible with your particular vehicle, and carry out basic checks to ensure that they too are not badly worn. In particular, on distributors, ensure that the main spindle cannot be moved from side to side more than just perceptibly (if it can, the bearings are worn and properly setting the points gap/dwell angle and ignition timing will be impossible). With regard to carburettors, similarly check to make sure that there is minimal sideways play between the throttle spindle and the body of the unit. If there is excessive movement, the carburettor is worn, the result being air leaks and erratic running.

CHECKS ON RUNNING GEAR COMPONENTS

Always take very great care when purchasing 'hardware' for the steering, suspension and braking systems, which are obviously vital for safety.

Although many outlets sell 'reconditioned' components on an 'exchange' basis, the quality of workmanship and the extent of the work carried out on such units can vary greatly. Therefore, if buying a rebuilt unit, always check particularly carefully when buying. It has to be said that, wherever possible, reconditioned units are best obtained from main agents, or from reputable specialist suppliers. Always talk to fellow owners before buying - they may be able to direct you to a supplier offering sound parts at reasonable prices. When buying, always enquire about the terms of the guarantee (if any!).

In any event, the following notes should help you make basic checks on some of the commonly required components:

BRAKES (NEW parts ONLY): Look for boxes bearing the markings of your cars manufacturer, or one of the few top brake companies. If buying at an autojumble or car boot sale, inspect the contents of the box and reject any obviously rusty stock.

STEERING: Ball joints and constant velocity joints - buy new, again rejecting any moisture-damaged stock. Steering racks are available as exchange units. Ensure that you rotate the operating shaft fully from lock to lock, feeling for any undue free play, roughness, stiffness, or 'notchiness' as you do so. Reject any units showing signs of any of these problems, or - of course - oil leaks or split gaiters.

SUSPENSION: Never buy shock absorbers second-hand. They are not too expensive when new but their condition can never be guaranteed when used and, in any case, you should always replace them in pairs; both fronts or both rears together.

TYRES: For the ultimate in long life, roadholding and wet grip, brand new radial tyres from a reputable manufacturer offer the best solution by far. Remoulds are available at lower initial cost, but life expectancy is not as long as with new tyres. Even low price 'budget range' tyres seem usually not to last as long as tyres with major brand names. Take advice from your tyre supplier on which tyres are expected to give most wear and remember that the cheapest in the short run may not be the cheapest over the longer term.

It is true that secondhand tyres can offer an inexpensive short-term solution to keeping a car on the road, but beware. Such tyres may have serious, hidden faults. Hundreds of thousands are imported from the continent, where tyre laws are more stringent than in the U.K. However, if you purchase such covers, you are taking a risk in that you have no knowledge of the history of the tyres or what has happened to them, how they have been repaired, and so on. Our advice - very strongly given - is to stick to top quality, unused tyres from a reputable manufacturer. They may cost a little more, but at least you will have peace of mind, and should be able to rely on their performance in all road and weather situations. After all, your life - and those of other road users - could depend on it!

SAVING MONEY

Finally, if you want to buy quality and save money, you must be prepared to shop around. Ring each of your chosen suppliers with a shopping list to hand and your car's personal data from the Auto-Biography at the front of this book in front of you. Keep a written note of prices, whether the parts are proper 'brand name' parts or not and - most importantly! - whether or not the parts you want are in stock. Parts expected 'soon' have been known never to materialise. A swivel pin in the hand is worth two in the bush! (Bad pun!)

Please read all the information contained in the following XX pages before carrying out any work on your car.

CHAPTER 3
SERVICE INTERVALS STEP-BY-STEP

Everyone wants to own a car that starts first time, runs reliably and lasts longer than the average. And there's no magic about how to put your car into that category, it's all a question of thorough maintenance! If you follow the Service Jobs listed here - or have a garage or mechanic do it for you - you can almost guarantee that your car will still be going strong when others have fallen by the wayside... or the hard shoulder. Mind you, we would be among the first to acknowledge that this Service Schedule is just about as thorough as you can get; it's an amalgam of all the maker's recommended service items plus all the 'Inside Information' from the experts that we could find. If you want your car to be as well looked after as possible, you'll follow the Jobs shown here, but if you don't want to go all the way, you can pick and choose from the most essential items in the list. But do bear in mind that the Jobs we recommend are there for some very good reasons:

- body maintenance is rarely included in most service schedules. We believe it to be essential.

- preventative maintenance figures very high on our list of priorities. And that's why so many of our service jobs have the word "Check..." near the start!

- older cars need more jobs doing on them than new cars - it's as simple as that - so we list the jobs you will need to carry out in order to keep any car, older or new, in fine fettle.

USING THE SERVICE SCHEDULES

At the start of each Service Job, you'll see a heading in bold type, looking a bit like this:

☐ **Job 25. Adjust spark plugs.**

Following the heading will be all the information you will need to enable you to carry out that particular Job. Please note that different models of car might have different settings. Please check **Chapter 8, Facts and Figures**. Exactly the same Job number and heading will be found in the Service History chapter, where you will want to keep a full record of all the work you have carried out. After you have finished servicing your car, you will be able to tick off all of the jobs that you have completed and so, service by service, build up a complete Service History of work carried out on your car.

You will also find other key information immediately after each Job title and in most cases, there will be reference to an illustration - a photograph or line drawing, whichever is easier for you to follow - usually on the same page.

If the Job shown only applies to certain vehicles, the Job title will be followed by a description of the type of vehicle to which the Job title applies. For instance, Job 31 applies to "**US and Export Cars Only**" - and the information in bold tells you so.

Other special headings are also used. One reads **OPTIONAL**, which means that you may wish to use your own discretion as to whether to carry out this particular Job or whether to leave it until it crops up again in a later service. Another is **INSIDE INFORMATION**. This tells you that here is a Job or a special tip that you wouldn't normally get to hear about, other than through the experience and 'inside' knowledge of the experts at the A1 Mini & Metro Centre, who have helped in compiling this Service Guide. The third is **SPECIALIST SERVICE**, which means that we recommend you to have this work carried out by a specialist. Some jobs, such as setting the tracking or suspension are best done with the right measuring equipment while other jobs may demand the use of equipment such as an exhaust gas analyser. Where we think you are better off having the work done for you, we say so!

SAFETY FIRST!
The other special heading is the one that could be the most important one of all! SAFETY FIRST! information must always be read with care and always taken seriously. In addition, please read Chapter 1 Safety First! at the beginning of this book before carrying out any work on your car. There are many hazards associated with working on a car but all of them can be avoided by adhering strictly to the safety rules. Don't skimp on safety!

Throughout the Service Schedule, each 'shorter' Service Interval is meant to be an important part of each of the next 'longer' Service Interval, too. For instance, under **1,500 Mile Mechanical and Electrical - Around the Car**, Job 16. you are instructed to check the tyres for wear or damage. This Job also has to be carried out at 3,000 miles, 6,000 miles, 9,000 miles, and so on. It is therefore shown in the list of extra Jobs to be carried out in each of these 'longer' Service Intervals but only as a Job number, without the detailed instructions that were given the first time around!

The 'Catch-up' Service

When you first buy a used car, you never know for sure just how well it's been looked after. Even one with a full service history is unlikely to have been serviced as thoroughly as one with a Porter Publishing Service Guide history! So, if you want to catch-up on all the servicing that may have been neglected on your car, just work through the entire list of Service Jobs listed for the 36,000 miles - or every thirty six months service, add on the 'Longer Term servicing' Jobs, and your car will be bang up to date and serviced as well as you could hope for. Do allow several days for all of this work, not least because it will almost certainly throw up a number of extra jobs - potential faults that have been lurking beneath the surface - all of which will need putting right before you can 'sign off' your car as being in tip-top condition.

The Service History

Those people fortunate enough to own a new car, or one that has been well maintained from new will have the opportunity to keep a service record, or 'Service History' of their car, usually filled in by a main dealer. Until now, it hasn't been possible for the owner of an older car to keep a formal record of servicing but now you can, using the complete tick list in **Appendix 4, Service History**. In fact, you can go one better than the owners of those new cars, because your car's Service History will be more complete and more detailed than any manufacturer's service record, with the extra bonus that there is space for you to keep a record of all of those extra items that crop up from time to time. New tyres; replacement exhaust; extra accessories; where can you show those on a regular service schedule? Now you can, so if your battery goes down only 11 months after buying it, you'll be able to look up where and when you bought it. All you'll have to do is remember to fill in your Service History in the first place!

RAISING A CAR - SAFELY!

You will often need to raise your car off the ground in order to carry out the Service Jobs shown here. To start off with, here's what you must never do - never work beneath a car held on a jack, not even a trolley jack. Quite a number of deaths have been caused by a car slipping off a jack while someone has been working beneath. On the other hand, the safest way is by raising a car on a proprietary brand of ramps. Sometimes, there is no alternative but to use axle stands. Please read all of the following information and act upon it!

When using car ramps:

(**I**) Make absolutely certain that the ramps are parallel to the wheels of the car and that the wheels are exactly central on each ramp.

Always have an assistant watch both sides of the car as you drive up. Drive up to the end 'stops' on the ramps but never over them!

Apply the hand brake firmly, put the car in first or reverse gear, or 'Park', in the case of an automatic.

I

(**II**) Chock both wheels remaining on the ground, both in front and behind so that the car can't move in either direction.

INSIDE INFORMATION - wrap a strip of carpet into a loop around the first 'rung' of the ramps and drive over the doubled-up piece of carpet on the approach to the ramps. This prevents the ramps from skidding away, as they are inclined to do, as the car is driven on to them.

II

III

IV

V

VI

On other occasions, you might need to work on the car whilst it is supported on an axle stand or a pair of axle stands. These are inherently less stable than ramps and so you must take much greater care when working beneath them. In particular:

- ensure that the axle stand is on flat, stable ground, never on ground where one side can sink in to the ground.

- ensure that the car is on level ground and that the hand brake is off and the transmission in neutral.

- raise the car with a trolley jack - invest in one if you don't already own one; the car's wheel changing jack is often too unstable. Place a piece of cloth over the head of the jack if your car is nicely finished on the underside. Ensure that the floor is sufficiently clear and smooth for the trolley jack wheels to roll as the car is raised and lowered, otherwise it could slip off the jack.

(**III**) Place the jack beneath the Mini's front subframe when raising the front of the car.

(**IV**) ... and place the axle stands beneath the front subframe rear body-mounts.

(**V**) At the rear of the car, place the jack head beneath the rear body jacking points.

(**VI**) If, for any reason, you can't use the location points recommended here, take care to locate the top of the axle stand on a strong, level, stable part of the car's underside: you should never use a movable suspension part (because the part can move and allow the axle stand to slip) or the floor of the car (which is just too weak).

Just as when using ramps - only even more importantly! - apply the hand brake firmly, put the car in first or reverse gear (or 'Park', in the case of an automatic) and chock both wheels remaining on the ground, both in front and behind.

Be especially careful when applying force to a spanner or when pulling hard on anything, when the car is supported off the ground. It is all too easy to move the car so far that it topples off the axle stands. And remember that if a car falls on you, *YOU COULD BE KILLED!*

Whenever working beneath a car, have someone primed to keep an eye on you! If someone pops out to see how you are getting on every quarter of an hour or so, it could be enough to save your life!

Do remember that, in general, a car will be more stable when only one wheel is removed and one axle stand used than if two wheels are removed in conjunction with two axle stands. You are strongly advised never to work on the car with all four wheels off the ground, on four axle stands. The car would then be very unstable and dangerous to work beneath.

When lowering the car to the ground, remember to remove the chocks, release the hand brake and place the transmission in neutral.

500 Miles, Weekly or Before a Long Journey

These are the regular checks that you need to carry out to help keep your car safe and reliable. They don't include the major Service Jobs but they should be carried out as an integral part of every 'proper' service.

500 Mile Mechanical and Electrical - The Engine Bay

Job 1. Engine oil level.

Check the engine's oil level with the car on level ground.

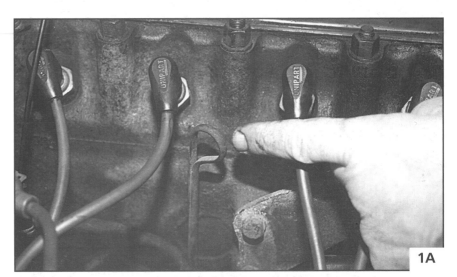

1A

1A. The Mini's oil dipstick is at the front of the engine. Lift out the dipstick, wipe it clean with a clean cloth, push it back in and lift it out again. Take a look at the level of the oil on the dipstick. You might have to do it two or three times before you can see a clear reading – the oil on the stick sometimes 'smears' as the stick is pulled out.

1B. The oil level should be somewhere between the MAX and MIN levels. Make sure that the dipstick is pushed right back in when replacing it and when 'dipping' it to discover the oil level.

1C. The Mini's filler cap is on the top of the rocker cover, on the top of the engine. Both metal and plastic caps twist-and-lift off.

Also, check the ground over which the car has been parked, for evidence of oil or other fluid leaks. (If any leaks are found, do not drive the car without first establishing where the leaks have come from - they could come from a major failure in the braking system.)

1B

Job 2. Clutch fluid level.

> **SAFETY FIRST!**
> **If clutch fluid should come into contact with the skin or eyes, rinse immediately with plenty of water.**

2. Check/top up clutch fluid reservoir. The level should be just at the bottom of the filler neck.

INSIDE INFORMATION: i) Check the ground on which the car has been parked, especially beneath the engine bay and inside each road wheel, for evidence of oil, clutch or brake fluid leaks. If any are found, investigate further before driving the car.

1C

2

ii) Clutch fluid will damage painted surfaces if allowed to come into contact. Take care not to spill any, but if there is an accident, refit the master cylinder cap and wash off any accidental spillage immediately with hot soapy water.

☐ Job 3. Brake fluid level.

SAFETY FIRST!
i) If brake fluid should come into contact with the skin or eyes, rinse immediately with plenty of water.
ii) The brake fluid level will fall slightly during normal use, but if it falls significantly below the bottom of the filler cap neck (or in the case of later Minis, below the MIN line), stop using the car and seek specialist advice.
iii) If you get dirt into the hydraulic system it can cause brake failure. Wipe the filler cap clean before removing.
iv) Use only new brake fluid from an air-tight container. Old fluid will absorb moisture and this could cause the brakes to fail when carrying out an emergency stop or other heavy use of the brakes - just when you need them most and are least able to do anything about it, in fact!.

3A

3A. Check/top up the brake fluid reservoir. The level should be just at the bottom of the filler neck on early models or to the MAX line on later models.

3B. Later Minis have transparent brake master cylinder reservoirs, with the latest type shown here. Be careful not to damage the wiring fitted to the cap when unscrewing - it's not easy!

INSIDE INFORMATION: i) Check the ground on which the car has been parked, especially beneath the engine bay and inside each road wheel, for evidence of oil, clutch or brake fluid leaks. If any are found, investigate further before driving the car.
iii) Brake fluid will damage painted surfaces if allowed to come into contact. Take care not to spill any but if there is an accident, refit the master cylinder cap and wash off any accidental spillage immediately with hot soapy water.

3B

LATER MODELS ONLY

Test the brake fluid warning light and its circuit. Switch on the ignition and release the handbrake. When you press the flexible contact cover in the centre of the filler cap, the warning light should illuminate. If it does not and the fluid level is satisfactory, consult your specialist or dealer.

4A

☐ Job 4. Battery electrolyte.

> **SAFETY FIRST!**
> *i) The gas given off by a battery is highly explosive. Never smoke, use a naked flame or allow a spark to occur in the battery compartment. Never disconnect the battery (it can cause sparking) with the battery caps removed.*
> *ii) Batteries contain sulphuric acid. If the acid comes into contact with the skin or eyes, wash immediately with copious amounts of cold water and seek medical advice.*
> *iii) Do not check the battery levels within half an hour of the battery being charged with a battery charger. The addition of fresh water could then cause the highly acid and corrosive electrolyte to flood out of the battery.*

4A. The battery can be found beneath a cover under the carpet in the boot on Saloon models; beneath the seat on Estate/Traveller models and behind the seat on Vans and Pick-ups. A fibre cover protects the battery and this should be lifted away.

Unless the battery is a 'sealed for life' unit, remove the battery caps or cover and, with the car on level ground, check the level of the electrolyte - the fluid inside each battery cell. You often can't see it at first, use an inspection lamp or flashlight and tap the side of the battery to make the surface of the electrolyte ripple a little, so that you can see it. The plates inside the battery should just be covered with electrolyte. If the level has fallen, top up with distilled water, NEVER with tap water! Dry off the top of the battery. If the battery terminals are obviously furred, refer to Job 101.

4B

4B *INSIDE INFORMATION: i) When water is mixed with the acid inside the battery, it won't freeze. So, in extremely cold weather, run the car (out of doors) so that you put a charge into the battery and this will mix the fresh water with the electrolyte, cutting out the risk of freezing and a cracked battery case.*

ii) Here's how to check the strength, or specific gravity, of the battery electrolyte. You place the end of a hydrometer into the battery electrolyte, squeeze and release the rubber bulb so that a little of the acid is drawn up into the transparent tube and the float, or floats, inside the tube (small coloured beads are sometimes used) give the specific gravity. If a battery goes flat because the car has been left standing for too long, use a small battery charger to re-charge the battery, following the maker's instructions and disconnecting the battery on your Mini first. A battery that goes flat too rapidly can be checked by a garage - they may well check the specific gravity of the electrolyte in each cell in order to establish whether one or more has failed but since garages often tell you that you need a new battery anyway, it might be worth investing in a hydrometer and testing the cells yourself. Otherwise, you could try disconnecting the battery and seeing if it still goes flat. If not, suspect a wiring fault allowing the current to drain away but do be aware that some car alarms will drain a car battery in around a week. They are designed primarily for cars that are used almost every day, rather than classic or special interest cars that may not be used so often.

5

☐ Job 5. Washer reservoir.

5. Check/top up the windscreen washer reservoir.

6A

☐ Job 6. Coolant system.

SAFETY FIRST!
i) The coolant level should be checked WHEN THE SYSTEM IS COLD. If you remove the pressure cap when the engine is hot, the release of pressure can cause the water in the cooling system to boil and spurt several feet in the air with the risk of severe scalding. ii) Take precautions to prevent anti-freeze coming in contact with the skin or eyes. If this should happen, rinse immediately with plenty of water.

6A. Carry out a visual check on all coolant system and other hoses in and around the engine bay for leaks.

6B. Top up with a mixture of 50% anti-freeze and water until the level is just beneath the filler neck on the radiator or to the correct reading on cars fitted with a "water level" indicator plate..

6B

500 mile Mechanical and Electrical - Around the Car

☐ Job 7. Check horns.

7. Try the horn button. If the horns fail to work, examine the wiring to the horns, or the horns themselves.

SPECIALIST SERVICE: Horn wiring and connections can be more complex than they appear at first. For instance, on some models, both terminals at the horn should be 'live'! If there is no obvious problem with wiring connections, have the horn, the circuitry and the switches checked over by a specialist.

7

Job 8. Windscreen washers.

8. Check the operation of the windscreen washers. If one of them fails to work, check that the pipes have not come adrift and then check the jet; clear it with a pin. Some jets are adjustable by inserting a pin and twisting the jet inside its rubber housing.

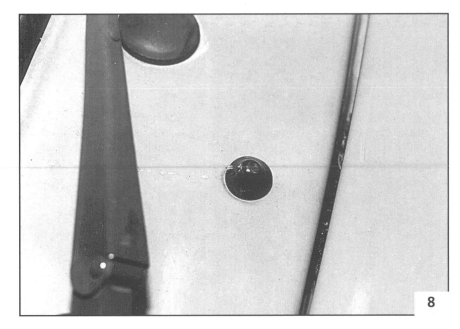

8

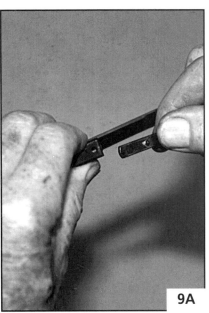

9A

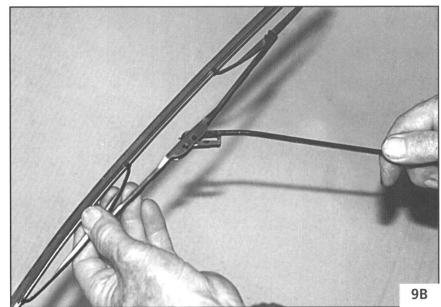

9B

Job 9. Windscreen wipers.

9A. Check that the wiper blades are not torn, worn or damaged in any way. Give each blade a wipe clean with methylated spirit (industrial alcohol). Many wiper arms are held in place with a peg and spring. Gripping the blade pivot between finger and thumb, push down on the arm and pull the blade away.

9B. Alternatively, a horseshoe fitting is used where the blade is turned through 90° ...

9C. ... and slipped out of the arm.

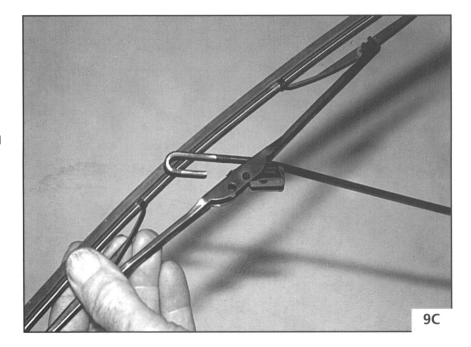

9C

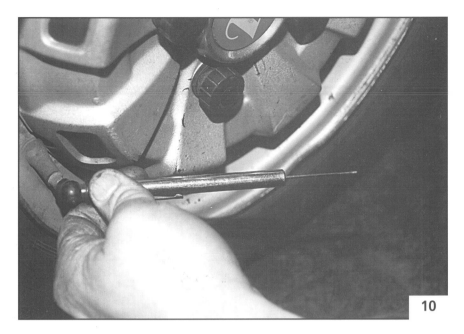

10

☐ **Job 10. Tyre pressures.**

> *SAFETY FIRST!*
> *Incorrectly inflated tyres wear*
> *rapidly, can cause the car's*
> *handling to become dangerous*
> *and can even cause the car to*
> *consume noticeably more fuel.*

10. Use a reliable tyre pressure gauge to check the tyre pressures on the car, but never after driving the car which warms up the tyres considerably and increases their pressures.

☐ **Job 11. Check headlamps and front sidelamps.**

SPECIALIST SERVICE: It is not possible to set headlamps accurately at home. In **Chapter 7, Getting Through The MoT**, we show how to trial-set your headlamps before going to the MoT Testing Station (in the UK) but this method is not good enough unless you are going to have the settings re-checked by a garage with proper headlamp beam checking equipment.

11A. The components for a sealed beam set-up are the simplest to deal with. The beam is set by turning in and out screws shown at numbers 11A.11 and 11A.12. *Illustration, courtesy Rover Cars.*

11B. Headlamp rims often appear to be 'welded' to the lamp unit but perseverance always pays. First remove the retaining screw.

11C. Then pull the rim away and lift up, freeing it from a lip at the top of the headlamp base-plate. On Clubman models remove the four screws and lift off the grille side extension.

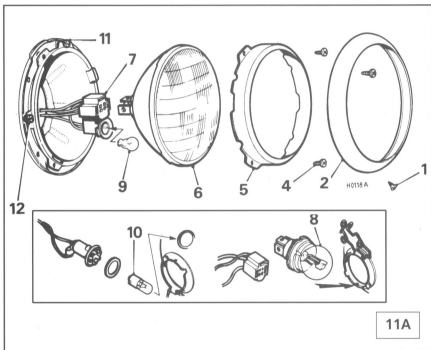

11A

11B

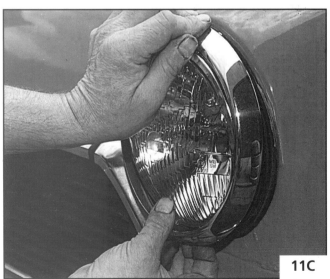

11C

500 MILE/WEEKLY SERVICE

11D. After removing the three screws holding the inner rim ...

11E. ... the unit inside will slip to the floor and break, if you're not careful!

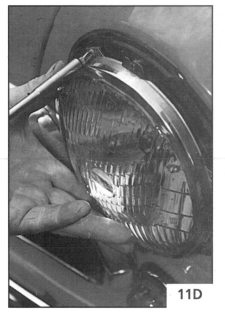

11D

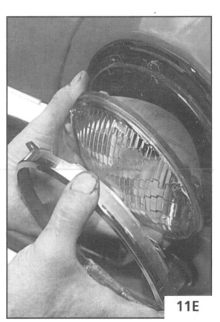

11E

11F. Sealed beam units just plug straight out and in again. (All models incorporate the sidelamp in the headlamp via a separate bulb).

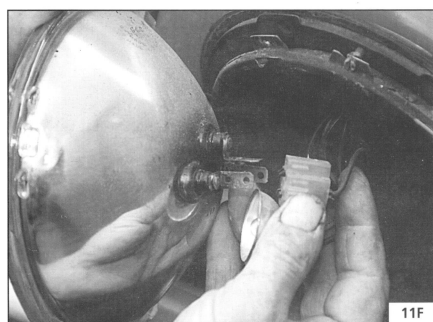

11F

11G. To replace a sidelamp, remove the headlamp as explained. On later models (illustrated), the bulb is a push fit. Earlier models are on a separate bulb holder and the bulb is a bayonet push in and twist type.

Where a replaceable bulb type, rather than a sealed beam headlamp is fitted, remove the headlamp as explained previously and disconnect the wiring plug. Lift up the retaining spring clip and withdraw the bulb (hold the bulb with a clean cloth, not your fingers). Fit the new bulb ensuring that the locating pip on the bulb rim engages correctly with the lamp unit and re-engage the spring clip. If the bulb glass is inadvertently touched with your fingers, wipe it clean with methylated spirit.

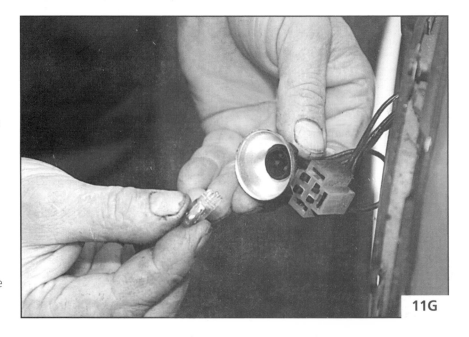

11G

12A

12B

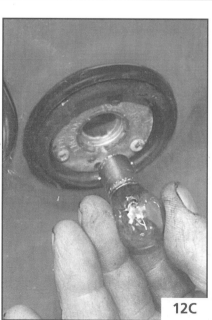

12C

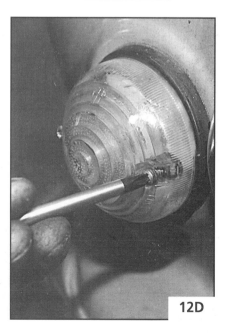

12D

☐ **Job 12. Check front indicators.**

Check the front indicator bulbs and replace if necessary.

12A. On early models, prize out the chrome retaining bezel ...

12B. ... and pull the indicator lens away from the rubber base.

12C. The bayonet type bulb is removed by pushing in slightly and twisting out. Replacing the lens can be a little tricky as the bezel will be extremely reluctant to return to its seat. A little water and washing-up liquid helps promote a smooth action when persuading the rubber lip to engulf the chrome bezel.

12D. Later models use more conventional screws. Simply release the two securing screws, and remove the bulb in the same fashion as in 12C.

INSIDE INFORMATION: If a bulb refuses to budge, try gripping with a piece of cloth or wrapping with a piece of masking tape - it provides a lot more grip and reduces the risk if the bulb glass breaks. If the bulb comes free of its brass ferrule, carefully break it away and push one side of the ferrule in with a screwdriver (lights/indicators turned off!). Spray releasing fluid behind the bulb base and leave for a while. Then work the base free by gripping the side that you have pushed in, using a pair of long-nose pliers.

Certain models are fitted with direction indicator side repeater lamps in the front wings. To change the bulb in these, slide the unit to the right and ease it away. Twist out the bulb holder and remove the bulb. *Illustration, courtesy Rover Cars*

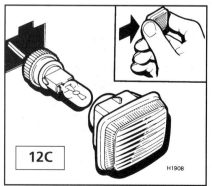

12C

H1908

Job 13. Check rear sidelamps.

13A. Check/replace rear sidelamp, stop lamp and indicator bulbs and clean the lenses. All Mini models have a lens secured to the base with screws. Elf/Hornet models bulb holders are accessed through the boot. Locate the bulb holders at the back of the light unit and pull clear (the holder is retained in the light unit by a series of sprung clips). Make sure that the sealing rubber is not kinked when the lens is replaced.

13B. Note that the rear tail lamp/stop lamp bulbs (lower) have a pair of offset pegs, so that they can't be fitted the wrong way round. This might explain why a new bulb won't go back in - but it's easy when you notice it!

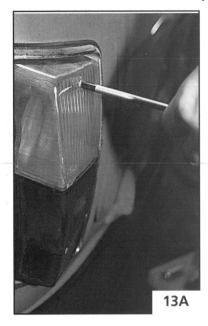

13A

13B

Job 14. Number plate lamps.

14A. Check the rear number plate lamps, replace the bulbs if necessary and clean out the lenses. A single screw retains early models ...

14B. ... but later models use two bulbs retained in holders secured by two screws (four in total). The bulb holder is pushed in slightly and then lowered down. The festoon bulb is pushed against the brass retaining spring contact and lifted out.

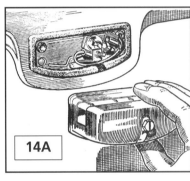

14A

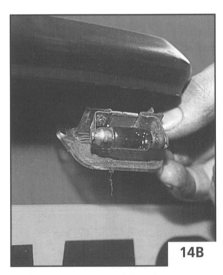

14B

Job 15. Reversing lamps.

Check the reversing lamps, if fitted, replace the bulbs if necessary and clean the lenses. Also check any auxiliary lamps, such as fog lamps, that may have been fitted as original equipment or as accessories, in which case they are still supposed to function correctly, by law.

1,500 Miles - or Every Month, Whichever Comes First

1,500 Mile Mechanical and Electrical - Around the Car

Job 16. Check tyres.

16A. Check the tyres for tread depth, using a tread depth gauge and note that in the UK, the minimum legal tread depth is 1.6 mm. However, tyres are not at their safest at that level, particularly in the wet, and you might want to replace them earlier.

16B. Also check both sides of each tyre for uneven wear, cuts, bulges or other damage in the tyre walls. Raise each wheel off the ground, using an axle stand, otherwise you won't be able to see the inside of each tyre properly and nor will you be able to check that part of the tread that is in contact with the ground. This tyre is showing lots of minor cracking on the side wall and should be replaced.

SAFETY FIRST!
Tyres that show uneven wear tell their own story, if only you know how to speak the language! If any tyre is worn more on one side than another, consult your specialist Mini centre or tyre specialist. It probably means that your suspension or steering is out of adjustment - possibly a simple tracking job but conceivably symptomatic of suspension damage or rear-end corrosion, so have it checked. If a tyre is worn more in the centre or on the edges, it could mean that your tyre pressures are wrong, but once again, have the car checked.

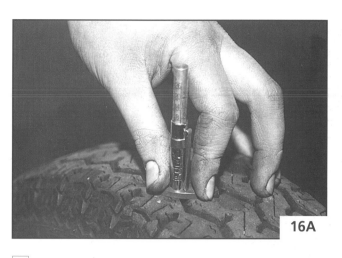

16A

16B

Job 17. Check spare tyre.

Check the tread depth, check for damage, check the wear pattern and the tyre pressure on the spare wheel, too. You should inflate the spare to the maximum recommended for high speed or high load running. Then, if you have a puncture whilst on a journey, you'll be okay. It's always easier to carry a tyre pressure gauge with you and let some air out than put some in!

1,500 Mile Bodywork and Interior - Around the Car

Job 18. Wash bodywork.

Wash paintwork, chrome and glass with water and a suitable car wash detergent, taking care not to get 'wax-wash' on the glass. Finish by washing the wheels and tyre walls. Leather the paintwork dry. Use a separate leather on the glass to avoid transfer of polish from paintwork.

Job 19. Touch-up paintwork.

Treat stone chips or scratches to prevent or eliminate rust. Allow ample time for new paint to harden before applying polish.

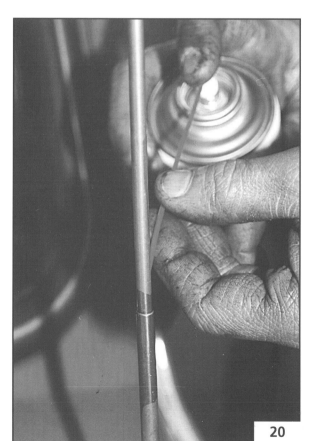

20

Job 20. Aerial/antenna.

20. Clean the sections of an extending, chrome plated aerial mast. Wipe a little releasing fluid (not oil - it will attract dirt) onto the surface and work in and out a few times.

Job 21. Valet interior.

Use a vacuum cleaner to remove dust and grit from the interior trim and carpets. Those cheap 12 volt vacuum cleaners are generally a waste of money so if you can't get your domestic cleaner to the car, take the car to a garage with a self-service valeting facility. Proprietary upholstery cleaners can be surprisingly effective and well worthwhile if the interior has become particularly grubby. Very bad stains, caused by grease, chocolate or unidentified flying brown stuff are best loosened with white or methylated spirit before bringing on the upholstery cleaner - but first test a bit of upholstery that you can't normally see, just in case either of the spirits removes upholstery colour.

Seat belts should be washed only with warm water and a non-detergent soap. Allow them to dry naturally and do not let them retract, if they're the inertia reel type, until completely dry.

☐ **Job 22. Improve visibility!**

Use a proprietary brand of windscreen cleaner to remove built-up traffic film and air-borne contaminants from the windscreen. Wipe wiper blades with methylated spirit to remove grease and contaminants.

1,500 Mile Bodywork - Under the Car

SAFETY FIRST!
Wear goggles when clearing the underside of the car. Read carefully the information at the start of this chapter on lifting and supporting the car.

23A

23B

23C

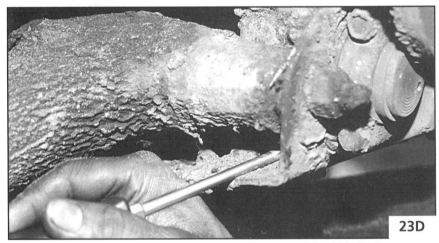

23D

☐ **Job 23. Clean mud traps.**

23A. Hose the underside of the car (if particularly muddy) and allow to dry before putting in the garage ...

23B. ... or scrape and wire brush off dry mud. Preferably, wear gloves because mud can force itself painfully behind finger nails!

23C. Clean out the main mud traps behind the headlamps and under the wings. This is a favourite gathering point for mud, which holds in moisture and salt and, of course, causes corrosion in a big way especially in headlamps and sidelamps, as well as the wing, front valance and flitch (engine bay) panel.

23D. A peculiarity to all Minis is this area around the rear radius arm. The crevice is snug enough for a mud poultice to do its worst! Rust will form in a very important part of the subframe making the Mini extremely dangerous. Always scrape it clean. That goes for every part of the rear subframe, particularly where the Metalastik mount meets the bodyshell.

3,000 Miles - or Every Three Months, Whichever Comes First

3,000 mile Mechanical and Electrical - The Engine Bay

First carry out Jobs 2 to 6.

24A

☐ **Job 24. Adjust spark plugs.**

24A. Number the spark plug HT leads to avoid confusion when refitting, then carefully pull them off the plugs. Remove the spark plugs using a proper plug socket with a rubber insert. This prevents the plug from dropping on the floor and breaking, and also prevents the socket from leaning over and breaking the plug's insulator as it is unscrewed.

24B. Check the spark plugs to ensure that they are in good condition (see colour illustrations on page 65) and also check that i) the round terminal nut is tight - tighten with pliers - and ii) that the gap is correct. Clean them up with a wire brush applied vigorously!

24C. Check the gap with a feeler gauge - the gauge should just go in, making contact and meeting just the smallest resistance from both sides, but without being forced in any way. Lever the longer earth (ground) electrode away to open the gap - but take great care not to move or damage the centre electrode or its insulation - and tap the electrode on a hard surface to close it up again. If in doubt, throw 'em out and buy new. Running with damaged or worn out plugs is a false economy - although having said that, don't change them for the sake of it. Look for evidence of electrode erosion, insulator staining, damage - or just old age.

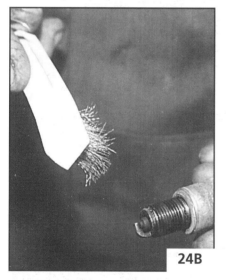

24B

24C

24D. On later models a water shield is fitted in front of the ignition components and, on this type of shield, it is removed by turning the two thumb clips at the top, and one at the bottom. Replacement clips are available if, as on this car, a Heath Robinson alternative to the proper clip has been used.

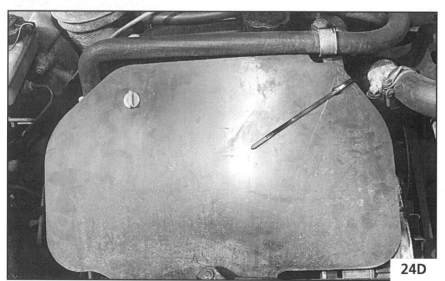

24D

3,000 MILE SERVICE

24E. Alternatively, on some models a plastic cover is fitted in front of, or over, the distributor or you may encounter a combination of all types in a previous owner's attempt to keep the very vulnerable Mini ignition system dry.

Make sure that the threads are clean then screw the plugs back by hand. Finally tighten them to the torque setting given in **Chapter 8, Facts and Figures**. Carry out the next Job before refitting the HT leads.

☐ Job 25. Check HT Circuit.

25A. Check the condition of the distributor cap and rotor arm and the security of wiring connections to the distributor. Removing a Mini's distributor cap is a tricky business due to its location at the front of the engine behind the grille. Try levering the tops of the cap clips with a screwdriver, but take great care that the bottom of the clip doesn't jump off the distributor body, possibly losing the clip somewhere. Don't apply excessive pressure to the cap with the screwdriver, it may break. Leave the plug leads in place on the distributor so that you can't confuse where they go. Disconnect the HT lead that comes from the coil if you want to take the cap away and into the daylight.

25B. Check the rotor tip for burning or brightness. If it's bright, it suggests that the distributor bushes may have worn out and that means its reconditioned distributor time - available from your Mini specialist. If the distributor rotor can move about, allowing its tip to brush against the contacts inside the distributor cap, the distributor accuracy will be way out too, which means that your car will run badly, uneconomically and may fail the emissions part of the MOT test.

25C. If this has been happening, the contacts will also be bright and you can expect to see quite a bit of brass or aluminium dust inside the distributor cap. Black dust in any quantity suggests that the top (carbon) contact has worn away - it should protrude from the centre of the cap and move in and out freely under light spring pressure. Also check for any signs of 'tracking' between the cap contacts. This will appear as a thin black line visible on the inside or outside of the cap between the contacts. These tracking lines are paths letting the spark run to earth instead of down the HT lead where it should be going. If you have any of these problems, fit a new cap.

24E

25A

25B

25C

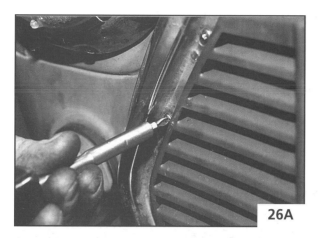

26A

☐ Job 26. The Distributor.

26A. One of the prices to pay for the compactness of a Mini is that some parts are tucked away and hard to get at. For the time it takes and the hassle saved, removing the grille is a tremendous help. It's secured to the front panel by a number of cross-head screws and once these are out, the grille can be lifted away. Now, if your car is so fitted, remove the water shield either by releasing the clips, undoing the screws, or slipping off the cover, according to type.

26B. With the grille out of the way, the once hidden distributor suddenly becomes accessible and in full vision from the front of the car.

26C. Once the distributor cap has been removed, first remove the rotor arm (26C.1) by pulling it off the centre rotor shaft. You're not changing the points at this stage, that comes later in the service schedule but with the ignition turned off, use a screwdriver to open the points up (26C.2) and see if they are badly pitted or burned. If there is any evidence of such marks, replace the points as shown in Job 70. and replace the condenser as well because a faulty condenser will cause the points to burn. Since the heel on the points can wear down, you'll have to adjust the points gap. Turn the engine over by pressing on the fan belt and turning the fan, which will rotate the distributor shaft cam (26C.6). Stop turning when the heel on the points (26C.14) is at the top of the cam lobe (26C.3). Now slacken the screw (26C.8).

26B

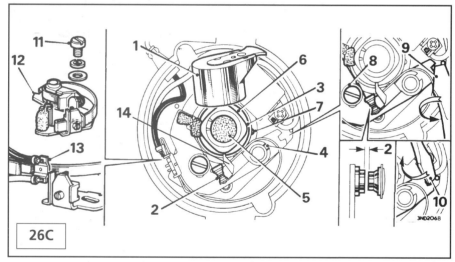

26C

26D. By inserting a screwdriver between the 'V'-shape in the base plate and the 'V' in the points (26C.9 and 26C.10) you will be able to open and close the points gap. Here you can see a feeler gauge inserted into the points gap. Adjust the gap until the feeler gauge makes contact with both sides of the points at once - a tricky business it's easy to close the points up too far so that they snap shut as you pull out the feeler gauge and it's equally easy to leave them too far apart because it's difficult to discern when the feeler gauge is actually in contact. Still, you have to persevere!

26D

You should also take this opportunity to lubricate the distributor taking enormous care not to get grease or oil on to the distributor points or any other electrical components. Very lightly smear the cam (26C.6) with a small amount of grease or petroleum jelly. Add a few drops of oil to the felt pad in the top of the cam spindle (sometimes missing but add a few drops of oil anyway) but do not oil the cam wiping pad fitted to later models. If you accidentally get any oil or grease onto the contact breaker points, wipe them clean with a cloth dampened with methylated spirits. Add another three or four drops between the contact plate and the cam spindle (26C.6) so that the oil runs down into the body of the distributor beneath the base plate. If this hasn't been done for some time, it's a good idea to use a can of releasing fluid with an injector nozzle to spray a small quantity beneath the base plate and into the body of the distributor. The centrifugal weights inside the distributor can seize and this would cause the engine to lose power.

26E. The most accurate way of setting the points gap is by using a dwell meter - they can be bought quite inexpensively from motor accessory stores. See the instructions with the meter for its correct use.

☐ Job 27. Generator belt.

27A. The generator belt should have about ½ inch (12 mm.) of free movement on its longest length (this shot is not on its longest length, that is between the crankshaft pulley and water pump or more easily, the generator. However, that shot would have been impossible and the one shown is by way of illustration). The free movement you are looking at is towards and away from the pulley on the water pump, not side to side.

27B. The generator belt should also be checked carefully for wear. If you see any signs of cracking or fraying or if the driving surfaces of the belt look polished, renew it. Unfortunately, the modern type of toothed belt can only be properly checked by taking it off. Examine the inside of the belt all the way around, bending it back to front and looking for cracking.

INSIDE INFORMATION: Since this type of belt is so difficult to check without taking it off the car, and since the car is not drivable for very far without a belt fitted, it pays to always carry a spare with you. (And the tools to fit it!).

27C. Adjustment of the belt is the same whether fitted with a dynamo or alternator. Slacken the rear mounting bolt ...

27D. ... the front bolt ...

27E. ... and the mounting nut and the adjuster nut, from below.

27F. So that you don't cause any damage to an alternator, use a piece of wood rather than metal to lever the generator until the belt has the correct degree of tension. With an alternator, lever against the thick end bracket and not any other part. Dynamos, with their steel casing, are not so susceptible to damage.

INSIDE INFORMATION: If you slacken off all of the bolts and nut just so that the generator can move when levered, but not so far that it can twist on the top mounting bolts, you will be able to place a socket spanner on the adjuster nut, holding it in place with one hand while you lever on the

26E

27A

27B

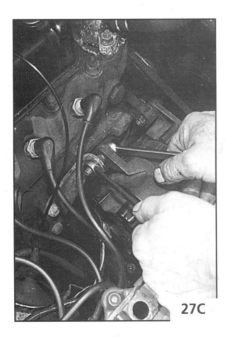

27C

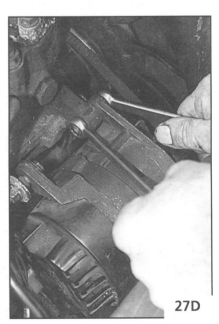

27D

27E

27F

piece of wood between the generator and engine block with the other. The socket spanner should stay in place while you loosen it in order to check the tension of the belt, and then you can rapidly tighten the adjuster nut, holding the generator in place. The three remaining bolts can then be tightened separately. DO NOT OVERTIGHTEN THE BELT because all that will do is to cause the generator bearings and possibly the water pump bearings to fail prematurely and the belt will become stretched.

☐ Job 28. SU carburettors.

OPTIONAL: SU carburettors in particular tend to go out of tune quite rapidly, especially if they are past their first flush of youth! If you wish to adjust them, follow Job 76 in the 6,000 mile service.

☐ Job 29. Check air filters.

Broadly, there are three types of air filters fitted to Minis. Early cars use a cleanable composite filter: early Mini Coopers an oil wetted gauze filter while later cars have a renewable paper element. As Mini Coopers ran with twin carburettors, two air filter elements are fitted. Remove the air filter housing(s) and check the condition of the element(s). Early composite filters are just tapped to loosen the dust and then blown out. Try to use an external air source such as a foot pump if compressed air is not available. Early Mini Cooper gauze type elements should be washed thoroughly with paraffin or a proprietary engine cleaner and allowed to dry. The gauze should then be lubricated sparingly with engine oil. All later cars with paper elements are inspected, and if there is anything more than a trace of soil, they should be replaced. In all cases, examine the rubber seal/gasket and replace if there is any doubt.

29A. On the majority of models, two wing nuts secure the filter housing to the carburettor, shown here on single carburettor model. Early models are slightly different in that the housing is fitted to the back of the carburettor with one wing nut holding the housing. A breather pipe attaches itself to the filter housing from the engine rocker cover. Later models also have a hot air intake duct and this should also be eased off. The lid of the filter can simply be eased off using a wide blade screwdriver.

29B. Mini Coopers have two cleaner elements.

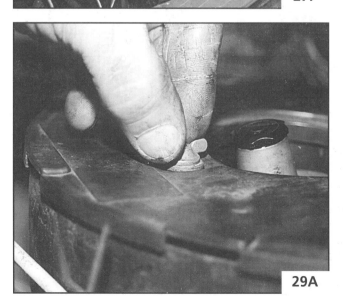

29A

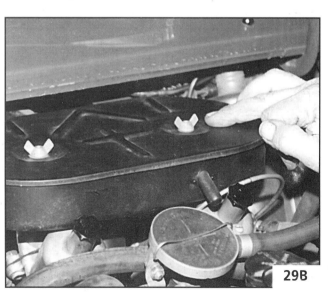

29B

On the latest fuel-injected models, the air cleaner lid is secured with three screws and a series of retaining clips. Once removed, the lid is simply lifted off.

29B. This filter is showing much abuse and will be replaced immediately. Check that the new filter is of the right size and type before fitting.

29C. Always examine the rubber seals/gaskets before refitting.

29D. Take this opportunity to examine all breather hoses as they are usually hidden by the air filter housing.

Early Mini Coopers used a mesh filter. Maintenance of these types is restricted to tapping out and loosening dust and then blowing through with an air line (a foot pump is fine).

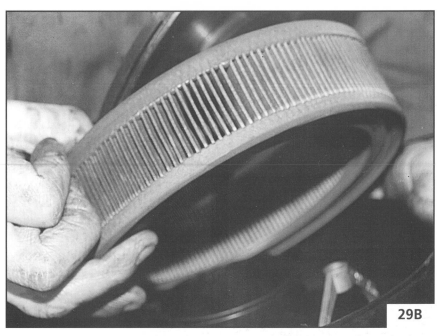

29B

☐ Job 30. Top-up carburettor dash pots.

Top up the SU carburettor dashpots with the correct grade of oil. Unscrew the dashpot cap and pull out the plunger. The dashpot contains a damper which prevents the fuel flow needle in the carburettor from fluttering and allows more petrol to come through when you accelerate hard - performance and fuel economy will be better if the dash pots are not allowed to run dry. Use ordinary engine oil, nothing thicker. Very thin oil tends to disappear too quickly!

INSIDE INFORMATION: Some SU carburettors tend to consume oil very quickly for a variety of reasons, some to do with driving style, some to do with general wear. If your carburettors are like this, check the oil more frequently than every 3,000 miles.

30A. Remove the carburettor piston damper and check the oil level...

30B. ...which should be about ½ inch (13 mm) above the carburettor piston rod (lifted here for clarity).

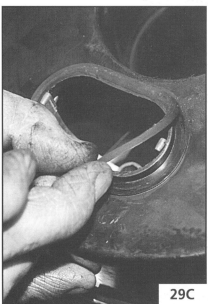

29C

29D

30A

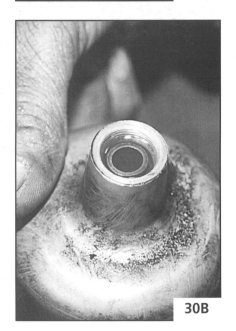

30B

☐ **Job 31. Check drive belts.**

JAPANESE AND CERTAIN EXPORT CARS ONLY.

Check the condition and adjustment of the air pump drive belt if your car is fitted with emission control equipment and an air pump. There should be ½ in. (12 mm) of movement at the longest section of drive belt visible between the pulleys.

Check belts for cracking on their inner faces and any signs of severe wear such as cords showing through the edges of the belt or polishing on the inner faces of the belt. Replace if any evidence of wear is found. For toothed belts, see comments under 27.

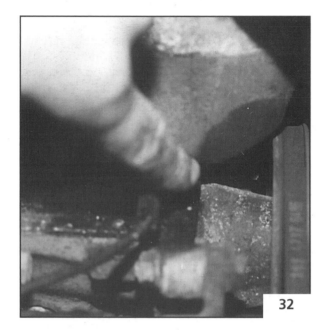

32

☐ **Job 32. Pipes and Hoses.**

32. Carry out a visual check on all flexible and rigid pipes and hoses in and around the engine bay for leaks. Not easily seen is the by-pass hose (between the cylinder head and water pump) the general location of which is shown here. The best way to check this hose is to grope around and feel for any leaks. If one is apparent, the job is a little outside the scope of the home tinkerer and help from a Mini specialist should be sought. Concertina replacement hoses are available but their life span is suspect.

3,000 mile Mechanical and Electrical - Around the Car

First carry out jobs 7 to 17.

☐ **Job 33. Handbrake travel.**

INSIDE THE CAR, check the handbrake. It should be mounted securely, it should stay in the 'on' position - the ratchet can sometimes wear, allowing the brake to slip 'off', and the release mechanism can sometimes seize inside the lever, which prevents the ratchet from holding. If undue movement of the handbrake itself is felt, it may be that the mounting bracket or base is cracked. It any of these faults are evident, seek advice from your Mini specialist.

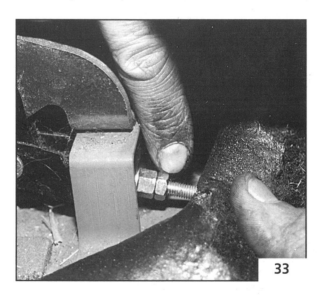

33

You should also check the handbrake to see if it has to be pulled too far before it operates correctly. Ideally, it should be fully on after three or four 'clicks' of the ratchet. If it's not, don't adjust the handbrake itself until the rear brakes are correctly adjusted - see Job 47. When the rear brakes are properly adjusted, and with the rear of the car raised and securely supported, you may then adjust the hand brake cable(s).

> **SAFETY FIRST!**
> *Don't work beneath a car supported on axle stands with someone else sitting in the car trying the hand brake. It's too risky that their movements will cause the car to fall off the axle stands. Make sure that you are well clear of the raised car when someone's inside it. Read carefully the information at the start of this chapter on lifting and supporting the car.*

33. Early cars have a separate cable to each wheel, later cars run a single cable from the handbrake lever. In either case, loosen the lock-nut and turn the adjusting nut (illustrated) half a turn at a time until the slack in the handbrake cable is such that the brake is on fully after three or four clicks. Also, make sure that with the handbrake released, both rear wheels are free to turn without binding. If you find that the rear brake shoes are in good condition but all adjustment is used up on the cable(s), then it is time to visit your Mini specialist for new cable(s).

Lower the rear of the car to the ground on completion.

3,000 mile Mechanical and Electrical - Under the Car

> **SAFETY FIRST!**
> *Raise the front of the car off the ground after reading carefully the information at the start of this chapter on lifting and supporting the car.*

☐ Job 34. Steering rack.

34A. Turn the steering wheel fully to the left; check the right hand steering rack gaiter for leaks and tears: squeeze and pinch the gaiter hard. Turn the steering to the right, check the left hand gaiter in the same way. As can be seen in the picture, this gaiter is split and leaking lubricant and will need to be replaced immediately.

34B. You will now have to remove the track-rod end from the steering arm - see Job 35 - so that the gaiter can be replaced. Do so straight away since, without oil in the rack, its life expectancy will be very poor indeed! Take out the small nut and screw holding the retaining clip in place at each end of the old gaiter and fit the new gaiter. Some gaiters are held with metal or plastic clips which have to be cut off.

34C. Using an oil can, inject fresh oil (early models SAE 90EP, or semi-fluid grease later models) into the gaiters to compensate for that lost (obviously the steering rack shown is one removed from the car for illustration only). You can add more later on, as the oil feeds across the rack, by removing the clip once again.

☐ Job 35. Track rod ends.

35A. Check the rubber boot on each track rod end (TRE). If torn, renew the complete track rod end. In theory, you can replace the boot but it's a false economy for the following reasons. i) Chances are that the old TRE will be worn because the boot has split and because of the resulting absence of lubricant, and ii) the TRE has to be removed from the steering arm in any case. This can be such a devil of a job to carry out that you might as well get it over with and fit a relatively inexpensive, new TRE whilst you're at it.

35B. The tapered shank system gives a very positive location but it also makes the ball joint very difficult to remove. There are ball joint removal tools (one of several types shown here) available from your local motorists' store and there is the traditional

34A

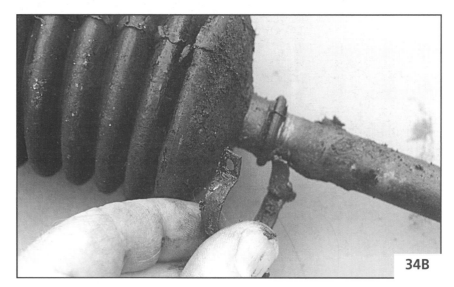

34B

34C

3,000 MILE SERVICE

35A

35B

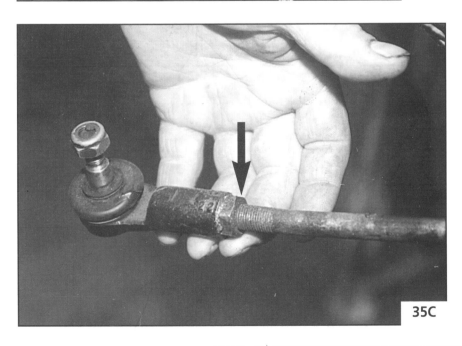

35C

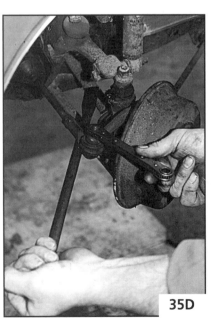

35D

way of doing the job. With the latter, you hold one hammer against one side of the eye (on the end of the steering arm, fitted over the taper) and hit the other side sharply with a hammer. This deforms the eye enough to loosen the taper. Theoretically! In practice, you may have to use a removal tool and a pair of hammers - and to strike the eye repeatedly until a good, sharp blow shocks the joint free. You will probably cut the rubber bellows on the ball joint as you hammer, so you will have to renew it even if you are just dismantling for another job.

35C. Before you start, count the number of visible exposed threads on the steering track rod up to the nut that locks the track rod end in place (arrowed). You will have to remove this nut as well as the TRE if you're doing this job to replace a steering rack gaiter, and it's very important that the nut goes back in the same position as before. Slacken this nut, remove the other nut holding the TRE to the steering arm (knock back the lock tab first on disc brake models) then remove the TRE as just described.

35D. *INSIDE INFORMATION: When you put it all back together and come to tighten the new locknut holding the track rod end to the steering arm, you'll probably find that the balljoint shank turns, making it impossible to tighten the nut. Try levering the TRE upwards using a long bar engaged with the front subframe. This will cause the tapered shank to lock in the steering arm allowing the nut to be tightened.*

36A

36B

☐ Job 36. Constant velocity joint boot.

36A. Turn the right wheel to full lock and turn slowly inspecting the constant velocity (CV) joint boot for cracks or tears. Pinch the boot to make sure that it is in first class condition. Repeat for the left hand side. If a defect is found then the car should be taken to a Mini specialist immediately. A loss of lubricant in the constant velocity joint will lead to extreme wear and could prove very dangerous. It is of course, an MOT failure.

36B. On later models, carry out the same check on the inner constant velocity joint boots at the transmission end of the driveshaft.

☐ Job 37. Steering clamp bolt.

37. Check the tightness of the steering clamp bolt situated at the base of the steering column (inside the car). A single bolt secures the shaft from the steering wheel to the rack and pinion unit.

☐ Job 38. Drain engine oil.

If you're not draining the oil at this time, don't forget to carry out Job 1 instead, but wait until the car has been lowered to the ground, so that it's level for checking the oil.

> **SAFETY FIRST!**
> *Refer to the section on **ENGINE OILS** in Chapter 1 Safety First! before carrying out the following work.*

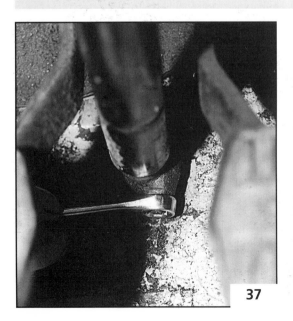

37

38

Warm the engine up just a little, but not so much that the oil becomes scalding hot - running the engine for just so long that it will idle off the choke should do it - so that the oil becomes warm and will therefore run more freely.

38. Place an oil drain container in place beneath the sump with several sheets of newspaper beneath and protecting the surrounding area. Unscrew the oil drain plug with a ring spanner but beware! especially if the bolt is so tight that you have to use an extension on your spanner - an unsafe thing to do but something that is occasionally unavoidable.

INSIDE INFORMATION: Note that the oil used on the Mini doubles for the transmission lubricant and this includes the automatic. You will need a container with a capacity of at least 5 litres. A 5 litre plastic oil can with one side cut out will be sufficient.

SAFETY FIRST!
Oil drain plugs are often so tight that they seem to have been fitted by a gorilla with toothache. i) Take care that the spanner does not slip causing injury to hand or head. (Use a socket or ring spanner - never an open ended spanner - with as little offset as possible, so that the spanner is as near to the line of the bolt as possible.) ii) Ensure that your spanner is positioned so that you pull downwards, if at all possible. iii) Take even greater care that the effort needed does not cause the car to fall on you or to slip off the stands - remember those wheel chocks!

Remove the oil drain plug and drain out the oil. Leave the car for several minutes for the oil to drain fully. Replace plug but be certain to use a new drain plug washer, available from your accessory shop or parts specialist.

Job 39. Remove oil filter.

Before removing the oil filter, move the drain container so that it is situated beneath the oil filter. Mini oil filters come in two broad types: the renewable element canister type with a steel casing and the disposable type. All models are fitted facing down EXCEPT, the automatic transmission cars, these are horizontal and are always the renewable element type.

39A. Release the centre bolt that passes through the centre of the canister type of oil filter. (This picture shows an engine removed from the car for clarity). You may find that the steel casing will remain 'glued' to the filter housing. Let the oil drain from the filter and then give the casing a slight nudge but be ready to support it when it does release as the paper filter is pushed against the housing with a spring which, although is low tension, will push the casing down.

39B. Pour any residual oil into the drain container but don't just tip the container upside down and let the contents fall - you will need to retain the innards.

39C. Almost certainly stuck to the bottom of the old filter will be a large washer.

39A

39B

39C

39D

39E

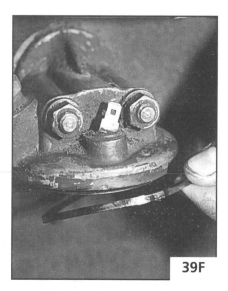

39F

39D. Beneath the washer is the spring referred to earlier. These sit on the inside of the container.

39E. On the outside, and towards the head of the bolt is a rubber seal and a washer. If you're extremely lucky, the rubber sealing ring between the container and the filter housing will have come away with the container but don't bank on it.

39F. In the majority of cases, the sealing ring will remain in the filter housing and will need to be prized out. A point from an old school drawing compass is ideal, as is a sharpened dart point. Scrape out any hardened or glued-in sealing ring that may remain.

39G

39G. Disposable oil filters rarely come off by hand so a number of tools are available on the market to assist. Shown here (again an engine removed from the car for clarity) is a belt wrench but they come in other forms such as chain or three pronged finger. Most fit a 1/2 inch socket drive. It only needs a jolt to free the seal and then the filter will spin off.

☐ Job 40. New oil filter.

40A. Thoroughly clean all components in the renewable element type container and make sure that all parts go back in the way they were removed. Apply a little grease or engine oil to the sealing ring and place in the lip of the housing. Grease should help the ring with the battle against gravity. Push the container against the spring and make sure that the lip sits squarely against the ring before finally tightening the long centre bolt.

40B. When fitting a disposable type of oil filter, wipe the sealing ring (40B.1) with a little grease or fresh engine oil.

40C. Fit the new filter using firm hand pressure only. Using the removal tool may distort the filter and render the sealing qualities useless.

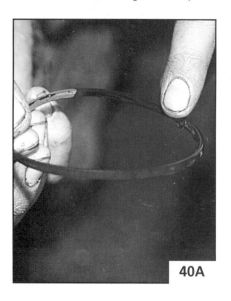

40A

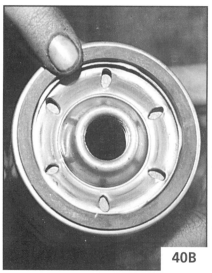

40B

40C

41

☐ Job 41. Pour fresh oil.

41. Pour in the fresh oil but do give the oil a chance to sink into the engine otherwise the surplus will run over the filler neck and run down to the exhaust manifold giving off an enormous amount of smoke when the engine runs.

Lower the car to the ground. Run the engine for a minute or so and then turn it off.

☐ Job 42. Check oil level.

Check the engine oil level and top up as necessary. See Job 1 if you need to understand the dipstick markings.

☐ Job 43. Check for oil leaks.

Run the engine for a minute or so and check beneath the car and especially around the oil filter and drain plug for leaks. Switch off the engine and allow the oil to settle before re-checking the oil level and topping up if necessary.

SAFETY FIRST!
Raise the front of the car off the ground once again, after reading carefully the information at the start of this chapter on lifting and supporting the car.

☐ Job 44. Check front brake pads.

SAFETY FIRST! and **SPECIALIST SERVICE:** Obviously, a car's brakes are among its most important safety related items. Do not dismantle your car's brakes unless you are fully competent to do so. If you have not been trained in this work, but wish to carry out the work described here, we strongly recommend that you have a garage or qualified mechanic check your work before using the car on the road. See also the section on BRAKES AND ASBESTOS in Chapter 1, for further important information.

44A. If your car is fitted with disc brakes to the front, you can check the condition of the brake pads without carrying out any dismantling - but only if you know what you are looking for! Looking at the front of the calliper (this one has been removed and fastened to a bench for clarity), check the distance between the disc and the pad metal backing plate. The gap in the middle should be filled with friction material - the stuff

44A

that wears away during braking. The manufacturers recommend that the minimum permissible disc pad thickness before they are replaced is ⅛th inch (1.6 mm.) but you should allow for the fact that you won't be checking the brakes again for further 3,000 miles or three months. The brake pads illustrated are well beyond the point where replacement is necessary and will in fact soon have no friction material left. Those who ignore the checks will become aware of the situation when a grating sound is heard from the front wheels, caused by the metal pad backing plate pushing on the disc. It's very common for one pad to wear down more quickly than the other so you should always take the thickness of the most worn out pad as your guide.

On the other hand, if one of the pads does not appear to be working at all (look for one pad very much thicker than the other or, if possible, one side of the disc shinier than the other). **SPECIALIST SERVICE**, have a garage check the callipers. One of the calliper pistons may have seized.

There is no facility for adjusting the front brakes since they adjust themselves automatically as the pads wear down but the fact that the pads do wear accounts for the fact that the brake fluid level goes down whilst you're using the car. The significance of this fact becomes apparent later, in the *Inside Information* on page 42.!

44B. First step in removing the old brake pads, should they need it, is to pull out the two split pins that hold the two spring clips in place. Note that the ends of the split pins will have been opened out and that you need to squeeze them flat with your pliers.

44C. before the split pin can be pulled out.

44D. With the split pins removed, lift away the retaining spring plate.

SAFETY FIRST!
If the ends of the split pins show any signs of breaking off, which will happen after the split pins have been closed and re-opened a number of times - fit new split pins. These are special items made specifically for your car so purchase them from your Mini specialist.

44E. It will be difficult to pull out the brake pads because of the action of using the brakes will have kept them in close proximity to the brake discs. Use a pair of grips between the metal backing plate and the outside of the calliper to ease the pad away from the brake disc.

44F. You can now pull out the pads quite easily, together with the anti-rattle shim, if fitted. If you are fitting new pads, you'll probably have to push the pistons right the way back into the calliper, bearing in mind the following information about brake fluid being expelled from the top of the master cylinder.

You should also clean out the inside of the calliper in which the friction pad assemblies lie and scrape off any traces of dirt or rust from each piston.

INSIDE INFORMATION: Inside the brake callipers, as you will see when you pull out the pads, there is a piston on each side of the disc which pushes against the brake pad when you apply the brakes. The piston is itself pushed out by the hydraulic fluid which is forced down the brake pipe from the master cylinder. As you push the brake pads back against the piston, brake fluid will be pushed back up the pipe and into the master cylinder. Because you will need to push the pistons even further back into the calliper before fitting new pads; i) Take a thin piece of lint-free cloth, moistened with brake cleaner or fluid and clean all around the piston (clean around the back like using dental floss).

44B

44C

44D

44E

44F

44G

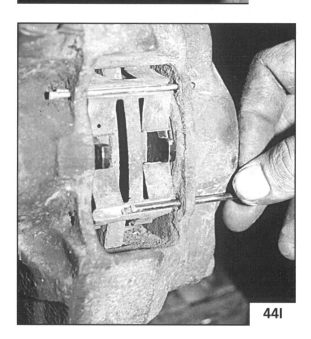

44H

44I

44G. Slide each new pad into the calliper just to make sure that each one
moves freely, scraping dirt out of the insides of the callipers if necessary. If
you are refitting previously fitted pads, it is permissible to use a file - lightly! -
to remove any rust that may have built up on the edge of each steel backing
pad.

44H. Now smear a little more of that brake grease - but only a very small
amount - on to the back of the pad, in other words on the back of the metal
backing plate NOT on the friction surface of the pad, which is the part that
pushes against the brake disc. Now the new pads can be fitted into place,
together with the anti-rattle shim, where applicable, and the spring plate seen
in 44D held down against the pads ...

44I. ... while the split pins are slid back into place. Use a screwdriver to open
up the ends of the 'legs' on the split pins so that they cannot slip back out
again.

Note that when the brakes are applied for the first time, the pedal will travel
much further than normal until the pads reach their operating position. Only
then will the brake pedal distance normalise. This will only take two or three
applications of the pedal.

☐ **Job 45. Check front brake shoes.**

First read the SAFETY FIRST! and SPECIALIST SERVICE note at the start of Job 44.

45A

45A. On Minis fitted with drum brakes at the front, it will be necessary to remove the brake drum to look at the brake shoes. As these brakes are fully adjustable, it helps to slacken the adjusters off to allow the brake drum to ease over the shoes. Early models have one adjuster per wheel, later models have two. The adjusters have a square head and are threaded into the adjuster unit (early models) or attached to the brake backplate (later models). Clean all around the adjuster with a wire brush and apply a little releasing fluid. Proper brake adjusting spanners are available although a 5⁄16th AF open ended spanner will work just as well. Where a single adjuster is fitted, rotate the adjuster anti-clockwise (when looking at the backplate) to slacken. On later models with two adjusters, Rotate each adjuster AGAINST the forward rotation of the wheel.

INSIDE INFORMATION: Mini brake adjusters are notorious for seizing solid! They're also notorious for the squared adjuster shaft being rounded off by ham-fisted mechanics who use the wrong tools on an adjuster that has become stiff and arthritic. If the brake adjuster on your car has become rounded off, there may be nothing for it but to renew the brake adjuster. On most models this means renewing the complete brake backplate assembly, although on cars with twin adjusters, pattern part replacement

45B

adjuster kits are available. If you are a novice at mechanical work, either regard this job as a SPECIALIST SERVICE item, or have a trained mechanic check the work over before the car is used on the road.

45B. The drum is secured to the hub by one or two cross head screws. Their location makes them vulnerable to road soil and can prove difficult to remove. In this shot an impact driver is being used as a precaution against damaging the screw head by a slipping screwdriver. If the screws have been 'butchered' in a previous life, replace them. The drum can now be slid over the brake shoes but it may need a little 'persuasion' with a soft faced mallet.

45C. Examine the brake shoes for friction material wear. The minimum permissible thickness above the rivets (or from the metal backing if they are of the bonded type) is 0.06 in (1.52 mm). If there is any oil or brake fluid contamination then the shoes must be replaced regardless of how much material is left. Ignore house-wives tales of boiling the shoes in washing powder - it doesn't work! Always replace the shoes on BOTH wheels if a replacement set is needed. While in the area, peel back the rubber boots on the wheel cylinders and check for any fluid leaks. If any is present, have the wheel cylinder replaced – SPECIALIST SERVICE.

45C

If the brake shoes are to be replaced, make a careful note of EXACTLY where and how the pull-off springs hold the shoes, as they do vary. Ascertain which way around the shoes are located on the adjusters and wheel cylinders. Only when you are sure, release the springs.

45D

45D. It is likely that a hair spring locates one end of the shoe to a wheel cylinder.

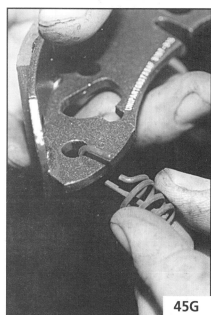

45E

45E. With this released, the shoes can be levered off the wheel cylinders, pivot end first and thus the tension lessened on the springs ...

45F. ... making their removal easier.

> **SAFETY FIRST! Brake dust is extremely hazardous if inhaled. ALWAYS wear a protective mask available at most stores for minimal cost. When fitting new shoes make sure that your hands are clean and free of oil/grease.**

Clean away all traces of brake dust using a proprietory spray-on brake cleaner. Apply a little high melting point brake grease to the brake adjusters and to the backplate where it is in contact with the brake shoes. Follow this with a little on the pivot areas on the adjuster and wheel cylinder.

45F

45G

45G. Where fitted, locate the hair spring in the wheel cylinder end of the new brake shoes. Fit one pull-off spring first, especially if it is of the reversed hook type. Manoeuvre that side into position around the hub before introducing the second spring.

45H. When that is in place, lever both sides home using a stout screwdriver against the central hub. Be prepared for the springs to 'bounce' off a few times. Your patience will be rewarded.

45I. Ensure that the brake shoes locate over the adjusters and, where fitted, re-engage the hair springs with the hole in the wheel cylinder pistons.

45H

45I

45J. Before refitting the brake drum, examine the inside face. If it is scored or cracked then it should be resurfaced, a job that can be done through your Mini specialist or at a local machine shop. There is a limit to the amount that cam be 'skimmed' so be prepared to replace the drum with a new one if necessary. Fit the drum over the shoes so that the screw hole(s) line up with those on the hub and fully tighten the screws. On early models with a single adjuster, adjust the brakes by turning the squared adjuster clockwise (when looking at the brake backplate) until the wheel is locked. Now back it off until the wheel can be rotated without excessive binding. On models with two adjusters, turn each adjuster in the FORWARD direction of the wheel rotation. As the adjuster winds in, a series of clicks will be felt. When the adjuster locks, wind it back one click at a time until the wheel spins freely. Repeat on the other adjuster. On all models, Press the brake pedal to centralise the shoes and then re-adjust if necessary. The drum may bind slightly but this is perfectly acceptable as the new shoes will have to bed in first.

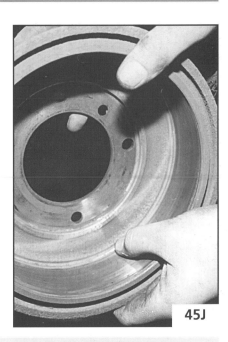

45J

SAFETY FIRST! Note carefully that new brake shoes won't work effectively as they should until they have 'bedded in'. Moreover, they can become glazed if the brakes are applied very hard within the first few hundred miles of running after fitting new brake shoes. For the first few hundred miles, therefore, you should avoid braking hard unless you have to, such as in an emergency, and allow extra braking distance because of the fact that the brakes won't work quite as effectively - you may have noticed that the brake drums will have become slightly scored and grooved and the new brake shoes have to take the shape of the brake drum before they will work as well as they are able to.

Job 46. Lubricate front grease points.

46A. Greasing the front suspension and other areas is a job often neglected. It may be that a grease gun is absent from many tool boxes. The importance cannot be over emphasised. Neglect here only promotes accelerated wear and could lead to a dangerous situation where suspension components could actually shear. This view shows the lower swivel pin being greased.

46B. The upper swivel is done in exactly the same fashion.

46C. A further grease nipple is fitted to the upper inner wishbone fulcrum, so easy to find but it's surprising that many people are unaware of its existence.

INSIDE INFORMATION: It's sometimes difficult to get grease to go through the grease nipples. Push the grease gun firmly onto the grease nipple - the nozzle on the end of the grease gun is spring loaded so it should clip into place - and hold the grease gun square on the grease nipple to give the grease the best chance of going into the joint. If you still find it impossible to get grease through the grease nipple, try unscrewing it and with the grease nipple held in a vice or a self-grip wrench - grip the spanner flats, not the thread - see if you can persuade grease to go through it. If not, fit a new grease nipple and try again. New ones will be available from your parts supplier although high street stores may not stock them.

Now lower the front of the car to the ground and raise the rear after reading carefully the **SAFETY FIRST!** information at the start of this chapter on lifting and supporting the car.

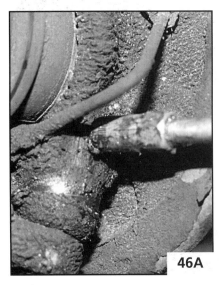

46A

46B

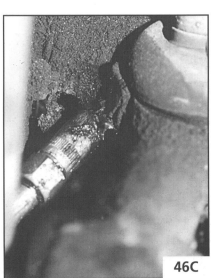

46C

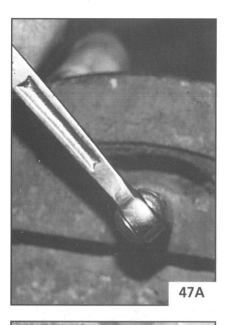

47A

47B

Job 47. Check rear brakes.

First read the SAFETY FIRST! and SPECIALIST SERVICE note at the start of Job 44.

47A. Before attempting to remove a rear brake drum, make sure that the handbrake is fully released. Slacken off the brake adjuster situated at the rear of the brake back-plate by turning in an anti-clockwise direction (viewed from the rear of the backplate). Remove the drum as described in 45B. and examine the wheel cylinders and brake shoes as described in 45C.

47B. See how close this friction material is to the rivets in the picture. Note that a single wheel cylinder is fitted to the rear and that handbrake levers pass through the brake shoes. Should these require replacement make a careful note of the spring locations and the way the shoes are fitted for reassembly. Lift the brake shoes off the adjuster pivot end and remove the return spring. Then lift the shoes from the cylinder end and negotiate away from the handbrake levers.

47C. Clean away all traces of dust paying heed to the precautions stressed in 45. Apply a **very small** amount of high melting point brake grease to the brake adjusting wedges and to the backplate where it is in contact with the brake shoes.

47C

47D. Follow this with a little on the pivot areas on the adjuster and wheel cylinder. Re-assemble the brake shoes in the reverse order of the disassembly making sure that no grease comes into contact with the friction material and that all springs are fitted correctly. Before refitting the brake drum, examine the inner face as described in 45J. As there is only one brake adjuster, turn this in a clockwise direction, one click at a time, until the drum locks. Slacken the adjuster until the drum spins freely.

Job 48. Lubricate rear suspension.

48. There is one grease point on each side of the car serving the radius arm pivot. This is accessed from the side of the car at the front of the rear wheel arch. On early models there is a small metal cover with a rubber grommet in the centre (if it's still there!). Hook out this grommet for access to the grease nipple.

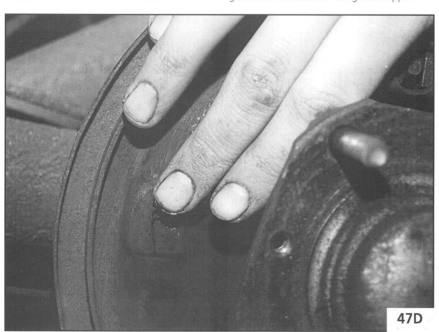

47D

48

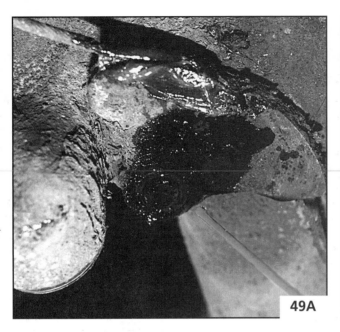

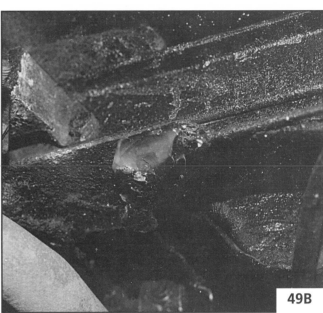

49A

49B

☐ **Job 49. Lubricate handbrake cable swivel and guide channels.**

49A. The handbrake cable is an exposed cable, pivoting on a swivel located on the radius arm. It's ability to 'seize' at the drop of a hat accounts for many handbrake faults. Not only should the cable be greased where it sits in the swivel but the swivel pivot point itself should be kept well greased. If you find that yours has seized, then apply a liberal dose of penetrating oil and rock backwards and forwards to free. In extreme cases, it may be necessary to release the cable from the lever on the rear brake backplate to get more leverage on the swivel. Once this has happened to you, your servicing will be such that it will never happen again!.

49B. Apply a dab of grease where the handbrake cable makes its final turn on the rear sub-frame towards the handbrake lever. If the cable is seized here, it is a simple matter of levering up the tags and freeing the cable.

Lower the car to the ground.

3,000 mile Mechanical and Electrical - Road Test

☐ **Job 50. Clean controls.**

Clean the door handles, controls and steering wheel; they may well have become greasy from your hands while you were carrying out the rest of the service work on your car. Start up the engine while you are sitting in the driver's seat.

☐ **Job 51. Check instruments.**

Before pulling away, and with the engine running, check the correct function of all instruments and switches.

☐ **Job 52. Throttle pedal.**

Check the throttle pedal for smooth operation. If the throttle does not operate smoothly, turn off the engine and check the cable itself for a cracked or broken casing, kinks in the casing, or fraying at the cable ends, especially where the ends of the cable 'disappear' into the cable 'outer'. If you find any of these faults, replace the throttle cable.

☐ **Job 53. Handbrake function.**

Check the function of the handbrake as described under Job 33. But this time, add a further check. An experienced mechanic will be able to engage first gear and let the clutch just a little at a time until the clutch 'bites' and strains against the hand brake - not too much; just enough to let him know that the brakes are working, and without travelling more than three or four feet (1 metre) or so. If you're not an experienced driver or mechanic and there's some risk that you might strain the car's mechanical components, try turning the engine off, pulling the handbrake on, putting the gearbox in neutral, getting out of the car - only do this on level ground! and see if you can push the car with the handbrake on. If, in the first test, the car moves blithely away, unhindered by the effect of the handbrake, or in the second, if the car moves at all, you've got major problems with the rear brakes. The most likely reason is that the brakes are 'oiled' because a brake hydraulic wheel cylinder is leaking brake fluid onto the brake shoes. This requires SPECIALIST SERVICE, unless you are an experienced mechanic. THE CAR SHOULD NOT BE DRIVEN until repairs have been carried out.

Job 54. Brakes and steering.

> **SAFETY FIRST!**
> *Only carry out the following tests in daylight, in clear dry conditions when there are no other traffic users about and no pedestrians. Use your mirrors and make sure that there is no traffic following you when carrying out the following brake tests.*

Only a proper brake tester at an MoT testing station will be able to check the operation of the brakes accurately enough for the MoT test, but you can rule out one of the worst braking problems in the following way. Drive along a clear stretch of road and, gripping the steering wheel fairly lightly between the thumb and fingers of each hand, brake gently from a speed of about 40 mph. Ideally, the car should pull up in a dead straight line without pulling to one side or the other. If the car pulls to the left (when being driven on the left-hand side of the road) or to the right (when being driven on the right-hand side of the road, such as in the USA), it might be that there is no problem with your brakes but that the camber on the road is causing the car to pull over. If you can find a stretch of road with no camber whatsoever, you may be able to try the brake test again or failing that, find a one-way-street where you can drive on the 'wrong' side of the road and see if pulling to one side happens in the opposite direction. If it does not, then you've got a problem with your brakes. Before assuming the worst, check your tyre pressures and try switching the front wheels and tyres from one side of the car to the other. If the problem doesn't go away, seek SPECIALIST SERVICE.

The second test is to ensure that the self-centring effect on the steering works correctly. If the steering stiffens up over a period of time, you can easily get used to it so that you don't notice that it doesn't operate as it should. After going round a sharp bend, the steering should tend to move back to the straight-ahead position all by itself without having to be positively steered back again by the driver. This is because the swivel pins are set slightly ahead of the centre line of the wheels so that the front wheels behave rather like those on a supermarket trolley - or at least those that work properly! If the swivel pins have become stiff internally because of rust or if new ones have been fitted badly, the steering will be stiff and no self centring will be evident. Alternatively, the steering rack could be dry due to a loss of lubricant caused by a split gaiter (see Job 34). Whichever the case, you've got a problem with the steering and should seek a little more of that SPECIALIST SERVICE, unless you're experienced enough and feel capable of diagnosing and rectifying these problems yourself, using your workshop manual.

Now, if you're ready to begin the road test proper, you can check the function of the brakes and the self-centring effect of the steering.

3,000 mile Bodywork and Interior - Around The Car

First carry out Jobs 19 to 22.

Job 55. Wash and wax the bodywork.

Wash the bodywork as described in Job. 18. Then, using a quality car wax, follow the instructions taking care not to get the wax on the windscreen or other glass.

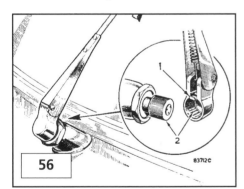

56

Job 56. Wiper blades and arms.

56. Check the operation of the windscreen wipers and correct position of 'sweep'. The wiper arms push onto splines (56.2). The Mini handbook recommends that the spring clip is depressed (56.1) but in practice, it is usually enough to fold back the arm, grasp near the splines and pull off with a slight rocking movement. Put on a smear of grease before refitting to prevent seizing up.

Job 57. Check windscreen.

Check the windscreen for chips, cracks or other damage - see *Chapter 7, Getting Through The MOT* for what is, and is not, acceptable according to UK regulations.

Job 58. Rear view mirrors.

Check your rear view mirrors, both inside and outside the car, for cracks and crazing. Also ensure that the interior rear view mirror is soundly fixed in place since they can come loose and when they do, the vibration can get so bad that you can't tell whether you're being followed by a long distance truck or one of the boys in blue!

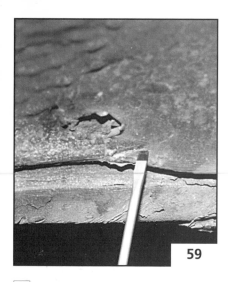

☐ Job 59. Check floors.

59. Lift the carpets to check for water accumulation beneath them, (including the boot and spare wheel well). Find and eliminate sources of water leaks before the smell of rotting carpet drives you to it - by which time the problem of rotting steel will have joined the list. Look at windscreen seals, rear door seals (where applicable) and boot lid seals. Look at door seals and window runners on sliding window models. Look for - and hope you don't find - rust holes in the floor. Leaks are best found with the inside of the car dry and, if necessary, the carpets taken out. Have somebody play a hose on one area of the car at a time whilst you go leak hunting.

☐ Job 60. Chrome trim and badges.

Rust can easily start to form behind badges and in the holes where badges are mounted. Apply water dispersant behind chrome trim and badges.

3,000 mile Bodywork - Under The Car

First carry out Job 23.

Job 61. Inspect underside.

61. When dry, inspect the underside of the car for rust and damage. Renew paint, underbody sealant and wax coating locally as necessary. This picture shows evidence of having 'bottomed' or run over something, raising the floor a little. Not dangerous in itself, but it has caused a fault in the underseal coverage. Old-fashioned bitumen type underseal goes brittle and comes loose anyway, this only exasperates the problem. Water will soon penetrate this area and form a breeding ground for corrosion. Scrape off any such loose underseal and paint on wax coating in its place, when dry.

6,000 Miles - or Every Six Months, Whichever Comes First

6,000 mile Mechanical and Electrical - The Engine Bay

First carry out Jobs 2 to 5, 25, 27, and 29 to 32.

The first part of this section is to be carried out with the engine cold, partly for safety reasons (the risks involved in handling hot components) and partly for comfort and ease of working.

☐ Job 62. Cooling system.

62. Check the cooling and heating systems for leaks and all hoses for condition and tightness. Look at the ends of hoses for leaks - check the clamps for tightness and pinch the hoses to ensure that they are not starting to crack and deteriorate. If you don't want a hose to burst and let you down in the worst possible place, change any hose that seems at all suspicious. Not easily seen is this by-pass hose (between the cylinder head and water pump) shown here for clarity on an engine removed from the car. The best way to check this hose is to grope around and feel for any leaks. If one is apparent, the job is a little outside the scope of the home tinkerer and help from a Mini specialist should be sought. Concertina replacement hoses are available but their life span is suspect. The Mini heater hose goes through the bulkhead and makes its connection inside the car, so don't overlook that check-point or you could have scalding water squirting over your ankles.

INSIDE INFORMATION: When you have to replace hoses, don't waste your time trying to undo tiresome clamps in the conventional way if it proves troublesome. The Worcester Mintro Centre simply cut through the hose clamp with a small hacksaw and then make a long-ways cut into the hose against the pipe with a sharp knife. Off pops the hose and you've saved time and those knuckles. Go easy on the pipe though, if the knife cuts too deep and scores the stub end, it could be the source of an irritating leak.

63

☐ Job 63. Coolant check.

63. Use a hydrometer to check the specific gravity of the coolant. The tester will show by way of a reading or possibly with coloured balls. If the level is below the recommended amount, top up the system with anti-freeze until the correct specific gravity is obtained. Of course the engine will have to be run for the newly introduced anti-freeze to mix thoroughly otherwise a false reading will be obtained. If you have any doubt over the period that the old mix has been in the car, drain and refill with fresh. The recommended concentration is between 25%-50% depending on the winter temperature.

INSIDE INFORMATION: Some owners think that there is little to be gained by using anti-freeze in their cast-iron block Mini all the year round, particularly in those parts of the world where frost is not a problem. Wrong! Anti-freeze to a concentration of 25% not only gives protection against around -13 degrees Celsius (9 degrees Fahrenheit) of frost. It also helps to stop the radiator from clogging and so helps to keep the car running cooler in hot weather. Owners also forget that there is aluminium in, or rather on, the Mini engines (water pump etc.) and that it does corrode. Use anti-freeze and cut down on one common problem - heater valve corrosion, seizure and failure. A 50% mix, by the way, gives protection down to -36 degrees Celsius (-33 degrees Fahrenheit).

☐ Job 64. Heater valve.

64. Talking of which (Job 63), check the heater control valve for correct operation and lubricate, with releasing fluid if seized, with thin oil if working. Ditto the control cable, adding oil or fluid to the ends before working the heater control open and shut a good few times. See how this neglected example is beginning to fur up.

64

☐ Job 65. Check water pump.

Check water pump for leaks - the first sign of failure - by looking for water leaks or stains around the spindle. So hidden is the pump, that it will be almost impossible to do this visually, so the best you can do is to feel around the pump and check your hands for water. Any problems should be dealt with by your Mini centre as much has to be dismantled to get access to the pump. Early models have a grease nipple fitted to the centre spindle. Take this opportunity to pump a little grease into the spindle.

66

☐ Job 66. Accelerator controls.

66. Lubricate the accelerator control linkage at the carburettors and the throttle pedal pivot, in the recesses of the footwell. Use spray-on lubricant or white silicone grease, so as not to spoil your shoes with dripping oil - it stains leather!

Job 67. Dynamo bearings.

67. Lubricate the dynamo bearings with a few drops of oil (early models). Take care not to over oil or to get oil inside the body of the dynamo.

67

Job 68. Fit new spark plugs.

OPTIONAL: Fit new spark plugs, with the correct gaps. Some leave spark plugs in place for longer, but there is always the risk that the insulation will break down and lower the performance of the plug even though it may appear perfect in every other way. Never leave them in place for longer than 12,000 miles, even with regular cleaning and adjustment as described elsewhere in the schedule.

When fitting new spark plugs, ensure that the threads in the cylinder head are free enough for you to screw the plugs in as far as their seats - engine cold - by hand. If there are any obstructions, SPECIALIST SERVICE – have your Mini specialist chase out the threads with a proper spark plug thread chasing tool.

Job 69. Distributor advance.

SAFETY FIRST!
You will have to reach into a running engine to carry out this check. Keep away from the fan and drive belts and from the car's ignition system. Wear no jewellery or loose clothing.

69. Check that the distributor vacuum advance is operating. The mechanism can seize or the rubber diaphragm that responds to the pressure in the inlet manifold can split. If the vacuum advance does not work properly, engine performance and economy will suffer. Run the engine until it is warm enough to run off the choke and then, with the engine still running, pull the vacuum advance hose or pipe off the distributor vacuum unit and seal the hose end with your thumb. Reconnecting the hose should cause a slight increase in the engine speed - not to be confused with the effect of covering and uncovering the hose end, which may also separately cause a change in engine speed.

INSIDE INFORMATION: An even more reliable way to check the vacuum advance is to disconnect the vacuum advance hose from its connection on the carburettor and wipe clean the end of the hose. Now suck on the hose, while you watch the contact breaker points (distributor cap removed). If the vacuum unit is in good condition you'll feel resistance when you suck, and also see the distributor baseplate and points move slightly. If nothing happens, the rubber diaphragm inside the vacuum unit is likely to be punctured (a common occurrence) and a new vacuum unit will be needed. Refit the vacuum hose and distributor cap after making this check.

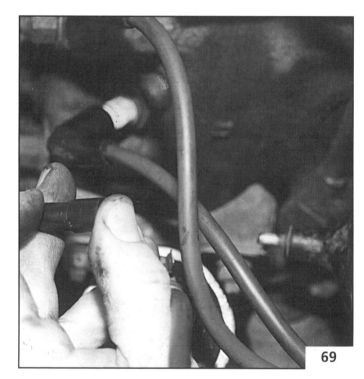

69

Job 70. Renew cb points.

70A. As contact breaker (cb) points are used they invariably deteriorate causing a steady and indiscernible drop off in performance. They're such inexpensive items that it is best to renew them at 6,000 miles although not necessarily at six months since it is purely use that causes them to deteriorate. Job 26 showed how to remove the distributor cap and rotor arm and also illustrated the later type Lucas distributor type 45D. The earlier 25D4 distributor shown in the line drawing 70A has only minor differences from the later type. Some models between '78-80 and '82 on used a Ducellier distributor, recognisable by an external condenser. All 1.3 models from '91 on use electronic ignition making distributor points redundant.

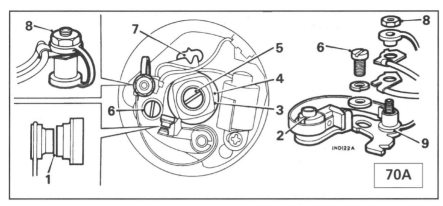

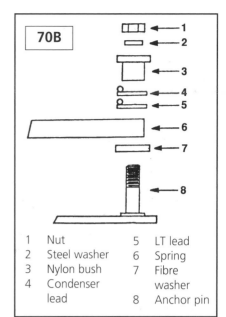

70A

70B

1	Nut	5	LT lead
2	Steel washer	6	Spring
3	Nylon bush	7	Fibre
4	Condenser		washer
	lead	8	Anchor pin

70B. You can see here the correct order in which the various connections have to be made to the new distributor points as they are fitted. Note that the fixing screws (70A.6) and its two washers are not supplied with the new points but are part of the distributor fittings, so be careful not to lose this screw!

70C. Another inexpensive item and one that is well worth fitting every time points are renewed is the condenser (70A.10). Note that the fixing screw that holds the condenser in place is even smaller and easier to lose than the screw for fixing the points in place. If you have straight-point and cross-point magnetic screwdrivers, use them for removing these screws but do take care not to drop the washers.

70D. Alternatively, unscrew the nut (70A.8) holding the wiring connections to the contact breaker points ...

70E. ... and remove those connections.

70F. Then undo the screw (70A.6) with your screwdriver ...

70G. ... whilst lifting the old contact breaker points and take off the points, screw and washers all in one piece (70A.9). Similarly, when removing the condenser, lift the condenser as you remove the screw and take the screw out of the hole in the end of the condenser when you've got it safely out of the engine bay.

70C

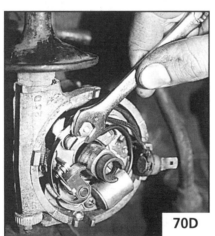

70D

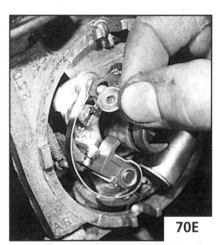

70E

70F

70G

Before offering up the new points, remember to lubricate the distributor as shown in Job 26. and in addition, put a very small amount of grease on the pivot post shown in Job 26 (26B.4).

70H. The only significant difference when fitting points to the later Lucas 45D distributor is the simpler method of connecting the internal wiring. There's no tiny nut and washers to lose since the connections just clip together.

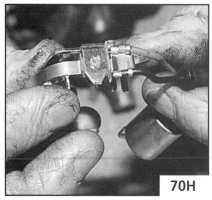

70H

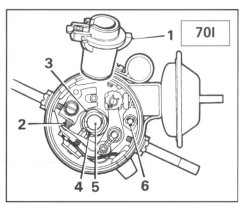

70I

70I. The Ducellier distributor, although common in basic detail to the Lucas, varies in its construction. To remove the cb points, first disconnect the low tension lead at its terminal. Then, with a screwdriver or long nose pliers, remove the circlip and washer securing the moving contact assembly to the pivot base and lift away (Job 70H). A single screw with its vulnerable washer retain the adjustable contact breaker plate to the base plate. Take great care not to drop the screw and washer, lift the plate away. Adjustment of the cb points is carried out in the same way as the Lucas type. Changing the condenser couldn't be easier. A single screw holds it in its external position and the wire is a straightforward push connecter. *Illustration, courtesy Rover Cars.*

Follow the instructions under Job 26 for setting the points gap.

SPECIALIST SERVICE: Have a specialist with the appropriate equipment check the voltage drop between the coil CB terminal and the earth (ground).

Now run the engine to ensure that the ignition has been reassembled correctly. If it hasn't the car probably won't start at all or will run very badly - if so check that the plug leads are in the correct order, that the points are opening correctly and that the electrical connections to the points are correct - it's all too easy to fit one of the wires to the insulator on the points incorrectly!

☐ Job 71. Check ignition timing.

71A. To establish the precise point at which a spark occurs we need to open a window into the ignition circuit and find out exactly when the points begin to open, breaking the circuit and sending a spark down a plug lead to the spark plug. It is essential that this spark occurs at precisely the right time. There is a timing scale on later models (shown in degrees before top dead centre BTDC) and a notch on the crankshaft pulley (radiator end).

71B. On earlier cars, an access hole to the flywheel shows the scale on the flywheel (or torque convertor) ...

71C. ... but this can only be seen with a mirror.

71D. On early models this is the inspection plate position and the timing marks on the flywheel *(Illustration, courtesy Rover Cars)*. Each engine type is designed to run efficiently at a predetermined point (see **Chapter 8, Facts and Figures** for the ignition timing setting for your car). The pointers on the timing scale equate to 4 degrees BTDC until '0' is reached (TDC). Looking through the access hole on the flywheel cover of manual transmission models (71A.4), the mark 1/4 indicates TDC with preceding marks 5 and 10 providing the BTDC points. On automatics, the marks are at 5 degree intervals either side of the '0' TDC mark, again viewed through the flywheel cover access hole. It is possible to check the timing without the engine running using a simple test light (although post '76 models cannot, as no figures are quoted).

71A

71B

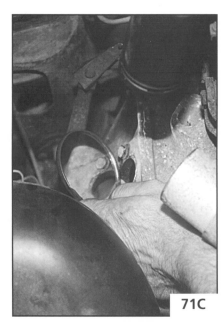

71C

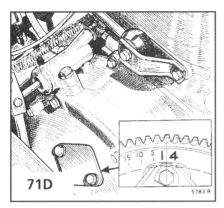

71D

71E

but by far the most efficient method is to use a stroboscopic timing light (71A.5). This device clips over the plug lead to No. 1 cylinder with two other leads to the battery. When the engine runs, a 'stroboscopic' light is triggered at the precise point in unison with the spark plug. Aiming the light at the timing marks has the effect of freezing the action long enough to

check that the pulley notch and timing pointer meet. To further enhance this, a little dab of white paint (typist's correction fluid works perfectly and dries immediately) on the appropriate pointer or flywheel/torque converter scale, and on the pulley notch, will make the marks even more visible. Disconnect the vacuum advance pipe at the distributor and plug the pipe end. The engine should be set to run at the correct rpm figure as shown in *Chapter 8, Facts and Figures* (most timing lights incorporate an RPM indicator) and the timing checked.

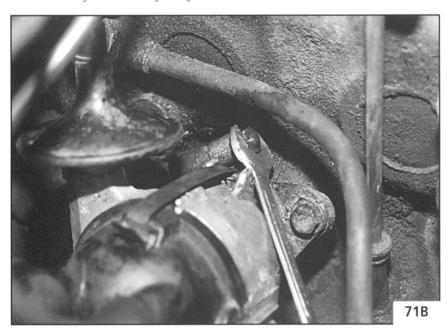

71B

71F. Should the timing need to be corrected, the distributor needs to be rotated to alter the point at which the contact breaker points just open. At the base of the distributor is a clamp plate with either a locknut or retaining bolt. Loosen this, not too much so that the distributor is sloppy but enough that it will move when pressure is applied. Start the engine and let it run until it settles at the correct rpm (adjust if necessary). Aim the timing light at the timing marks and rotate the distributor (the direction depends on whether the timing is out in retard or advance) until the timing marks align. Switch off the engine and re-tighten the clamp. Re-check the timing again in case the act of tightening the clamp has disturbed the distributor. Alternatively, on the Lucas 25D4 distributor, provision is made for fine adjustment by means of the knurled vernier adjustment wheel opposite the vacuum unit. Turning this adjustment wheel has the same affect as rotating the distributor body and is useful when the timing is only out by a couple of degrees. *For safety's sake, don't try adjusting the distributor with the engine running!*

Job 72. Valve clearances.

Adjust the valve clearances, with the engine hot or cold but not in-between (although it will be jolly uncomfortable to work on when hot!). It is best to remove the spark plugs (ignition off) when carrying out this work since the engine will have to be turned over several times. Now this is tricky. Turn the engine by moving the fan belt with your hands, gearbox in neutral (take care not to trap your hands in the pulleys). Valve clearances are made when each valve is in the fully closed position. The only way of being sure of this is to follow a mechanics rule that says that each valve will shut when another particular valve is fully open - and you can see that they are open because the rocker will have 'rocked', pushing the valve right down. Try it; it's easy!

INSIDE INFORMATION: Mechanics know which valves relate to which by the 'rule of nine' for 4-cylinder engines. Here's how it works: The Mini engine has two valves per cylinder making eight in all. Start counting from the radiator end. When No. 1 is open, No. 8 will be closed (1+8=9). When No. 2 is open, No. 7 will be closed (and 2+7=9 again, of course). Follow the rule right through and you can identify which 'open' valve relates to which 'fully closed' one, right the way through.

72. Setting tappets is easy! First, remove the rocker cover secured by two bolts that pass through grommets and lift away. Undo the locknut, which allows the centre screw to be moved in and out, changing the valve clearance. Use a feeler gauge to establish when the gap is exactly 0.012 in. (0.305mm) - it should be a tight sliding fit - and tighten the locknut as the screw is held tight. You will probably find that the last turn of the locknut also tightens the screw further, no matter how hard you hold the screwdriver. Try edging the gap open a touch to allow for the fact but check with a feeler gauge when the locknut is tight to ensure that the gap is correct.

72

☐ Job 73. Rocker cover gasket.

73A. Thoroughly clean the inside and fit a new gasket ...

73B. ... and grommets to the rocker cover. Don't make the common mistake of over-tightening the cover - it causes leaks - just 'nip' the nuts down onto the top of the cover.

Drive the car for several miles until it reaches its normal operating temperature. Check the rocker cover again for leaks.

73A

73B

☐ Job 74. Fit fuel filter.

SAFETY FIRST! Disconnect the battery and read the precautions given in Chapter 1, Safety First! before doing any work on the fuel system.

OPTIONAL: If your car was not fitted with a fuel filter (most Mini's weren't), you are strongly recommended to fit one. In-line filters are easily obtainable from car accessory stores - follow the fitting instructions on the pack.

☐ Job 75. Fuel connections.

75. Check the carburettor connections (and fuel filter if fitted) and fuel pipes at the front of the car, in the engine bay, for chafing, leaks and corrosion.

75

☐ **Job 76. Set carburettors.**

SAFETY FIRST! Please read the information contained in Chapter 1, Safety First! especially that relating to the safety hazards surrounding petrol (gasoline). In addition, note that you will have to run the car with the air filter(s) removed. There is the slight risk of a flashback through the carburettor(s), so don't get your face or clothing too close. Also, have a suitable workshop-sized fire extinguisher to hand, in case the worst should happen. If a fire should break out, turn off the ignition - and thus the engine and fuel pump - immediately, so that no more petrol can be pumped through. Because of the fire risk, however slight, and because of the very strong danger from exhaust fumes, carry out this next part of the work out of doors.

CARS WITHOUT EMISSION CONTROL EQUIPMENT ONLY

Many owners shy away from the idea of adjusting their own carburettors and, while they certainly look complicated, it's a job that can be carried out at home with the simplest of tools, although a couple of inexpensive special tools will make all the difference. An external tachometer and a carburettor balancer for twin carburettors are a great help. It's also important that the ignition timing is set correctly, the contact breaker points and plugs are in good shape and that the valve clearances are correct. The colour of the exhaust gives an idea if the carburettor(s) need adjustment. Light whitish grey is too weak, sooty and black to rich. A mid-grey is the ideal. You should also check that your carburettors are not too badly worn. With the air filter(s) removed, turn the butterfly until it is open and try moving the spindle on which it turns. If there is a lot of play in the spindle, consider swapping your carburettor(s) for reconditioned units - they are available from your Mini specialist, both new and reconditioned.

Excluding the newest of Mini's (SU HIF 44, 38 or fuel injection), carburation is by SU HS2 or SU HS4 types (see **Chapter 8, Facts and Figures** for your model), with twin units fitted to Mini Cooper versions. Two types of direct adjustment are possible, idle speed and mixture. One further adjuster screw sets the choke cam to increase idle speed when the choke is operated. All carburettors are adjusted in the same way. The job is done twice (one for each carburettor) on Coopers, after which, both are synchronised (easier than you think). Later cars are fitted with tamperproof seals over the idle speed screw and mixture adjusting nut. These can easily be prized away with a small screwdriver and discarded.

76A

76A. It helps to have the carburettor piston sliding up and down nicely before attempting any adjustment. Try yours, pushing your finger inside the mouth of the carburettor and lifting the piston as far as it will go. When you release the piston, it should slide down smoothly and end with a slight 'clunk'. It's worth cleaning the inside of the dashpot to help with the rise and fall of the piston. The dashpot is secured by two screws and although it will go back any way, mark the position of the dashpot to the carburettor body with a felt tip pen - things have a habit of working better the same way they came off. Lift the dashpot off the carburettor but allow the piston to fall back in place. It will do so easily as there's a big lazy spring inside. Clean the inside with engine degreaser or a carburettor cleaner available at all spares stores. Lightly oil the inside and return to the carburettor.

INSIDE INFORMATION: If your piston doesn't slide down with a smooth movement, ending in a small 'clunk', it could also be that the jet in the base of the piston is not centred correctly. This job is more than a service item and you should seek SPECIALIST SERVICE help at your Mini Centre.

SAFETY FIRST!
The Mini's carburettor(s) is situated at the back of the engine and requires you to lean across. As it will be at operating temperature, be extremely careful to avoid the hotter parts such as the exhaust manifold (situated under the carburettor and close to the mixture adjusting nut).

76B. To adjust the mixture, bring the engine to operating temperature and make sure that the choke is fully released. Early models (HS2) have a piston lifting pin at the side of the carburettor. Lifting this (about 1/32 in. (1 mm) after contact with the piston) will give an indication of the mixture. If the engine speed gains appreciably, the mixture is too rich. If it slows or stops altogether then the diagnosis is too weak. A slight increase or no change at all, is pretty well spot on.

76B

SINGLE CARBURETTORS:

76C. If adjustment to the mixture is required, rotate the jet adjustment nut (76C.2), (clockwise when viewed from below to weaken, anti-clockwise will richen) until the fastest, smoothest (fast is not necessarily smooth) engine speed is reached. Make this adjustment one flat of the nut at a time. It is quite possible that the idle speed has now altered. Turn the throttle adjusting screw (76C.4) in the appropriate direction to obtain the correct engine idle speed as given in ***Chapter 8, Facts and Figures***. Finally, adjust the fast idle screw (76C.1) by pulling the choke out about ¼ in (6mm). Then turn the fast idle screw until the engine runs at about 1,000 rpm. *Illustration, courtesy Rover Cars*

The HS2 carburettor
1   Fast-idle adjusting screw
2   Jet adjusting screw
3   Connection , control rod (auto. transmission)
4   Throttle adjusting screw
5   Piston lifting pin
6   Jet lock nut (not used for normal tuning)

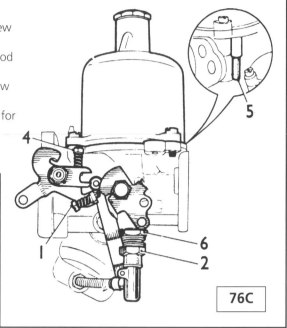

76C

76D. On later HIF carburettors, mixture adjustment is by the mixture adjustment screw (76D.1) - turn it by small increments in or out until the fastest, smoothest engine speed is obtained. Now set the idle speed using the throttle adjusting screw (76D.2). Finally adjust the fast idle speed by pulling out the choke until the arrow on the carburettor fast idle cam is aligned with the adjustment screw. Turn the adjusting screw (76D.3) as necessary to obtain the specified fast idle speed. *Illustration, courtesy Rover Cars*

76E. TWIN CARBURETTORS: There's no mystique about twin carburettors, they're just two carburettors joined by spindles to operate as one. Before any adjustments can be made, they should be freed from each other by slackening the spindle clamps on the throttle and choke linkages illustrated. (engine removed from car - you try taking a photograph behind a Mini engine in situ!)

76F. It would be really helpful to buy a carburettor balancer such as the type marketed by Gunson's used here. This accurately measures the air flow through each carburettor and takes the guess work out of the job, although a trained ear could judge the 'hiss' of the inlet air. All balancing meters fit onto the carburettor intake and measure the ingoing air velocity on a scale. First check that each carburettor is running at the same speed by placing the balancer over the intake of one carburettor, then the other. Turn the throttle adjusting screws as necessary until the intake air passing through each carburettor is the same, as indicated on the balancer scale. Once they're balanced, turn the throttle adjusting screws on both carburettors by the same amount so that the idle speed is as specified in ***Chapter 8, Facts and***

76D

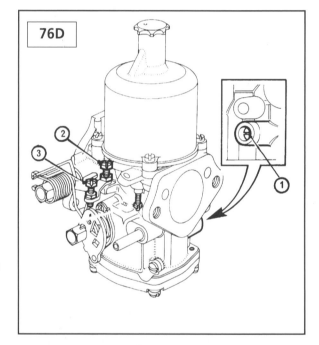

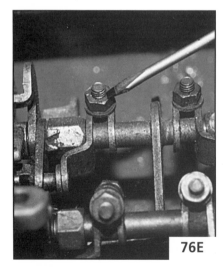

76E

76F

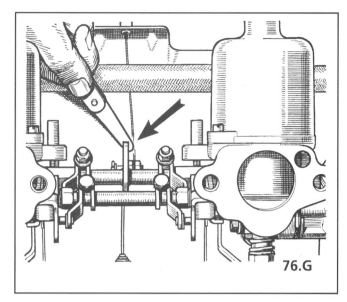

76.G

Figures. Turning both the screws by equal amounts alters the tickover while keeping the carburettors in balance. Carry out the mixture adjustments as explained in 76C. Re-check the idle speed and when satisfied, re-tighten the spindles ensuring that there is a small gap between the peg at the end of the spindle and the lower part of the fork. The gap size is not critical but that both are identical is.

76G. So that the throttle butterfly is not loaded, check that the clearance under the throttle stop is 0.012 in (0.3mm). Use a feeler gauge. *Illustration, courtesy Rover Cars.*

☐ Job 77. Exhaust emissions.

SPECIALIST SERVICE: Have a properly equipped garage carry out an exhaust gas emissions check, especially for carbon monoxide (CO) and unburned hydrocarbons. But note the comments under 'Getting Through The MOT' regarding the difficulty of persuading SU carburettors to pass the UK's emission regulations.

☐ Job 78. Check clutch return stop.

78. On all but the latest Minis, compensation for wear of the clutch friction material is taken up by adjustment of the clutch return stop situated at the very end of the engine/transmission unit on the off-side. Disconnect the clutch lever return spring and push the lever away from the engine taking up all free play and insert a 0.020 in. (0.50 mm) feeler gauge. If adjustment is needed, loosen the inner lock-nut and turn the adjuster until the correct clearance is achieved. Re-tighten the lock-nut and refit the clutch lever return spring.

6,000 mile Mechanical and Electrical - Around The Car

First, carry out Jobs 7 to 17 then 33.

☐ Job 79. Adjust headlamps.

It is possible to adjust your own headlamps but not with sufficient accuracy. Badly adjusted headlamps can be very dangerous if they don't provide you, the driver, with a proper view of the road ahead or they dazzle oncoming drivers. Older drivers·and those with poor eyesight can become disorientated when confronted with maladjusted headlights. SPECIALIST SERVICE: Have the work carried out for you by a garage with beam setting equipment. Any MoT testing station in the UK will be properly equipped.

☐ Job 80. Front wheel alignment.

SPECIALIST SERVICE: Have the front wheel alignment checked and tested. Wheel alignment will go 'out' through regular use and especially if you go over a pothole or a kerb. The car will become less stable and tyres will wear out much more quickly. This is not work that can be carried out at home. Special alignment equipment is required.

☐ Job 81. Rear ride height.
RUBBER SUSPENSION CARS ONLY

81. *INSIDE INFORMATION: Measure the rear trim (ride) height, between the centre of the rear hub to the wheel arch edge, comparing one side with the other. If they are different, it is possible that the knuckle joint at the end of the rubber cone spring has worn. SPECIALIST SERVICE: This is not work that can be carried out*

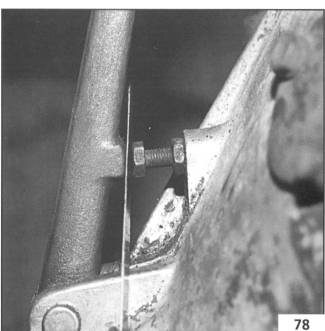

78

81

at home, visit your local Mini specialist for help.

HYDROLASTIC SUSPENSION CARS ONLY

Owners of cars fitted with hydrolastic suspension should keep a careful note on the trim (ride) height as described earlier. As the system is fully sealed requiring no maintenance, a significant drop in the ride height indicates a leak in the system. SPECIALIST SERVICE: Only a main dealer or Mini specialist will have the equipment to carry out any repairs and re-charge the system. Should the ride height be completely lost, it is permissible to drive a short distance at low speed exercising extreme care.

☐ Job 82. Front ride height.

82

82. Carry out the same instructions as in Job 81. Cars fitted with hydrolastic suspension are measured for trim (ride) height at the front. The distance between the centre of the front hub to the wheel arch edge should be 13.5 in. (343 mm) Ò 0.37 in (9.5 mm).

☐ Job 83. Check wheel nuts.

Check tightness of the road wheel nuts making sure that the nuts run freely up and down each stud. Many people over tighten wheel nuts which, in extreme cases, can be dangerous.

6,000 mile Mechanical and Electrical - Under The Car

> First carry out Jobs 34 to 46.

> **SAFETY FIRST! Raise the front of the car off the ground after reading carefully the information at the start of this chapter on lifting and supporting the car.**

☐ Job 84. Front fuel lines.

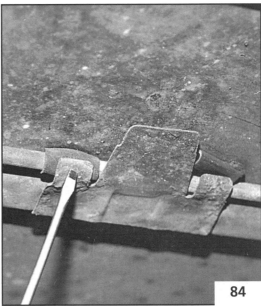

84

84. Check the fuel lines beneath the front of the car. Most corrosion takes place beneath the pipe clips where it cannot easily be seen. There should be a rubber protective sleeve between the pipe and clip as shown. That to the right has slipped and the pipe can now chafe against the clip. Moisture can rest quite happily between the rubber and the pipe doing its worst. A spray of underbody wax wouldn't come amiss here.

☐ Job 85. Front brake lines.

Check all brake lines beneath the front end of the car for corrosion - once again, especially behind pipe clips where most corrosion takes place - and check all flexible pipes for chafing and perishing.

85. *INSIDE INFORMATION: i) bend each flexible hose back on itself, especially near the unions. This will show up perishing and cracking in the pipe. ii) have an assistant press hard on the brake pedal while you look out for bulges in the flexible hoses. If you see ANY signs of weakness or deterioration in any of the pipes, stop using the car until they have been replaced.*

☐ Job 86. Exhaust manifold.

85

Check the exhaust manifold where it bolts to the downpipe, a week spot on the Mini. As the engine rocks backwards and forwards on acceleration and braking, this seal can easily be broken. Also check the front section of the exhaust pipe. Any faults can be rectified by one of the many chains of exhaust centres.

INSIDE INFORMATION: An excellent way of spotting leaks in the exhaust system is to hold a rag over the end of the exhaust pipe, while the engine is running on tickover. You'll hear any leaks loud and clear, as gases are forced through them.

Job 87. Front dampers or hydrolastic displacers.

87. Check for fluid leaks from the front dampers. If it is seeping, it will show from the top shroud. Also check the condition of the damper bushes. If they appear soft, spreading - or non-existent! - fit new ones. Faulty dampers must be replaced, always in pairs. Leaking hydrolastic displacers will normally be associated with a loss in the trim (ride) height. Any faults with the displacers is outside the normal servicing procedures and is definitely SPECIALIST SERVICE.

Job 88. Driveshaft couplings.

Early Minis used rubber driveshaft couplings to transmit the drive from the transmission to the driveshafts. As they are in direct line of fire from any oil leaks, inspect the rubber for any deterioration and check the tightness of the 'U' bolts. At the slightest sign of the rubber breaking up or perishing, have your Mini centre replace the couplings.

On automatic transmission Minis a universal joint coupling is used at the transmission end of the driveshaft. Check for wear of the couplings and check the tightness of the flange retaining bolts.

87

Job 89. Engine stabilisers.

89A. Inspect the engine stabiliser rubbers for wear by either levering with a stout screwdriver or grasping the top of the engine and rocking the unit backwards and forwards, noting any play in the rubbers. The bushes are in each end of an arm, one end of which is fixed to the cars bulkhead, the other to the engine block.

89B. Later models have a supplementary stabiliser bracket at the bottom of the engine/transmission unit. Examine these from beneath the car. Also check the bracket for cracks as this has proved to be a fairly common fault.

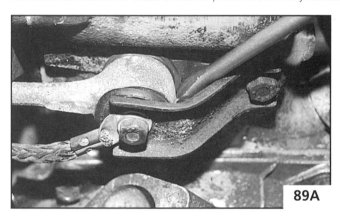
89A

89B

Job 90. Front subframe mounting rubbers.

90. The front subframe is secured to the main bodyshell by four Metalastik mounts. If these separate or split, the front end of the car will become extremely unstable and difficult to control. The mount shown here has actually parted from its metal facing and should be replaced immediately.

90

Job 91. Clutch hydraulics.

Check the clutch flexible pipe for perishing or cracks. It is unlikely that the rigid pipe will have corroded because of its location in the engine bay. Peel back the rubber boot from the slave cylinder and take a look for fluid leaks. Spotting a trickle early can save total failure later.

SAFETY FIRST! Lower the front of the car, then raise the rear of the car off the ground after reading carefully the information at the start of this chapter on lifting and supporting the car.

First carry out Jobs 47 to 49.

☐ Job 92. Check rear hub bearings.

Grasp the wheel at the top and bottom and rock it in and out checking for excess play or wear in the hub bearings. Now spin the wheel and check for any roughness which would also indicate that the bearing is on the way out. If any wear is detected, SPECIALIST SERVICE: have the bearings replaced by your Mini specialist or dealer.

☐ Job 93. Rear brake lines.

93

93. Check all the brake lines beneath the back end of the car for corrosion - once again, especially behind pipe clips where most corrosion takes place - and check all flexible pipes for chafing and perishing. This pipe had become bent and was actually touching the bracket with the cable rubbing against it each time the handbrake was applied. Very gently, it was eased out of harms way.

INSIDE INFORMATION: i) bend each flexible hose back on itself, especially near the unions. This will show up perishing and cracking in the pipe. ii) have an assistant press hard on the brake pedal while you look out for bulges in the flexible hoses. If you see ANY signs of weakness or deterioration in any of the pipes, stop using the car until they have been replaced.

☐ Job 94. Rear fuel lines.

94

94. Check the fuel pump (early models only where an electric pump is secured to the sub-frame) and fuel pipes - at the rear of the car - for chafing, leaks and corrosion. The pipe shown is beginning to rust and the protective rubber has slipped from the metal clip and is chafing against the pipe. If your fuel line is like this, have your Mini specialist replace it immediately.

☐ Job 95. Exhaust system.

95. Check the rear of the exhaust system for leaks and security of mountings.

☐ Job 96. Rear dampers or hydrolastic displacers.

95

Check for fluid leaks from the rear dampers. If it is seeping, it will show from the top shroud. Also check the condition of the damper bushes. If they appear soft, spreading - or non-existent! - fit new ones. Faulty dampers must be replaced, always in pairs. Leaking hydrolastic displacers will normally be associated with a loss in the trim (ride) height. Any faults with these is outside the normal servicing procedures and is definitely SPECIALIST SERVICE.

☐ Job 97. Check rear sub-frame mounts.

97. One of the most neglected areas beneath the Mini is the rear sub-frame mounts. Check all four, particularly around the metal where those at the front are bolted.

Lower the car to the ground.

97

6,000 mile Mechanical and Electrical - Road test

Carry out Jobs 50 to 54.

6,000 mile Bodywork and Interior - Around the Car

First carry out Jobs 18 to 22 and 55 to 60.

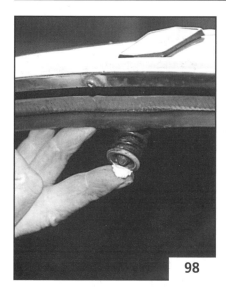
98

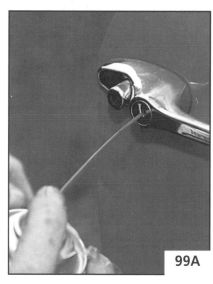
99A

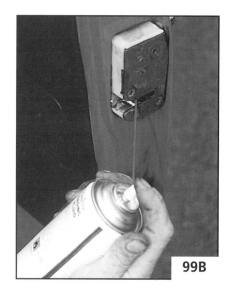
99B

☐ Job 98. Bonnet release.

98. Lubricate the bonnet release and safety catch using clean silicone grease so that you won't soil clothes when leaning into the engine bay. Lubricate the bonnet hinges too.

☐ Job 99. Door locks.

99A. Lubricate the door locks and hinges with silicone releasing fluid using an extension tube to direct the spray.

99B. Don't forget to lubricate the catch mechanisms on the doors.

99C. Also lubricate the door latches, using silicone grease where they can come into contact with clothes.

Note that early cars have external hinges. These operate by a small pin that eventually wears, allowing the door to 'drop', making it difficult to close. See your Mini specialist who can fit an oversized pin to your hinge.

☐ Job 100. Boot lock.

100A & B. Lubricate the boot lock, latch and hinges.

Do not lubricate the steering lock, except with a drop of oil on the end of a key to prevent the lock barrel from seizing.

99C

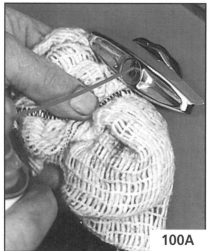
100A

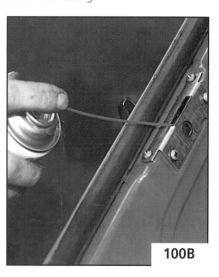
100B

☐ Job 101. Check battery connections.

Clean and grease the battery connections. Better still, use petroleum jelly or copper-impregnated grease.

Drive the car out of doors.

INSIDE INFORMATION: Despite what the manual tells you, the best way of cleaning old grease and corrosion from your battery terminals is a kettle full of water, recently boiled. Pour it slowly over each terminal and you'll see a bright, shiny surface appear from underneath the fur. Make sure that the battery caps or cover are firmly in place first. Due to the battery box construction, it may be necessary to remove the battery anyway but the hot water treatment still holds good. If the battery terminals are badly furred, it is likely that some corrosion will have taken place inside the clamps and indeed, it has been known for clamps to be almost completely eaten away inside although invisible from above. Disconnect the clamps, clean up the clamps and the outside of the terminal with a medium grit sandpaper. Apply petroleum jelly or copper-impregnated grease to the bottom of the clamp but it's best to leave the electrical connection dry and never apply ordinary grease to this area.

101

☐ Job 102. Seats and seat belts.

Check the condition and security of seats and seat belts. Tip the front seats forward and check that the seat diaphragm is intact; it has a tendency to tear from its fixings with the occupant sinking slowly to the floor. Shake each seat to check its security, pull hard on each length of belt webbing near where each section is fitted to the car, test each buckle. Check inertia reel belts. With most types, you can test by tugging; if you pull hard and quickly on the belt the reel should lock; with others the lock may only work under braking. Carry out a careful road test, in the daylight, under dry road conditions and with no other traffic or pedestrians about.

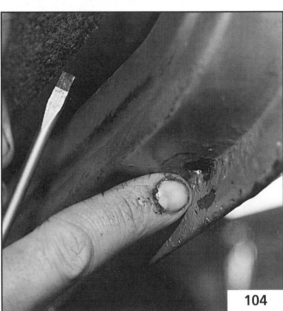

104

6,000 mile Bodywork - Under the Car

First, carry out Jobs 23 and 61.

☐ Job 103. Rustproof underbody.

Renew wax treatment to wheel arches and underbody areas. Refer to **Chapter 5, Rustproofing** for full details.

☐ Job 104. Clear drain holes.

104. Check and clear the drain holes in sills, doors, boot and those in the lower sill. This door is already showing signs of corrosion - easily avoided had the correct rust-proofing measures been taken.

12,000 Miles - or Every Twelve Months, whichever comes first

12,000 mile Mechanical and Electrical - Emission Control Equipment

To comply with the stringent overseas requirements, many Mini's were fitted with emission control equipment early in the production cycle, later to become more standardised as most markets adopted the various systems.

SPECIALIST SERVICE: Many emission control components are not serviceable without the correct specialist equipment such as a vacuum gauge, pressure gauge, exhaust gas analyser, distributor advance tester, carburettor piston loading tool and an engine oscilloscope, depending upon the model of car. Without describing every type of emission control system in detail, the following Job numbers list the components that can be tested or serviced at home. All should be carried out at the 12,000 miles/twelve months service interval.

SPARK PLUG CONDITIONS

You can learn a lot about the condition of an engine from looking at the spark plugs. The following information and photographs, reproduced here with grateful thanks to NGK, show you what to look out for.

1. Good Condition

If the firing end of a spark plug is brown or light grey, the condition can be judged to be good and the spark plug is functioning at its best.

4. Overheating

When having been overheated, the insulator tip can become glazed or glossy, and deposits which have accumulated on the insulator tip may have melted. Sometimes these deposits have blistered on the insulator's tip.

6. Abnormal Wear

Abnormal electrode erosion is caused by the effects of corrosion, oxidation, reaction with lead, all resulting in abnormal gap growth.

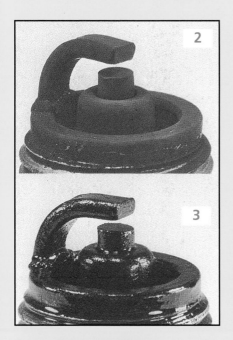

5. Normal Wear

A worn spark plug not only wastes fuel but also strains the whole ignition system because the expanded gap requires higher voltage. As a result, a worn spark plug will result in damage to the engine itself, and will also increase air pollution. The normal rate of gap growth is usually around 'half-a-thou.' or 0.0006 in. every 5,000 miles (0.01 mm. every 5,000 km.).

7. Breakage

Insulator damage is self-evident and can be caused by rapid heating or cooling of the plug whilst out of the car or by clumsy use of gap setting tools. Burned away electrodes are indicative of an ignition system that is grossly out of adjustment. Do not use the car until this has been put right.

2. Carbon Fouling

Black, dry, sooty deposits, which will eventually cause misfiring and can be caused by an over-rich fuel mixture. Check all carburettor settings, choke operation and air filter cleanliness. Clean plugs vigorously with a brass bristled wire brush.

3. Oil Fouling

Oily, wet-looking deposits. This is particularly prone to causing poor starting and even misfiring. Caused by a severely worn engine but do not confuse with wet plugs removed from the engine when it won't start. If the "wetness" evaporates away, it's not oil fouling.

12,000 MILE SERVICE

JAPANESE AND OTHER EXPORT CARS ONLY - fitted with a Crankcase Emission Valve System with Air Pump. Please note that this system will only work properly if the engine is generally kept in a proper state of tune.

☐ Job 105. Crankcase breather.

105A. Early cars are fitted with what can only be described as a token gesture emission device. Remove the spring clip and lift away the metal cover plate ...

105A

105B. ... followed by the diaphragm, metering valve and spring. Clean all the internal parts. Use methylated spirit (denatured alcohol) for the rubber parts and white spirit for the metal. INSIDE INFORMATION: If there are stuck-on deposits, try boiling the metal parts in an old saucepan first. If any parts are damaged, or if the diaphragm looks perished, replace. Reassemble, taking care that the metering valve fits correctly in its guides and that the diaphragm seats correctly.

INSIDE INFORMATION: If the breather pipes have become blocked, it is certain that the breather connections on the engine block will also be congested. As the connection is to the tappet chest behind the exhaust manifold, this really is a job for your Mini specialist.

105B

☐ Job 106. Oil filler cap.

106. Most models, including all UK cars with plastic oil filler caps, take in air through the oil filler cap, which contains an integral filter, in which case the filler cap should now be replaced. A blocked filler/filter cap will cause the car to burn oil, put out smoke and display several symptoms of a worn-out engine. A new cap comes a lot less expensive!

☐ Job 107. Inspect air injection pipes and hoses.

JAPANESE AND OTHER EXPORT CARS ONLY: Air is fed (under pressure) to the exhaust port of the combustion chamber. Inspect both the hoses and pipes for condition. If there is any doubt then have your Dealer or specialist give a second opinion and carry out any remedial work.

☐ Job 108. Renew fuel line filter.

JAPANESE AND OTHER EXPORT CARS ONLY: The fuel filter is fitted to the carburettor supply pipe and is replaced by releasing the two retaining clips. When refitting, make sure that either 'in' or a direction arrow, points towards the carburettor.

106

☐ Job 109. Renew charcoal adsorption canister.

JAPANESE AND OTHER EXPORT CARS ONLY: There are four hoses fitted to the canister; a vent hose at the bottom, two vapour hoses at the outer top and a purge hose to the centre top. With the hoses released, the retaining strap can be loosened and the canister lifted away. Note that the canister cannot be overhauled, but should be discarded and replaced. Once the new canister is fitted, detach the purge hose from the rocker cover and clean the restrictor orifice with a soft wire and finally refit.

☐ Job 110. Check operation of gulp valve.

JAPANESE AND OTHER EXPORT CARS ONLY - SPECIALIST SERVICE: As vacuum testing equipment is required for this job, consult your local Rover dealer.

☐ Job 111. Check operation of air diverter valve.

JAPANESE AND OTHER EXPORT CARS ONLY: Two types of diverter valve are fitted. One is vacuum operated and the other is cable controlled. The valve is fitted in line between the air pump and check valve. To check its operation, first disconnect the hose at the check valve end. Then run the engine and allow it to idle. Air pressure should be felt as the valve should then be open to the air pump. Opening the choke should divert the air supply and the pressure should be cut off. If air pressure can still be felt, then the valve is faulty and should be replaced. On early models, operated by cable, have your dealer check the cable adjustment before replacing the valve. Should a new valve be required, then SPECIALIST SERVICE, your Rover dealer will need to make the necessary adjustment.

Job 112. Test check valve.

JAPANESE AND OTHER EXPORT CARS ONLY: The check valve is a one way valve. To check, remove the valve from the air injection manifold by detaching the hose on one side and unscrewing the valve from the manifold union, taking care not to twist the union. Blow down the valve on each side. It should only allow air to pass through the 'inlet' end. If both sides give, then replace the valve.

Job 113. Air pump belt.

JAPANESE AND OTHER EXPORT CARS ONLY: All systems with an air pump. Change the air pump drive belt. When correctly tensioned, the belt should deflect by about 1/2 in. half way along the longest part of the belt between the pulleys. Check all pipes and connections for soundness. Replace if necessary. Faulty air pumps usually become excessively noisy. INSIDE INFORMATION: Try disconnecting the air pump belt then running the engine again, to see if the noise is actually coming from the pump. SPECIALIST SERVICE: If you suspect the air pump of any other fault, seek specialist advice for diagnosis.

Job 114. Emission system.

SPECIALIST SERVICE: Have a specialist run a check over the emission control and evaporative loss control systems for leaks and correct operation of all the valves and components that cannot be checked without specialist equipment.

12,000 mile Mechanical and Electrical - The Engine Bay

First carry out Jobs 2 to 5, 25, 27, 29 to 32, and 62 to 78.

115

118

Job 115. Oil leaks.

Check for engine/transmission oil leaks, especially around the back of the engine behind the exhaust manifold where the tappet cover can often leak, the rocker cover and the timing chain cover, especially the oil seal by the crankshaft pulley, buried down and hidden by the radiator.

115. A common and irritating source of leakage on later Minis (because it leaves oil stains on the driveway) is the gear selector rod oil seal. It's easily replaced though, by driving out the roll pin that secures the selector rod to the gear change shaft, then hooking out the old seal with a screwdriver. Carefully tap in a new seal then reconnect the selector rod.

Job 116. Clean radiator.

Carefully clean the front of the surface of the radiator fins. The Mini radiator is extremely well tucked away with cooling air fed from the engine compartment and exhausted under the front wing. You should be able to get a small soft hand brush at least part way between the inner wing and the radiator but some models are shielded making the job almost impossible.

Job 117. Grease water pump.

EARLY MODELS ONLY:
Lubricate the water pump by taking out the screw and adding a little grease.

Job 118. Remote brake servo filter.

118. Certain Mini Coopers and 1275 GT models are fitted with a remote brake vacuum servo unit. Remove the five screws securing the air valve cover and blow out the filter area (arrowed). This can be done with a foot-pump.

Job 119. In-line brake servo filter.

119. Later models are equipped with an in-line brake vacuum servo unit fitted between the engine bulkhead and the master cylinder. Ease back the rubber boot (119.1) covering the servo push-rod and hook out the old filter (119.2) from the end of the servo unit. Cut the new filter so it can be fitted over the push-rod and ease it back into the servo body. Refit the rubber boot. *Illustration, courtesy Rover Cars*

Job 120. Check cylinder compressions.

SAFETY FIRST! Take off the HT lead that runs from the coil to the distributor at the coil end so that there is no risk of sparks or an electric shock. Carry out this work outside, and make sure that the gearbox is in neutral.

SPECIALIST SERVICE: If your car is fitted with electronic ignition, do not disconnect any of the coil wiring without first ascertaining that damage will not be caused to the electronic ignition circuitry.

Ensure that the engine oil is up to the recommended level and that the engine is at running temperature. Remove the spark plugs.

120. Push the tester (or screw it in depending on type) against the first spark plug port. Have an assistant hold the throttle fully open while the engine is spun over on the starter motor and make a note of the maximum reading on the gauge. Repeat the operation on each cylinder. If the engine is in good condition, there should not be a variation of more than five to six p.s.i., or at the very most ten p.s.i., between each cylinder.

INSIDE INFORMATION: i) Low similar readings on two adjacent cylinders suggests a faulty head gasket between the two cylinders. ii) If one cylinder shows a higher reading than the other three, check the spark plug from that cylinder for oil or excessive carbon. Worn or broken piston rings could allow oil to be forced passed the rings to create a better seal - paradoxically, an indication that the engine is very heavily worn. iii) If you suspect worn or broken rings, pour a small quantity of engine oil in through the spark plug hole and carry out the check again. If there is a temporary increase in the p.s.i. reading, suspect the piston rings. If there is no increase, then the valves in the cylinder head are probably badly burnt.

12,000 mile Mechanical and Electrical - Around the Car

First carry out Jobs 7 to 17, 33, and 79 to 83.

Job 121. Test Dampers.

On non-hydrolastic cars only, bounce each corner of the car in turn in order to check the efficiency of the shock absorbers. If the car 'bounces' at all, the shock absorbers have had it. They should be replaced in pairs and efficient shock absorbers can make an enormous difference to your car's safety and handling.

Job 122. Alarm remote units.

If an alarm is fitted to your car, replace the battery in each alarm sender unit. Otherwise, as was once found by the Publisher, it is all too easy to be banished from your own car, if the battery 'dies' at an inopportune moment. Like in France. With the shops shut...

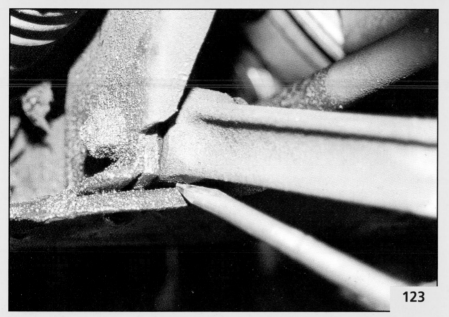

123

12,000 mile Mechanical and Electrical - Under The Car

First carry out Jobs 34 to 46, and 84 to 91.

SAFETY FIRST! Raise the front of the car off the ground after reading carefully the information at the start of this chapter on lifting and supporting the car.

☐ Job 123. Wishbone bushes.

123. Check the front suspension wishbone bushes for wear. The easiest way is to lever against the bush with a stout screwdriver. If wear is apparent, SPECIALIST SERVICE: have the job done by your Mini specialist as special tools will be involved to compress the suspension rubber cone or depressurise and repressurise the hydrolastic system.

☐ Job 124. Top and bottom swivel pins.

Check the swivel pins for wear by grasping the roadwheel at 12 o'clock and 6 o'clock and trying to rock it in and out. Any wear will be obvious as the hub assembly will visibly move and this will be from either the swivel pins or the front hub bearings. Have an assistant press down on the brake pedal, to lock the hub, and repeat the test. If the play is still there, it's the swivel hubs; if it's gone check the hub bearings.

126

☐ Job 125. Check front hub bearings.

The front hub bearings on a Mini are pre-loaded and not adjustable. Wear will be associated with a humming noise from the front, easing off when cornering with the load on the opposite wheel. With the car still raised and supported, check the front hub bearings for play. Grasp the wheel at the top and bottom (12 o'clock and 6 o'clock positions) and again side to side. Have an assistant look behind the wheel to see if there is any movement when you push and pull (you should feel it through the wheel anyway). If there is wear here, have the hub bearings replaced if necessary - SPECIALIST SERVICE.

☐ Job 126. Steering rack mountings.

126. From inside the car, lift the footwell carpets where you will see two nuts at the end of each footwell. These secure the rack and pinion steering to the bodywork. Check that the nuts are fully tightened.

☐ Job 127. Check free play.

Check free play at the steering wheel. See *Chapter 7, Getting Through The MOT* for details of what is acceptable.

☐ Job 128. Check ball joints.

Check for play in the ball joints at the inner ends of the steering rack and check the (outer) track rod ends. Turn the steering so that the road wheel turns in at the front. Grasp the wheel at both sides (as when checking the wheel bearings) and have an assistant look for play. Perhaps the easiest way is for your assistant to grip the steering at the ball joint and as you try to rock the wheel back and forth, they will 'sense' any play in the joints. SPECIALIST SERVICE: Should play be present, have the job looked at by your Mini specialist or Dealer.

Lower the front of the car to the ground.

> **SAFETY FIRST!**
> **Raise the rear of the car off the ground after reading carefully the information at the start of this chapter on lifting and supporting the car.**

Now carry out Jobs 47 to 49 and 92 to 97.

☐ Job 129. Check rear radius arm bearing.

129. To check the play in the rear radius arm bearing, grasp the rear hub and pull towards you as hard as possible (taking care not to pull too hard, bearing in mind that the car is resting on axle stands) and then push away from you all the while looking at the radius arm (at the grease point) for movement. If any is detected, SPECIALIST SERVICE have the fault remedied at your local Mini specialist.

Lower the car to the ground.

129

12,000 mile Mechanical and Electrical - Road Test

> Carry out Jobs 50 to 54.

12,000 mile Bodywork and Interior - Around the Car

> First, carry out Jobs 18 to 22, 55 to 60 and 98 to 102.

☐ Job 130. Seat runners.

Carefully lubricate the seat runners and hinges, preferably using non-staining silicone grease, taking care not to get grease onto the carpet or rubber mats.

☐ Job 131. Toolkit and jack.

Inspect the toolkit, wipe tools with an oily rag to stop them rusting and lubricate the jack, checking that it works smoothly. Also, check that the spare wheel retaining bolt hasn't rusted in. Remove it and lubricate the threads with a dab of grease.

12,000 mile Bodywork - Under the Car

> First carry out Jobs 23 and 61, bearing in mind that Job 132 entails a more thorough wax coating treatment.

☐ Job 132. Top-up rustproofing.

Renew the rust treatment to the underside of the car, box sections, sills, insides of doors and other hidden areas. Give the rear subframe a special look. See **Chapter 5, Rustproofing** for full details.

Now carry out Job 104 after Job 132.

24,000 Miles - or Every Twenty Four Months, Whichever Comes First

The Service Jobs mentioned below should be carried out in addition to the regular 12,000 mile/twelve month service Jobs shown previously. They cover the sort of areas that experience has shown can give trouble in the longer term or, in some cases, they cover areas that may prevent trouble from starting in the first place. Most of them don't appear on manufacturers' service schedules - but these are the sort of jobs which make all the difference between a car that is reliable, and one that gives problems out of the blue.

24,000 mile Mechanical and Electrical - The Engine Bay

133

☐ Job 133. Engine mountings.

133. Check the engine mountings, especially the one at the end of the clutch housing. The one illustrated is from a unit removed from the car. Try placing a jack beneath the engine/transmission unit (with a block of wood in-between) and lifting slightly. You should then be able to see if the rubber has parted from the metal. In this case, and indeed if the mounting looks swollen, replace immediately. SPECIALIST SERVICE: Replacing the mounting is an extremely awkward job. If you do not feel competent, entrust the work to your Mini specialist.

☐ Job 134. Refill cooling system.

SAFETY FIRST!
Only work on the cooling system when the engine is cold. If you try to drain a hot engine, the water inside can boil up as the pressure is removed, releasing spurting, scalding steam and water.

Every two years, the coolant should be drained from the cooling system, discarded and then replenished with fresh. This is to ensure that the anti-corrosion properties of the coolant are retained and you should also take the opportunity to flush out the cooling system, getting rid of any debris that may have built up in there. Before draining down the cooling system, turn the heater tap on to the fully open position and remove the radiator pressure cap. Now, the Mini has its own problem when draining. That is, later cars and those early cars with replacement radiators,

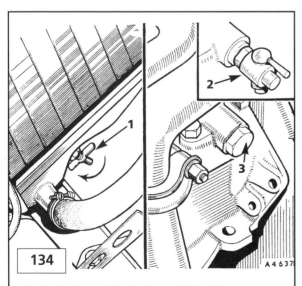

1   Drain tap or plug (early models only)
2   Drain tap in cylinder block (early cars only)
3   Drain plug in cylinder block

do not have a drain tap. Neither does the engine block, so prepare for some fiddly work. If drain taps or plugs are fitted, the one for the radiator is on the radiator base, nearest the grille (134.1) and the one for the cylinder block is on the rear of the engine just below the engine stabiliser bar (134.2 & 3). If no taps or plugs are to be found then you will have to disconnect the radiator bottom hose at its lowest point ie, the radiator connection. INSIDE INFORMATION: If the bottom hose has not been off for two years, the chances are that it will stick and need replacing anyway. Be prepared and have a spare hose on hand. Whilst the hose is tucked out of the way, it can be reached from above (just!). When you refit (or replace), arrange the clip so that it faces upwards and can be reached easily (although a long screwdriver will be needed). It will simplify the job for the next time.

Before refilling the system, flush it through. With the pressure cap still off, put a garden hose into the car's bottom hose and try to plug the gap between the small bore of the garden hose and the larger bore of the bottom hose (good luck!). Turn on the tap and run the water until no more sediment flows out of the radiator. Try turning the heater tap on and off so that the flow through the heater surges through it and helps to clear sediment from the heater itself. Now take the garden hose out and insert it into the bottom stub of the radiator and flush that out in the same way.
Illustration, courtesy Rover Cars

In order to refill the system, look in **Chapter 8, Facts and Figures** and establish the capacity of the cooling system of your car. Mix water and anti-freeze in a 50/50 solution (it can be as low as 25% but experience proves the larger mix to be on the safe side). After reconnecting the bottom hose, top-up the coolant. Replace the cap and run the engine for a minute or so checking for leaks around the disturbed hose.

INSIDE INFORMATION: Fill the system slowly and squeeze the bottom hose a few times during filling to expel any trapped air.

SAFETY FIRST!
Keep your hands away from the cooling fan and belts.

Stop the engine and carefully remove the radiator cap and top-up. Now you should run the engine, getting it up to full operating temperature and revving the engine rapidly on several occasions so that the water pump pushes the water round the system and removes any air locks. Wait for the water to cool down fully and then check the level once again. Take care to check the water levels after the first time you use the car on the road, allowing the water to cool down fully before taking the radiator pressure cap off.

Job 135. Radiator pressure cap.

Renew the radiator pressure cap - the spring weakens over time and the rubber seal perishes which reduces the pressure in the system which, in turn, allows the coolant to boil at a lower temperature.

Job 136. Drive belts.

136. Renew all drive belts (normally only one - the 'fan belt', unless the car has an air pump - JAPANESE AND CERTAIN EXPORT CARS ONLY). Another tricky job. Slacken off the dynamo/alternator (see Job. 27) and ease the belt over the pulley. It now has to be fed through the radiator fan by way of an access indent in the radiator metal cowl. Replacement is even more fiddly as once it has been fed over the fan, it then has to be fitted over the crankshaft pulley before the water pump and finally the dynamo/alternator. If you think it's bad in the workshop, try doing this on a country lane at night in the rain when your old belt broke because you couldn't face changing it at the correct service interval!.

136

24,000 mile Mechanical and Electrical - Under the Car

SAFETY FIRST!
Raise the car off the ground as necessary after reading carefully the information at the start of this chapter on lifting and supporting the car.

Job 137. Engine Flushing Oil.

On older engines, whose service history may be doubtful or unknown it's a good idea to clean out all the accumulated sludge that will have gathered in the sump over the years, using flushing oil. On later cars, that have had the benefit of regular oil changes, this operation probably won't be necessary.

After draining the engine oil in the normal way, leave the oil filter in place and refill the sump with engine flushing oil. Follow the instructions which come with the oil but in general, run the engine for a little while to allow the flushing oil to clean out the engine's oil passages. Drain off the flushing oil - don't run the car with the flushing oil in the sump; that's not what it's for! - and then carry out the remainder of **Job 38, Drain Engine Oil**, in the normal way for a regular 3,000 mile Service.

138

Job 138. Check brake discs.

To measure the brake disc thickness, undo the brake calliper retaining bolts, slide the caliper, complete with pads off the disc, and tie it up under the wheel arch using string or wire. Take care not to stretch the brake hydraulic hose.

138. Use a micrometer to measure the thickness of the brake discs. If the thickness varies considerably around various points on the discs, replace with new discs. If the discs are badly scored, you may be able to have an engineering shop skim them down for you. (Ask them to check that the discs run true before spending on them.) But you will probably find it less expensive, in the UK, to buy replacement discs.

Job 139. Brake callipers.

SAFETY FIRST! and SPECIALIST SERVICE: Obviously, a car's brakes are among its most important safety related items. Do not dismantle your car's brakes unless you are fully competent to do so. If you have not been trained in this work, but wish to carry out the work described here, we strongly recommend that you have a garage or qualified mechanic check your work before using the car on the road. See also the section on BRAKES AND ASBESTOS in Chapter 1, for further important information.

139. *INSIDE INFORMATION: See Job 44 for information on removing and replacing brake pads. When it is time to check the front pads, remove them and wash and scrape out the brake callipers, with proprietary brake cleaner, to reduce the risk of brake squeal and seizure.*

139

Job 140. Renew brake fluid.

First read the SAFETY FIRST! and SPECIALIST SERVICE note in the previous Job.

If this work is carried out in an unskilled manner, the car's braking system could fail totally. If the work is not carried out at all, the system could also fail. Brake fluid deteriorates over a period of time - it absorbs moisture from the air and then, under heavy braking, the water can turn to vapour, creating a vapour lock in the braking system and leaving the car without brakes. The brake fluid renewal procedures vary considerably between models, especially with later cars, and can be quite complex. Do not attempt to carry out this work without a workshop manual and a thorough understanding of what is involved. It may be best to invest in the cost of having this work carried out by a qualified Mini specialist or Rover dealership.

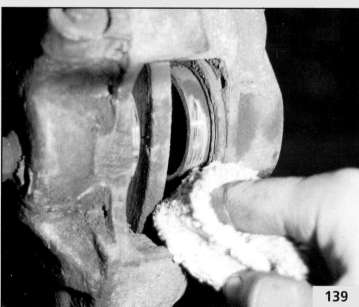

140

Job 141. Check brake drums.

First read the SAFETY FIRST! and SPECIALIST SERVICE note at the beginning of Job 139.

Examine the thickness and depth of wear of all brake drums. If excessively scored or worn thin (maximum diameter is often cast into the drum itself) or if any sign of cracking is found, replace. If you don't have sufficient experience to know whether the drums are excessively worn or not, take professional advice from a fully trained mechanic.

INSIDE INFORMATION: Tap the drum, suspended on a piece of string or a hook, to see if it rings true. If it produces a flat note, the drum is cracked and must be replaced: don't use the car until you have done so.

☐ Job 142. Brake back plates.

First read the SAFETY FIRST! and SPECIALIST SERVICE note at the beginning of Job 139.

INSIDE INFORMATION: Strip and clean the front (if applicable) and rear brake back plates using brake cleaner (to reduce risk of brake squeal and seizure) and clean out and lubricate the brake adjuster(s).

Lower the car to the ground.

24,000 mile Bodywork and Interior - Around the Car

☐ Job 143. Maintain window mechanism.

On cars with wind-up windows, lubricate the window control mechanism. Take off the door interior trim and lubricate with grease the window winder gear and in particular the channel in which the window runners move, and the toothed quadrant arm on which the winder handle operates.

143. On cars with sliding windows, examine the window channels and clean out. After a time, the windows will 'cut' down into the channel. Replacement is fairly straightforward but for some, may be SPECIALIST SERVICE.

143

☐ Job 144. Maintain door gear.

With the interior trim still off from Job 143, lubricate, with a dab of grease on each pivot point, the door lock and latch release gear, inside the door frame.

☐ Job 145. Lamp seals.

Remove the side lamp/indicator lenses, particularily the front indicators, and ensure that the seals are effective. If water has been getting in to the lights, remove the bulbs and smear a light coating of petroleum jelly inside the bulb holder to prevent rust. Renew the seal.

145

36,000 Miles - or Thirty Six Months, Whichever Comes First

Carry out all of the jobs listed under the earlier service headings before undertaking these additional tasks.

Job 146. Overhaul ignition.

Replace the distributor cap, high tension leads and condenser. Faulty leads and cap may look perfect but can be major contributors to poor starting in damp weather. Replace them before they start to go wrong and let you down! Take great care not to confuse the order in which the leads are fitted. Fold a piece of masking tape around each lead as you remove it and number it 1, 2, 3 or 4, starting from the front (radiator) end of the engine. Make a diagram of the distributor cap and write down the correct lead positions. You can now match the new to the old.

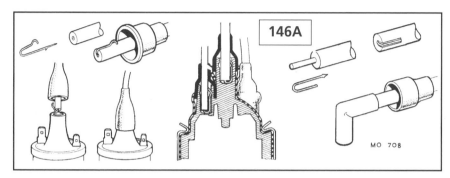

146A This is one of the later push-in types – ensure that all connections are pushed fully home. *Illustration, courtesy Rover Cars.*

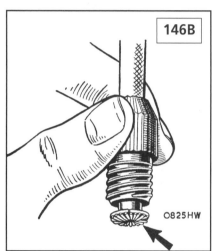

146B. Use the correct type of washer on earlier HT coil connections. Push the wires through the centre of the washer and spread them wide. *Illustration, courtesy Rover Cars.*

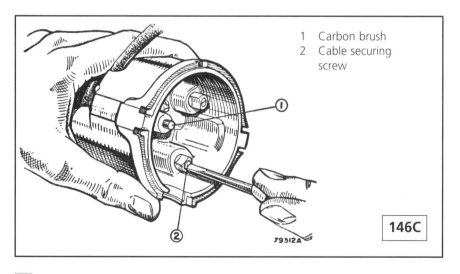

1 Carbon brush
2 Cable securing screw

146C. The HT leads are secured in the old-type of distributor cap by a screw in each contact. *Illustration, courtesy Rover Cars.*

Job 147. Clean float bowls.

Remove carburettor float covers, wriggle out the float and clean out any sediment in the bowls before it gets in the carburettor jets.

Share in the action and the spine-tingling sounds of the greatest cars ever built, from
The PP Video Collection

For motoring action, classic cars and motorsport, you can't beat high-quality video! We're proud to present the finest collection of classic and performance car video around. We are the only producers of the official Jaguar Cars film archive, and we have a licence to market the Audi AG footage and the Dunlop/SP Tyres collection, among others. As you will see, there's a fine range of classic and action motoring tapes: something for everyone, and at the right price too!

THE JAGUAR CARS ARCHIVE

Produced under licence from Jaguar Cars including the official Jaguar Cars Film Archive.

XJ220 – The Official Story	1 hr £10.99	PPV3142
The Jaguar XJR Racing Archive 1988-1992	1 hr £12.99	PPV3143
The XK120 Archive	1 hr £12.99	PPV3144
The History of Jaguar	90 min. £12.99	PPV3145
Jaguar V12 Archive	55 min. £12.99	PPV3138
Jaguar E-Type Archive	40 min. £12.99	PPV3139 and
Jaguar MK2 – Building a Legend	1 hr £12.99	PPV3117
The E-Type Jaguar Experience	1 hr £12.99	PPV3103

CLASSIC CAR TAPES

An all-round profile of some of the finest classic cars ever built. From the earliest Morgans to the latest Jaguars, including XJ220 – it's all here!

Mini The Legend	40 min. £12.99	PPV3136
Mini Goes Racing: 1961-1967	1 hr £14.99	PPV3129
Capri The Legend	30 min. £12.99	PPV3137
The MGB Experience	1 hr £12.99	PPV3101
Battle of the MGBs (Racing)	35 min. £14.99	PPV3104
The Porsche 911 Experience	1 hr £12.99	PPV3102
The Morgan Experience	1 hr £12.99	PPV3106
The VW Beetle Experience	1 hr £12.99	PPV3119
Quattro Racing in the USA	45 min. £14.99	PPV3134
Classic Car Greats! Performance Cars	50 min. £14.99	PPV3114
Ferrari Fever	1 hr £14.99	ESV4102

CLASSIC RACING "ARCHIVE" TAPES: *all filmed "at the time"... ALL the great names of motorsport, from* 1900 through to the '80s. (Also, see the Audi Quattro and race tapes listed above.)

Pre-War Motor Racing: 1900-'39	1 hr £12.99	PPV3105
Motor Racing '50s Style: '57 & '58	70 min. £14.99	PPV3115
Motor Racing '60s Style: '61 & '62	1 hr £14.99	PPV3107
Motor Racing '60s Style: '63 & '64	1 hr £14.99	PPV3108
Motor Racing '60s Style: '60 & '67	1 hr £14.99	PPV3109
Autocross '60s Style	1 hr £14.99	PPV3110
Motor Racing '70s Style: '70 & '71	1 hr £14.99	PPV3121
Prod. Car Racing: '73, '74 & '75	1 hr £14.99	PPV3127
Classic Saloon Car Action '70s	1 hr £14.99	PPV3128
The Phil Hill Story	30 min. £12.99	PPV3146

CLASSIC RACING – THE RETROSPECTIVES: *great events, rerun in later years with original cast of courses, cars and, often, the drivers themselves.*

Mille Miglia 1994	1 hr £12.99	ESV4108
Mille Miglia 1993	90 min. £14.99	ESV4106
Targa Tasmania 1994	90 min. £12.99	ESV4108
Carrera Panamericana 1990	1 hr £14.99	ESV4105
Vintage Formula Ones at the Nurburgring '88	1 hr £12.99	ESV4104

Vintage Racing Greats! – The Best of VSCC Events

1965 and 1966	1 hr £14.99	PPV3111
1969 and 1972	1 hr £14.99	PPV3112
1973 and 1974	1 hr £14.99	PPV3113

BARC PRODUCTION CAR RACING All the cut and thrust of Fast Production racing cars – the cars we can all identify with – at speeds we can only dream of!

Production Car Championships:

1993	1 hr £12.99	PPV3135
1992	1 hr £10.99	PPV3124

1991	1 hr £10.99	PPV3125
1990	1 hr £10.99	PPV3126
1989 Prod. Car 25-hour Race	1 hr £9.99	PPV3123

OTHER TITLES

Off-Road Driving School	1 hr £12.99	PPV3133
Classic Bike Action '53 & '64	1 hr £14.99	PPV3130
Motorcycle Racing Greats	1 hr £14.99	PPV3116
Skill-Guide to Gas Welding	1 hr £14.99	PPV3118
European Truck Trial 1994	55 min. £12.99	ESV4109
European Truck Trial 1993	55 min. £12.99	ESV4107
Trams, Tracks & Trolleys	1 hr £12.99	PPV3141
Steam Across Tasmania	2 hrs £14.99	PPV3147
Steam Across the EBR	90 mins. £14.99	PPV3148
Classic 'Bike Grand Prix 1994	1 hr £12.99	ESV4110

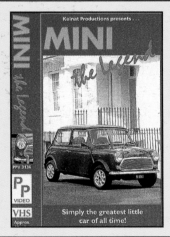

Mini – The Legend

Produced by Kelnat Productions. This video takes an affectionate look at the Mini's sporting heritage and includes interviews with Paddy Hopkirk and John Cooper. There's also up-to-date production line footage of the latest Mini Cooper and Cabriolet being built and driven off the line.

40 minutes. Price £12.99 + £1.50 P&P.

Mini goes Racing

Produced by David Roscoe. This video covers the golden years of Minis racing on circuit and grass. Some of the best known drivers, such as Paddy Hopkirk and Christabel Carlisle are seen in ding-dong competition. The racing is competitive and David Roscoe captures brilliantly the excitement, the interest and the zany humour of this racing era.

One hour. Price £14.99 + £1.50 P&P.

WHAT THE PAPERS SAY!

"Plenty of fascinating material for owners and enthusiasts alike." – **Practical Classics**

"A new temptation for Classic car enthusiasts." – **Garage News**

"Plenty of action footage from road and track both modern and vintage." – **Cars and Cars Conversions**

"The enthusiast tapes are everything you have always wanted to know and each has a history of the car." – **Auto Express**

"A lot of useful information is crammed into these watchable and well-made videos." – **Popular Classics**

CHAPTER 4
REPAIRING BODYWORK BLEMISHES

However well you look after your car, there will always be the risk of car park accident damage - or even worse! The smallest paint chips are best touched up with paint purchased from your local auto. accessory shop. If your colour of paint is not available, some auto. accessory shops offer a mixing scheme or you could look for a local paint factor in Yellow Pages. Take your car along to the paint factor and have them match the colour and mix the smallest quantity of cellulose paint that they will supply you with.

Larger body blemishes will need the use of body filler. You should only use a filler with a reputable name behind it, such as Isopon P38 Easy Sand and that's what we used to carry out this repair.

SAFETY FIRST!
Always *wear plastic gloves when working with any make of filler, before it has set. Always wear a face mask when sanding filler and wear goggles when using a power sander.*

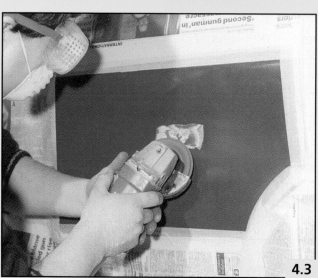
4.1

4.2

4.3

4.1 The rear of this car has sustained a nasty gash - the sort of damage for which you will certainly need to use body filler.

4.2 The first stage is to mask off. Try to find "natural" edges such as body mouldings or styling stripes and wherever you can, mask off body trim rather than having to remove it.

4.3 Isopon recommend that you remove all paint from the damaged area and for about 1 in. around the damaged area. Roughen the bare metal or surface with coarse abrasive paper - a power sander is best - and wipe away any loose particles. If you have access to professional spirit wipe, so much the better and the whole area should now be wiped down. If not, wipe over the area with white spirit (mineral spirit) and then wash off with washing-up liquid in water - *not* **car wash detergent.**

REPAIRING BODYWORK BLEMISHES

4.4 Use a piece of plastic on which to mix the filler and hardener, following the instructions on the can.

4.4

4.5 Mix the filler and hardener thoroughly until the colour is consistent and no traces of hardener can be discerned. It's best to use a piece of plastic or metal rather than cardboard because otherwise, the filler will pick up fibres from the surface of the card.

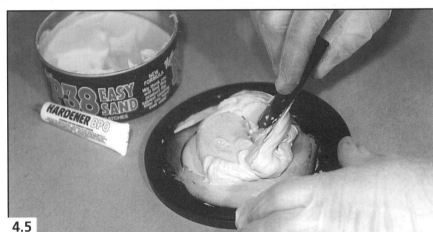

4.5

4.6 You can now spread the filler evenly over the repair.

4.7 If the damage is particularly deep, apply the paste in two or more layers, allowing the filler to harden before adding the next layer. The final layer should be just proud of the level required, but do not overfill as this wastes paste and will require more time to sand down. *(Courtesy Isopon)*

4.7

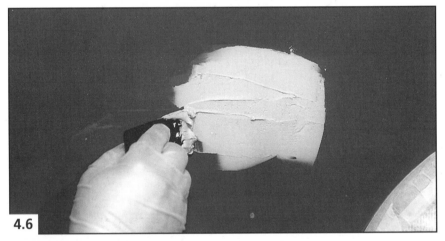

4.6

4.8 It is essential when sanding down that you wrap the sanding paper around a flat block. You can see from the scratch marks that the repair has been sanded diagonally in alternate directions until the filler is level with the surrounding panel but take care not to go deeply into the edges of the paint around the repair.

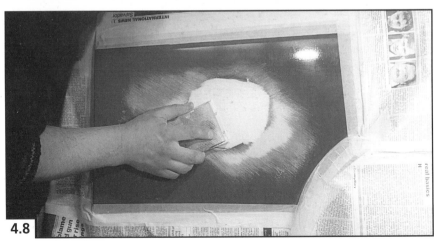

4.8

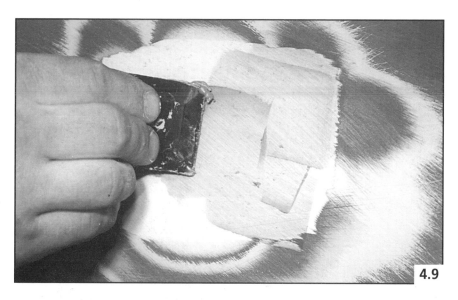

4.9 There will invariably be small pin holes even if, as in this case, the right amount of filler was applied first time. Use a tiny amount of filler scraped very thinly over the whole repair, filling in deep scratches and pin holes and then sanding off with a fine grade of sand paper - preferably dry paper rather than wet-or-dry because you don't want to get water on to the bare filler - until all of the core scratches from the earlier rougher sanding have been removed.

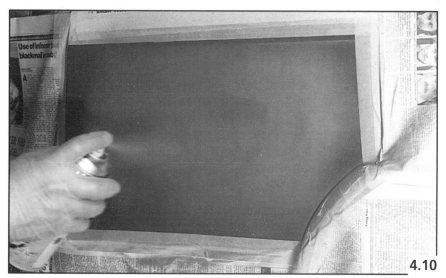

4.10 You can now use an aerosol primer to spray over the whole area of the repair but preferably not right up to the edges of the masking tape ...

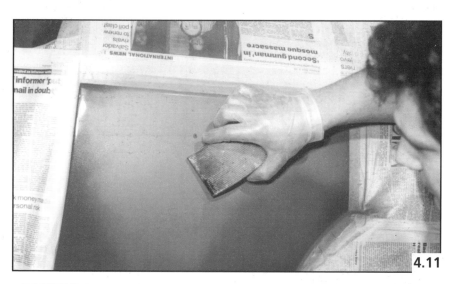

4.11 ... and you can now use wet-or-dry paper, again on a sanding block, to sand the primer paint since the Isopon is now protected from the water by the paint. If you do apply paint right up to the edge of the tape, be sure to 'feather' the edges of the paint, once it has dried off thoroughly (usually next day) so that the edges blend in smoothly to the surrounding surface, with no ridges.

SAFETY FIRST!

Always wear an efficient mask when spraying aerosol paint and only work in a well-ventilated area, well away from any source of ignition, since spray paint vapour, even that given off by an aerosol, is highly flammable. Ensure that you have doors and windows open to the outside when using aerosol paint but in cooler weather, close them when the vapour has dispersed otherwise the surface of the paint will "bloom", or take on a milky appearance. In fact, you may find it difficult to obtain a satisfactory finish in cold and damp weather.

4.12 Before starting to spray, ensure that the nozzle is clear. Note that the can must be held with the index finger well back on the aerosol button. If you let your finger overhang the front of the button, a paint drip can form and throw itself on to the work area as a paint blob. This is most annoying and means that you will have to let the paint dry, sand it down and start again.

4.13 One of the secrets of getting a decent coat of paint which doesn't run badly is to put a very light coat of spray paint on to the panel first, followed by several more coats, allowing time between each coat for the bulk of the solvent to evaporate. Alternate coats should go horizontally, followed by vertical coats as shown on the inset diagram.

4.14 If carried out with great care and skill, this type of repair can be virtually invisible. After allowing about a week for the paint to dry, you will be able to polish it with a light cutting compound, blending the edges of the repair into the surrounding paintwork.

4.12

Do note that if your repairs don't work out first time and you have to apply more paint on top of the fresh paint that you have already used, allow a week to elapse otherwise there is a strong risk of pickling or other reactions taking place. Also note that a prime cause of paint failure is the existence of silicone on the surface of the old paint before you start work. These come from most types of polish and are not all that easy to remove. Thoroughly wipe the panel down with white spirit before starting work and wash off with warm water and washing-up liquid to remove any further traces of the polish and the white spirit - but don't use the sponge or bucket that you normally use for washing the car otherwise you will simply introduce more silicones onto the surface!

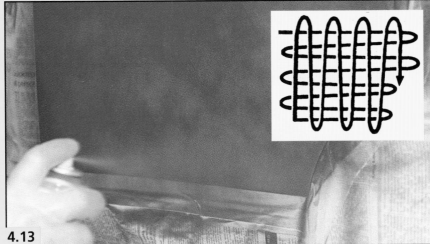

4.13

4.15 We are grateful to W. David & Sons Ltd, the makers of Isopon for their assistance with this section of the book and to CarPlan for their supply of the aerosol paints featured here. Isopon P38 is available in several different sizes of container and can easily be matched to the size of the repair that you have to carry out and all of the products shown here are readily available from high street motorists' stores.

4.14

4.15

CHAPTER 5 - RUSTPROOFING

When mechanical components deteriorate, they can cost you a lot of money to replace. But when your Mini's bodywork deteriorates it can cost you the car, if the deterioration goes beyond the point where the car is economic to repair. However, time and money spent on servicing and maintaining your car's bodywork will save you even more money in the long run than that spent on its mechanical components. You may have noticed several places in *Chapter 3, Service Intervals Step-by-Step* where checking the car's underbody and topping up its rust preventative treatment is called for. Here's how to carry out that preventative treatment in the first place and, of course, how to reapply it when the time comes. Please remember, however, that early and late models of Mini may have a few 'access' holes (they weren't put there for that, of course) in different places, so it isn't necessarily possible to be specific about which cars have to be drilled and which use existing holes.

Do take note of the fact that in Britain, the Automobile Association has carried out research into rustproofing materials and has found that inadequately applied materials do more harm than good. It appears that a car's body panels are forever in the process of rusting unless there is a barrier in place to keep out the air and moisture which are necessary to help the rusting process along. However, if that barrier is inefficiently applied, the rusting process seems to concentrate itself on the areas where the rustproofing is missing which speeds up the rusting and makes it worse in those areas. So do take great care that you apply the rustproofing materials used on your car as thoroughly as possible. It's not a question of quantity; more a question of quality of application - reaching every part of the car with a type of rustproofing fluid that "creeps" into each of the seams, into any rust that may have already formed on the surface and using an applicator that applies the fluid in a mist rather than in streams or blobs which unfortunately is all that some of the hand applicators we have seen seem to do.

Also, you should note that the best time to apply rustproofing materials to your car is in the summer when the warmer weather will allow the materials to flow better inside the hidden areas of the car's bodywork and, just as importantly, the underside of the car and the insides of the box sections will be completely dried out. In spite of what anyone says, you are better off applying rust preventative materials when the car is dry than when it is wet.

SAFETY FIRST!
Wear gloves, a face mask and goggles when applying rustproofing materials. Keep such materials away from your eyes but if you do get any into your eyes, wash out with copious amount of cold water and, if necessary, seek medical advice. All rustproofing materials are flammable and should be kept well away from all sources of ignition, especially when applying them. All such materials are volatile and in vaporised form are more likely to catch fire or explode. Do bear in mind that, if any welding has to be carried out on the car within a few months of rustproofing materials being injected into it, you must inform those who are carrying out the welding because of the fire risk. Cover all brake components with plastic bags so that none of the rustproofing material can get on to the brake friction materials and keep well away from the clutch housing and from exhaust manifold and system. Always carry out this work outside since the vapour can be dangerous in a confined space.

INSIDE INFORMATION: i) All electric motors should be covered up with plastic bags so that none of the rustproofing fluids get into the motors (these include power windows and power aerials) and all windows should be fully wound up when injecting fluid inside the door panels. ii) Ensure that all drain channels are clear (see Job 104 in **Chapter 3, Service Intervals Step-by-Step**) so that any excess rustproofing fluid can drain out and also check once again that they are clear after you have finished carrying out the work to ensure that your application of the fluid has not caused them to be clogged up, otherwise water will get trapped in there, negating much of the good work you have carried out.

☐ Job 1. Wash Underbody

You will need to wash the underside of the car before commencing work, scraping off any thick deposits of mud with a wooden scraper and also removing loose paint or underseal beneath the car. Here you can see a power washer being used - very efficient, but you'll have to leave the car for about a week in warm dry weather so that it dries out properly underneath. Some garages have car washing equipment on the forecourt that enables you to wash underneath the wheel arches where, of course, most of the heavy mud resides. All of the better rustproofing materials manufacturers make two types: one which is "thinner" and is for applying to box sections and another one which is tougher for applying to the undersides of wheel arches and anywhere that is susceptible to blasting from debris thrown up by the wheels.

Job 2. Equipment

Gather together all the materials and equipment you will need to carry out the work. Bear in mind the safety equipment you will need - referred to in Safety First! - see above. You will also need lifting equipment and axle stands - see **Chapter 1, Safety First!** for information on raising and supporting a car above the ground and also the Introduction to **Chapter 3, Service Intervals Step-by-Step**, for the correct procedures to follow when raising your car with a trolley jack. You will need copious amounts of newspaper to spread on the floor because quite a lot of the fluid will run out of the car and you may need to park your car over newspaper for a couple of days after carrying out this treatment. A combination of a large plastic sheet and newspaper works extremely well. Do remember that the vapour given off will continue for several days and you would be best parking the car out of doors for about a week after carrying out the work shown here. Probably the best known makes of rust preventative fluid in the UK are Waxoyl and Dinitrol. The later product came out top in a survey carried out by Practical Classics magazine and they also have the advantage that they produce an inexpensive application gun which does a proper job of atomising the fluid and putting a thorough misting inside each enclosed box section. If you don't own a compressor, you will have to hire one in order to power the Dinitrol applicator but the results will be better than can be obtained with any hand operated applicator. (Courtesy Frost Auto Restoration Techniques)

AROUND THE CAR

Job 3. Chrome Trim

Some rustproofing fluids are available in aerosol form and since they generally contain thinner fluid, they are probably best for injecting behind chrome trim such as the body mouldings on the Clubman Estate, which are particularly prone to rust on the steel panel where the securing clips hold the moulding. All Minis have some form of trim to 'decorate' the body seam. Water creeps in behind and starts the corroding process, this example shows the beginning.

Also remember to treat behind each of the bumpers and the insides of the over riders since all are particularly susceptible to corrosion.

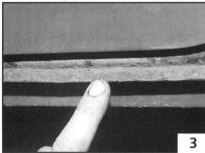

Job 4. Inside Doors

To do this job properly, you will have to remove the door trim although some firms, such as Before'n After Prestige featured here, drill a hole or utilise an existing hole, and bung it later, if necessary, with a rubber grommet. By taking the door trim off, you can see most of the areas and be confident that you get maximum coverage. Here (4A), the door trim is being eased back to gain better access. Although by using a flexible extension (4B), the direction of spray can be manipulated.

Job 5. Boot Lid and Rear Doors

You'll be able to get behind the supporting ribs in the boot lid and rear doors, although in the latter case, you will have to remove the trim panels. Ensure that the fluid is injected in vaporised form all along the inside of the pressings, especially the lower edges.

Job 6. Bonnet

There's little of a Mini bonnet and it has proved to be quite resilient over the years. Possibly the Clubman is a little more vulnerable. There are plenty of areas where you can insert a lance to ensure full coverage.

Job 7. Sills and Cross-member

As with most cars, the Mini's sills are essential to the strength of the car so it's important that you understand where they go. They are simple structures, but take time to work out their construction. Use every access point you can point a lance at. The lower seat belt mounting bolt provides a perfect entry point.

> **SAFETY FIRST!**
> **Do make sure that the seat belt bolt is replaced and fully tightened.**

However, it will be necessary to drill a hole (7A) to get access to the centre of the sill. Make sure that you clean away all swarf from the drilling and that you have the right sized grommet to match the size of the hole drilled. There is a cross-member where the seat hinges, and hole (7B) has thoughtfully been provided (although not for this purpose). Give the inside a thorough dowsing. The sill will need to be attacked from underneath as well. There are many of these drain pressings and all provide good access. At the end of each sill is a small hole blocked with a grommet (7C). Whip that out and give the inside a good dose - this

7A

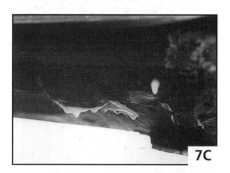

7B

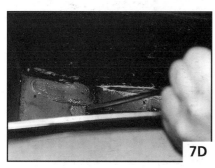

7C

7D

8

is the area in front of the rear sub-frame mount. Remove the lower trim inside the rear side panel pocket (a difficult shot but it does show the area) and make the best of a small hole provided (7D).

☐ Job 8. Door Hinge Posts

These are vertical box sections located behind the front wings. Peel back the carpet on the inner wheel arch and drill a hole into the door post (again, make sure that you have the right size of grommet for the drill), clearing away the swarf from the drill.

☐ Job 9. Front Bulkhead

There is an access point behind the dash sides where you can carry the penetration deeper although this is going to be messy. This continues the hinge post and invades the front bulkhead too.

☐ Job 10. Door Shut Pillars

One of the best vantage points here is through an opening behind the post. If your car does not feature this hole, then it's back to the drill.

☐ Job 11. Boot Floor

To avoid creating a sticky mess, it's best not to apply rustproofing materials over the whole of the boot floor, just over the seam edges. As the fuel tank occupies one side of the car (both sides in the case of the Cooper), you really have to get a flexible lance right down the back. Don't forget the box section where the boot hinges from. Depending on your model of Mini, you may have to drill a hole.

BENEATH THE CAR

☐ Job 12. Front Wheel Arches

Be extremely careful around the front nearside inner wing as the area is vented for air exit from the radiator. To get rustproofing fluid onto the radiator fins would have disastrous results. In this shot (actually unseen), a protective cardboard sheet has been secreted behind the vent panel and firmly fastened in place. It's no good just pushing a piece of card down expecting it to protect, the force of the nozzle will push it away and find a route to the radiator. Spray every part, particularly around the headlamps and the section behind the door post. The heavier type of fluid can be used on this application.

☐ Job 13. Front Valance

Beneath the front of the car, behind and below the bumper is an open valance and box section that secures the front sub-frame. Get into every crevice and give a liberal coating.

☐ Job 14. Rear Wheel Arches

This is a similar panel to that of the front wheel arch (Job 12), although of course, there is no worry about the radiator.

☐ Job 15. Rear Valance

This is a little more vulnerable than the front valance as it acts as a collection point for all the dirt and mud. It's access is very easy, so apply fluid to the entire area particularly the top seam.

☐ Job 16. Front Subframe

It is rare for a front subframe to 'rot out'; maybe stray engine oil protects it. Nonetheless, give it due protection.

☐ Job 17. Rear Subframe

If you do nothing else on a Mini, at least protect the rear subframe. It is possibly one of the most vulnerable areas on the car. In the picture (17A) you can see how the original paint is already beginning to fade from the outer edges. This one has been saved in time. There are many access holes (17B) to reach every point of its fairly intricate construction. Get right into the area between the rear bodywork and the front of the subframe.

☐ Job 18. Under Floor

Most of the underside of the Mini is of flat construction. Use the heavier black fluid to cover this area.

9

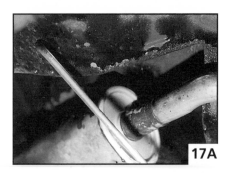

17A

Job 19. Engine Bay

INSIDE INFORMATION: i) Some car manufacturers coat the engine bay and the engine with protective clear (or yellow) wax when it is new. The wax is then washed off with a steam cleaner or with degreaser every two or three years and fresh wax applied. This makes the engine look dingy but protects metal surfaces against corrosion, screws against seizure, and helps to keep rubber supple. Provided that you kept the wax off manifolds, radiators and any other very hot areas and away from any cylinder - covering each item individually with taped-on plastic bags should do it - you could preserve the components in your engine bay in the same way. Check that the makers of whichever rustproofing fluid you select don't recommend against using their product for this purpose.

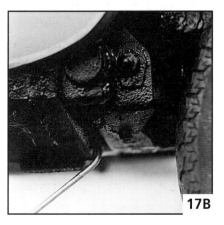

Job 20. The Mess

Its a mucky job but somebody has to do it. Using a large plastic sheet contains all the mess in one area that can be easily gathered together when the job is done.

17B

10

These sketches gives an idea (in the shaded areas) of where to apply the rustproofing for the best effect. Use this as a guide during your application. *(Courtesy of Car Mechanics Magazine)*

11

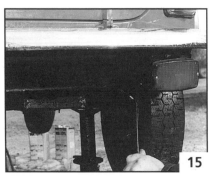

12

INSIDE INFORMATION: i) Most rustproofing fluids have the consistency of cold porridge. It can be diluted with white spirit but by far the best way is to warm it up a little. Place the can in a bucket and fill the bucket with boiled water. The rustproofing fluid will then reach a workable fluidity. It gets a little monotonous because as the water cools, so the fluid thickens. The only remedy being a change of water. NEVER heat up pressurised containers, such as aerosols, however! ii) Always buy any blanking grommets you may want to use - a dozen or so is usually enough - before you drill any holes in the car's underbody. As there are fewer sizes of grommets than drills, it's best to match the drill bit to the grommet size.

19

20

15

CHAPTER 6 - FAULT FINDING

This Chapter aims to help you to overcome the main faults that can affect the mobility or safety of your car. It also helps you to overcome the problem that has affected most mechanics – amateur and professional – at one time or another... Blind Spot Syndrome!

It goes like this: the car refuses to start one damp Sunday morning. You decide that there must be no fuel getting through. By the time you've stripped the fuel pump, carburettor, fuel lines and "unblocked" the fuel tank, it's time for bed. And the next day, the local garage finds that your main HT lead has dropped out of the coil! Something like that has happened to most of us!

Don't leap to assumptions: if your engine won't start or runs badly, if electrical components fail, follow the logical sequence of checks listed here and detailed overleaf, eliminating each "check" (by testing, not by "hunch") before moving on to the next. Remember that the great majority of failures are caused by electrical or ignition faults: only a minor proportion of engine failures come from the fuel system, follow the sequences shown here – and you'll have better success in finding that fault.

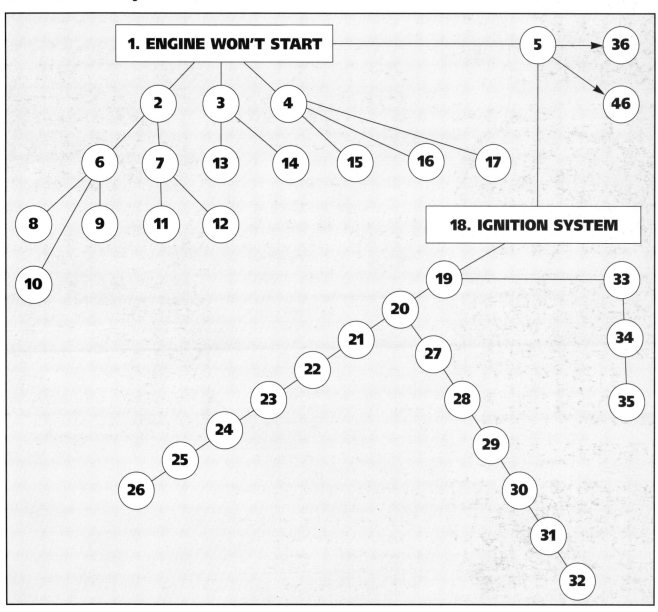

Before carrying out any of the work described in this Chapter please read carefully Chapter 1 Safety First!.

1. ENGINE WON'T START.

2. Starter motor doesn't turn.

3. Starter motor turns slowly.

4. Starter motor noisy or harsh.

5. Starter motor turns engine but car will not start.

6. Is battery okay?

7. Can engine be rotated by hand?

8. Check battery connections for cleanliness/tightness.

9. Test battery with voltmeter.

10. Have battery 'drop' test carried out by specialist.

11. If engine cannot be rotated by hand, check for mechanical seizure of power unit, or pinion gear jammed in mesh with flywheel - 'rock' car backwards and forwards until free, or apply spanner to square drive at front end of starter motor.

12. If engine can be rotated by hand, check for loose electrical connections at starter, faulty solenoid, or defective starter motor.

13. Battery low on charge or defective - re-charge and have 'drop' test carried out by specialist.

14. Internal fault within starter motor - e.g. worn brushes.

15. Drive teeth on ring gear or starter pinion worn/broken.

16. Main drive spring broken.

17. Starter motor securing bolts loose.

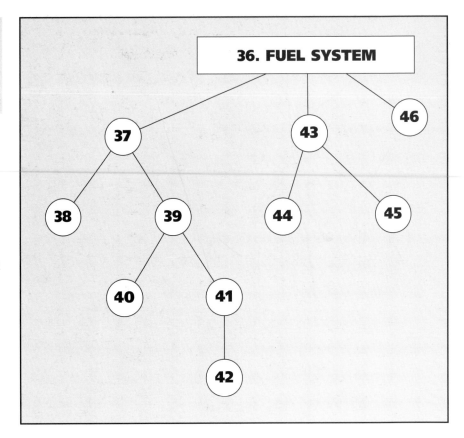

18. IGNITION SYSTEM.

19. Check for spark at plug (remove plug and prop it with threads resting on bare metal of cylinder block). Do not touch plug or lead while operating starter.

20. If no spark present at plug, check for spark at contact breaker points when 'flicked' open (ignition 'on'). Double-check to ensure that points are clean and correctly gapped, and try again.

21. If spark present at contact breaker points, check for spark at central high tension lead from coil.

22. If spark present at central high tension lead from coil, check distributor cap and rotor arm; replace if cracked or contacts badly worn.

23. If distributor cap and rotor arm are okay, check high tension leads and connections - replace leads if they are old, carbon core type suppressed variety.

24. If high tension leads are sound but dirty or damp, clean/dry them.

25. If high tension leads okay, check/clean/dry/re-gap sparking plugs.

26. Damp conditions? Apply water dispellant spray to ignition system.

27. If no spark present at contact breaker points, examine connections of low tension leads between ignition switch and coil, and from coil to contact breaker (including short low-tension lead within distributor).

28. If low tension circuit connections okay, examine wiring.

29. If low tension wiring is sound, is condenser okay? If in doubt, fit new condenser.

30. If condenser is okay, check for spark at central high tension lead from coil.

31. If no spark present at central high tension lead from coil, check for poor high tension lead connections.

32. If high tension lead connections okay, is coil okay? If in doubt, fit new coil.

33. If spark present at plug, is it powerful or weak? If weak, see '27'.

34. If spark is healthy, check ignition timing.

35. If ignition timing is okay, check fuel system (see 36).

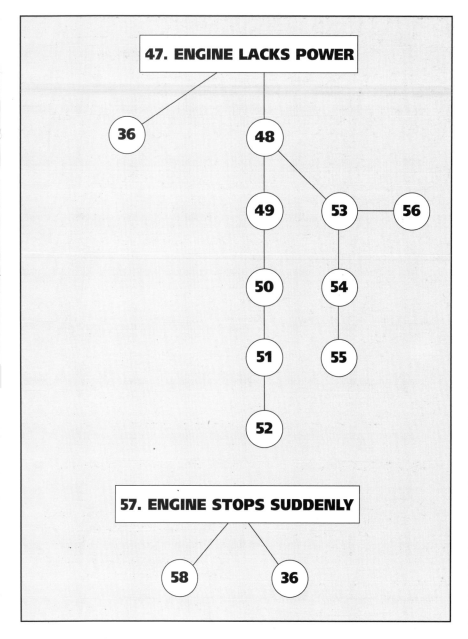

44. If the spark plugs are fuel-soaked, check that the choke linkage operates as it should and is not jammed 'shut'. Other possibilities include float needle valve(s) sticking 'open' or leaking, float(s) punctured, carburettors incorrectly adjusted or air filter totally blocked.

45. If the spark plugs are dry, check whether the float needle valve(s) are jammed 'shut'.

46. OTHER POSSIBILITIES. Severe air leak at inlet manifold gasket or carburettor gasket(s). Incorrectly set valve clearances. Leaking brake servo hose and/or connections.

47. ENGINE LACKS POWER.

48. OTHER POSSIBILITIES. Before following the rest of this sequence check that, if your car's carburation or fuel injection has an air inlet connected to a heater chamber on the exhaust manifold that: i) the pipe is in place and not split and, ii) any thermostatic valve or flap is operating correctly. If not the car can stop and restart intermittently because of inlet icing.

49. Engine overheating. Check temperature gauge for high reading.

50. Check for loss of coolant - WAIT UNTIL ENGINE HAS FULLY COOLED BEFORE ATTEMPTING TO REMOVE RADIATOR CAP. USE RAG TO PROTECT HANDS WHEN RELEASING CAP, AND KEEP FACE WELL CLEAR IN CASE COOLANT SPRAYS OUT. If low on coolant, check hoses and connections, water pump and cylinder block for leaks. Rectify and top up system.

51. If coolant level okay, check oil level. BEWARE - DIPSTICK AND OIL MAY BE VERY HOT.

52. If oil level okay, check for slipping fan belt, blocked radiator core/air grille, thermostat jammed 'shut', coolant hose obstructed, cylinder head gasket 'blown' (look for signs of mixing of oil and coolant), partial mechanical seizure of engine, blocked or damaged exhaust system.

53. If engine temperature is normal, check cylinder compressions.

54. If cylinder compression readings low, add a couple of teaspoons of engine oil to each cylinder in turn, and repeat test. If readings don't improve, suspect burnt valves/seats.

36. FUEL SYSTEM

Check fuel system for fuel at feel pipe to carbs. (Disconnect pipe and turn ignition 'on' very briefly, ensuring pipe is aimed away from hot engine and exhaust components).

37. If no fuel present at feed pipe, is petrol tank empty? (Rock car and listen for 'sloshing' in tank, as well as looking at gauge).

38. If tank is empty, replenish!

39. If there is petrol in the tank but none issues from the feed pipe, check for a defective fuel pump. (With outlet pipe disconnected AND AIMED AWAY FROM PUMP AND HOT EXHAUST COMPONENTS, ETC., turn ignition 'on' - pump should 'click' – or crank engine (later models with

mechanical pump) and fuel should issue from pump outlet).

40. If pump is okay, check for blocked filter or pipe, or major leak in pipe between tank and pump, or between pump and carb.

41. If the filter is clean and the pump fails to operate, check for 12 volts at electrical supply to pump (with ignition 'on').

42. If 12 volts evident at pump supply, check for sticking and/or dirty pump contact points. Tapping pump with a spanner may re-start it to 'get you home'; cleaning or replacing points is long-term answer.

43. If fuel is present at carburettor feed pipe, remove spark plugs and check whether wet with unburnt fuel.

55. If compression readings improve after adding oil as described, suspect worn cylinder bores, pistons and rings.

56. If compression readings are normal, check for mechanical problems, for example, binding brakes, slipping clutch, partially seized transmission, etc.

57. ENGINE STOPS SUDDENLY

58. Check in particular for electrical disconnections, running out of fuel, blown fuse protecting petrol pump, and for sudden ingress of water/snow onto ignition components, in adverse weather conditions.

59. Go to 5 and follow subsequent checking sequence.

60. LIGHTS FAIL

61. Sudden failure. Check fuses.

62. If all lamps affected, check switch and main wiring feeds.

63. If not all lamps are affected, check bulbs on lamps concerned.

64. If bulbs appear to be okay, check bulb holder(s), local wiring and connections.

65. If bulb(s) blown, replace!

66. Intermittent operation, flickering or poor light output.

67. Check earth (ground) connections(s).

68. If earth(s) okay, check switch.

69. If switch okay, check wiring and connections.

70. HORN FAILURE

71. If horn does not operate, check fuse, all connections and cables. Remove horn cover and check/clean contact breaker points with fine file, wiping clean with petrol-dampened rag. Check current consumption - should be 3.5 amps if all is well.

72. If horn will not stop(!), check for earthing of horn button or cable between button and horn unit.

73. FUEL GAUGE

74. Gauge reads 'empty' - check for fuel in tank.

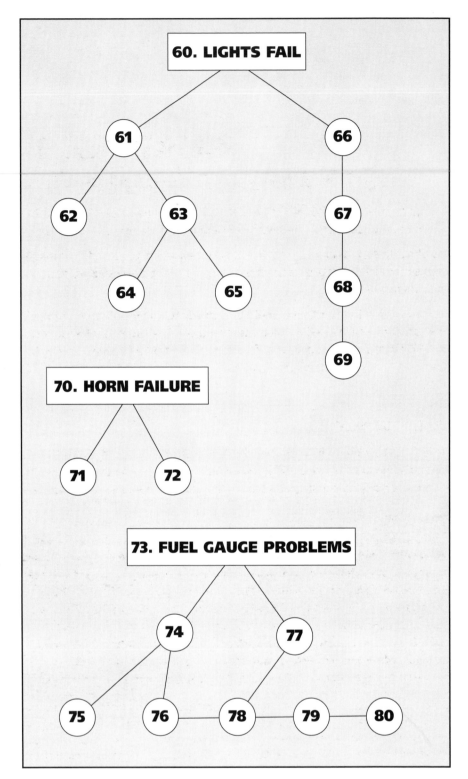

75. If not fuel present, replenish!

76. If fuel is present in tank, check for earthing of wiring from tank to gauge, and for wiring disconnections.

77. Gauge permanently reads 'full', regardless of tank contents. Check wiring and connections between tank sender unit and gauge.

78. If wiring and connections all okay, sender unit/fuel gauge defective.

79. With wiring disconnected, check for continuity between fuel gauge terminals. Do NOT test gauge by short-circuiting to earth. Replace unit if faulty.

80. If gauge is okay, disconnect wiring from tank sender unit and check for continuity between terminal and case. Replace sender unit if faulty.

CHAPTER 7
GETTING THROUGH THE MOT

Taking your beloved Mini for the annual MoT test can be rather like going to the dentist - you're not sure what to expect and the result could be painful - not only to your pocket! However, it needn't be like that...

This Chapter is for owners in Britain whose cars need to pass the 'MoT' test. The Test was first established in 1961 by the then-named Ministry of Transport: the name of the Test remains, even though the name of the government department does not!

The information in this Chapter could be very useful to non-UK owners in helping to carry out a detailed check of a car's condition - such as when checking over a car that you might be interested in buying, for instance. But it is MOST IMPORTANT that UK owners check for themselves that legislation has not changed since this book was written and that non-UK owners obtain information on the legal requirements in their own territory - and that they act upon them.

PASS THE MoT!

The aim of this chapter is to explain what is actually tested on a Mini and (if it is not obvious) how the test is done. This should enable you to identify and eliminate problems before they undermine the safety or diminish the performance of your car and long before they cause the expense and inconvenience of a test failure.

SAFETY FIRST!
The MoT tester will follow a set procedure and we will cover the ground in a similar way, starting inside the car, then continuing outside, under the bonnet, underneath the car etc. When preparing to go underneath the car, do ensure that it is jacked on firm level ground and then supported on axle stands or ramps which are adequate for the task. Wheels which remain on the ground should have chocks in front of and behind them, and while the rear wheels remain on the ground, the hand brake should be firmly ON. For most repair and replacement jobs under a car these normal precautions will suffice. However, the car needs to be even more stable than usual when carrying out these checks. There must be no risk of it toppling off its stands while suspension and steering components are being pushed and pulled in order to test them. Read carefully Chapter 1, Safety First! for further important information on raising and supporting the car above the ground.

The purpose of the MoT test is to try to ensure that vehicles using British roads reach minimum standards of safety. Accordingly, it is an offence to use a car without a current MoT certificate. Approximately 40 per cent of vehicles submitted for the test fail it, but many of these failures could be avoided by knowing what the car might 'fall down' on, and by taking appropriate remedial action before the test 'proper' is carried out. It is also worth noting that a car can be submitted for a test up to a month before the current certificate expires - if the vehicle passes, the new certificate will be valid until one year from the date of expiry of the old one, provided that the old certificate is produced at the time of the test.

It is true that the scope of the test has been considerably enlarged in the last few years, with the result that it is correspondingly more difficult to be sure that your Mini will reach the required standards. In truth, however, a careful examination of the car in the relevant areas, perhaps a month or so before the current certificate expires, will highlight components which require attention, and enable any obvious faults to be rectified before you take the car for its test.

If the car is muddy or particularly dirty (especially underneath) it would be worth giving it a thorough clean a day or two before carrying out the inspection so that it has ample time to dry. Do the same before the real MoT test. A clean car makes a better impression on the examiner, who can refuse to test a car which is particularly dirty underneath.

MoT testers do not dismantle assemblies during the test but you may wish to do so during your pre-test check-up for a better view of certain wearing parts, such as the rear brake shoes for example. See *Chapter 3, Service Intervals Step-by-Step* for information on how to check the brakes.

TOOL BOX

Dismantling apart, few tools are needed for testing. A light hammer is useful for tapping panels underneath the car when looking for rust. If this produces a bright metallic noise, then the area being tapped is sound. If the noise produced is dull, the area contains rust or filler. When tapping sills and box sections, listen also for the sound of debris (that is, rust flakes) on the inside of the panel. Use a screwdriver to prod weak parts of panels. This may produce holes of course, but if the panels have rusted to that extent, you really ought to know about it. A strong lever (such as a tyre lever) can be useful for applying the required force to suspension joints etc. when assessing whether there is any wear in the joints.

You will need an assistant to operate controls and perhaps to wobble the road wheels while you inspect components under the car.

Two more brief explanations are required before we start our informal test. Firstly, the age of the car determines exactly which lights, seat belts and other items it should have. Frequently in the next few pages you will come across the phrase "Cars first used ..." followed by a date. A car's "first used date" is either its date of first registration, or the date six months after it was manufactured, whichever was earlier. Or, if the car was originally used without being registered (such as a car which has been imported to the U.K. or an ex-H.M. Forces car etc.) the "first used date" is the date of manufacture.

Secondly, there must not be excessive rust, serious distortion or any fractures affecting certain prescribed areas of the bodywork. These prescribed areas are load-bearing parts of the bodywork within 30 cm (12 in.) of anchorages or mounting points associated with testable items such as seat belts, brake pedal assemblies, master cylinders, servos, suspension and steering components and also body mountings. Keep this rule in mind while inspecting the car, but remember also that even if such damage occurs outside a prescribed area, it can cause failure of the test. Failure will occur if the damage is judged to reduce the continuity or strength of a main load-bearing part of the bodywork sufficiently to have an adverse effect on the braking or steering.

The following notes are necessarily abbreviated, and are for assistance only. They are not a definitive guide to all the MoT regulations. It is also worth mentioning that the varying degrees of discretion of individual MoT testers can mean that there are variations between the standards as applied. However, the following points should help to make you aware of the aspects which will be examined. Now, if you have your clipboard, checklist and pencil handy, let's make a start...

THE 'EASY' BITS

Checking these items is straightforward and should not take more than a few minutes - it could avoid an embarrassingly simple failure...

LIGHTS:

Within the scope of the test are headlamps, side and tail lights, brake lamps, direction indicators, and number plate lamps (plus rear fog lamps on all cars first used on or after 1 April, 1980, and any earlier cars subsequently so equipped, and also hazard warning lamps on any car so fitted). All must operate, must be clean and not significantly damaged; flickering is also not permitted. The switches should also all work properly. Pairs of lamps should give approximately the same intensity of light output, and operation of one set of lights should not affect the working of another - such trouble is usually due to bad earthing.

Indicators should flash at between 60 and 120 times per minute (rev the engine to encourage them, if a little slow, although the examiner might not let you get away with it!) Otherwise, renew the (inexpensive) flasher unit and check all wiring and earth connections.

Interior 'reminder' lamps, such as for indicators, rear fog lamps and hazard warning lamps should all operate in unison with their respective exterior lamps.

Headlamp aim must be correct - in particular, the lights should not dazzle other road users. An approximate guide can be obtained by shining the lights against a vertical wall, but final adjustment may be necessary by reference to the beam checking machine at the MoT station - if necessary, you may have to ask the examiner to adjust the lights so that they comply.

Reflectors must be unbroken, clean, and not obscured - for example, by stickers.

WHEELS AND TYRES

Check the wheels for loose nuts, cracks, and damaged rims. Missing wheel nuts or studs are also failure points, naturally enough!

There is no excuse for running on illegal tyres. The legal requirement is that there must be at least 1.6 mm. of tread depth remaining, over the 'central' three-quarters of the width of the tyre all the way around. From this it can be deduced that there is no legal requirement to have 1.6 mm. (1/16th in.) of tread on the 'shoulders' of the tyre, but in practice, most MoT stations will be reluctant to pass a tyre in this condition. In any case, for optimum safety - especially 'wet grip' - you would be well advised to change tyres when they wear down to around 3 mm. (1/8th in.) or so depth of remaining tread.

Visible 'tread wear indicator bars', found approximately every nine inches around the tread of the tyre, are highlighted when the tread reaches the critical 1.6 mm. point.

Tyres should not show signs of cuts or bulges, rubbing on the bodywork or running gear, and the valves should be in sound condition, and correctly aligned.

Cross-ply and radial tyre types must not be mixed on the same axle, and if pairs of cross-ply and radial tyres are fitted, the radials must be on the rear axle.

WINDSCREEN

The screen must not be damaged (by cracks, chips, etc.) or obscured so that the driver does not have a clear view of the road. Permissible size of damage points depends on where they occur. Within an area 290 mm. (nearly 12 in.) wide, ahead of the driver, and up to the top of the wiper arc, any damage must be confined within a circle less than 10 mm. (approx. 0.4 in.) in diameter. This is increased to 40 mm. (just over 1.5 in.) for damage within the rest of the screen area swept by the wipers.

WASHERS AND WIPERS

The wipers must clear an area big enough to give the driver a clear view forwards and to the side of the car. The wiper blades must be securely attached and sound, with no cracks or 'missing' sections. The wiper switch should also work properly. The screen washers must supply the screen with sufficient liquid to keep it clean, in conjunction with the use of the wipers.

MIRRORS

If your Mini was first used before 1 August, 1978, it only needs to have one rear view mirror. Later cars must have at least two, one of which must be on the driver's side. The mirrors must be visible from the driver's seat, and not be damaged or obscured so that the view to the rear is affected. Therefore cracks, chips and discolouration can mean failure.

HORN

The horn must emit a uniform note which is loud enough to give adequate warning of approach, and the switch must operate correctly. Multi-tone horns playing 'in sequence' are not permitted, but two tones sounding together are fine.

SEAT SECURITY

The seats must be securely mounted, and the frames should be sound.

NUMBER (REGISTRATION) PLATES

Both front and rear number plates must be present, and in good condition, with no breaks or missing numbers or letters. The plates must not be obscured, and the digits must not be re-positioned to form names, for instance.

VEHICLE IDENTIFICATION NUMBERS (VIN)

Minis first used on or after 1 August, 1980 are obliged to have a clearly displayed VIN - Vehicle Identification Number (or old-fashioned 'chassis number' for older cars), which is plainly legible. See **Chapter 3, Buying Spares** for the correct location on your car.

EXHAUST SYSTEM

The entire system must be present, properly mounted, free of leaks and should not be noisy - which can happen when the internal baffles fail. 'Proper' repairs by welding, or exhaust cement, or bandage are acceptable, as long as no gas leaks are evident. Then again, although common sense, if not the MoT, dictates that exhaust bandage should only be a very short-term emergency measure. For safety's sake, fit a new exhaust if yours is reduced to this!

SEAT BELTS

Belts are not needed on Minis first used before 1 January, 1965. On cars after this date - and earlier examples, if subsequently fitted with seat belts - the belts must be in good condition (i.e. not frayed or otherwise damaged), and the buckles and catches should also operate correctly. Inertia reel types, where fitted, should retract properly.

Belt mountings must be secure, with no structural damage or corrosion within 30 cm. (12 in.) of them.

MORE DETAILS

You've checked the easy bits - now it's time for the detail! Some of the 'easy bits' referred to above are included here, but this is intended as a more complete check list to give your car the best possible chance of gaining a First Class Honours, MoT Pass!

INSIDE THE CAR

☐ 1. The steering wheel should be examined for cracks and for damage which might interfere with its use, or injure the driver's hands. It should also be pushed and pulled along the column axis, and also up and down, at 90 degrees to it. This will highlight any deficiencies in the wheel and upper column mounting/bearing, and also any excessive end float, and movement between the column shaft and the wheel. Rotate the steering wheel in both directions to test for free play at the wheel rim - this shouldn't exceed approximately 13 mm. (0.5 in.), assuming a 380 mm. (15 in.) diameter steering wheel. Look, too, for movement in the steering column couplings and fasteners, and visually check their condition and security. They must be sound, and properly tightened.

☐ 2. Check that the switches for headlamps, sidelights, direction indicators, hazard warning lights, wipers, washers and horn, appear to be in good working order and check that the tell-tale lights or audible warnings are working where applicable.

☐ 3. Make sure that the windscreen wipers operate effectively with blades that are secure and in good condition. The windscreen washer should provide sufficient liquid to clear the screen in conjunction with the wipers.

☐ 4. Check for windscreen damage, especially in the area swept by the wipers. From the MoT tester's point of view, Zone A is part of this area, 290 mm (11.5 in.) wide and centred on the centre of the steering wheel. Damage to the screen within this area should be capable of fitting into a 10 mm (approx. 0.5 in.) diameter circle and the cumulative effect of more minor damage should not seriously restrict the driver's view. Windscreen stickers or other obstructions should not encroach more than 10 mm (approx 0.5 in.) into this area. In the remainder of the swept area the maximum diameter of damage or degree of encroachment by obstructions is 40 mm

(approx. 1.6 in.) and there is no ruling regarding cumulative damage. Specialist windscreen companies can often repair a cracked screen for a lot less than the cost of replacement.

☐ 5. The horn control should be present, secure and readily accessible to the driver, and the horn(s) should be loud enough to be heard by other road users. Gongs, bells and sirens are not permitted (except as part of an anti-theft device) and two (or more) tone horns (which alternate between two or more notes) are not permitted at all. On cars first used after 1 August 1973, the horn should produce a constant, continuous or uniform note which is neither harsh nor grating.

☐ 6. There must be one exterior mirror on the driver's side of the vehicle and either an exterior mirror fitted to the passenger's side or an interior mirror. The required mirrors should be secure and in good condition.

☐ 7. Check that the hand brake operates effectively without coming to the end of its working travel. The lever and its mechanism must be complete, securely mounted, unobstructed in its travel and in a sufficiently good condition to remain firmly in the "On" position even when knocked from side to side. The 30 cm rule applies in the vicinity of the hand brake lever mounting.

☐ 8. The foot brake pedal assembly should be complete, unobstructed, and in a good working condition, including the pedal rubber (which should not have been worn smooth). There should be no excessive movement of the pedal at right angles to its normal direction (indicating a badly worn pedal bearing or pivot). When fully depressed, the pedal should not be at the end of its travel. The pedal should not feel spongy (indicating air in the hydraulic system), nor should it tend to creep downwards while held under pressure (which indicates a faulty master cylinder). However, on cars fitted with a vacuum servo unit, if the pedal is depressed and held in this position while the engine is started, it should dip slightly as the engine starts. This indicates that the servo is working properly.

☐ 9. Seats must be secure on their mountings and seat backs must be capable of being locked in the upright position when a seat lock is fitted (not earliest models).

☐ 10. On Minis first used on or after 1 January 1965, but before 1 April 1981, the driver's and front passenger's seats need belts, but these can be simple diagonal belts rather than the three-point belts (lap and diagonal belts for adults with at least three anchorage points) required by later cars. (For safety's sake, however, we do not recommend this type of belt.) Examine seat belt webbing and fittings to make sure that all are in good condition and that anchorages are firmly attached to the car's structure. Locking mechanisms should be capable of remaining locked, and of being released if required, when under load. Flexible buckle stalks (if fitted) should be free of corrosion, broken cable strands or other weaknesses.

☐ 11. Check that on retracting seat belts the webbing winds into the retracting unit automatically, albeit with some manual assistance to start with.

☐ 12. Note the point raised earlier regarding corrosion around seat belt anchorage points. The MoT tester will not carry out any dismantling here, but he will examine floor mounted anchorage points from underneath the car if that is possible.

☐ 13. Before getting out of the car, make sure that both doors can be opened from the inside.

OUTSIDE THE CAR

☐ 14. Before closing the driver's door check the condition of the inner sill. Usually the MoT tester will do this by applying finger or thumb pressure to various parts of the panel while the floor covering remains in place. For your own peace of mind, look beneath the sill covering, taking great care not to tear any covering. Then close the driver's door and make sure that it latches securely and repeat these checks on the nearside inner sill and door.

Now check all of the lights, front and rear, (and the number plate lights) while your assistant operates the light switches.

☐ 15. As we said earlier, you can carry out a rough and ready check on headlamp alignment for yourself, although it will certainly not be as accurate as having it done for you at the MoT testing station. Drive your car near to a wall, as shown. Check that your tyres are correctly inflated and the car is on level ground.

Draw on the wall, with chalk:

- a horizontal line about 2 metres long, and at same height as centre of headlamp lens.

- two vertical lines about 1 metre long, each forming a cross with the horizontal line and the same distance apart as the headlamp centres.

- another vertical line to form a cross on the horizontal line, midway between the others.

Now position your car so that:

- it faces the wall squarely, and its centre line is in line with centre line marked on the wall.

- the steering is straight.

- headlight lenses are 3.8 metres (12.5 ft) from the wall.

Switch on the headlamps' 'main' and 'dipped' beams in turn, and measure their centre points. You will be able to judge any major discrepancies in intensity and aim prior to having the beams properly set by a garage with beam measuring equipment.

Headlamps should be complete, clean, securely mounted, in good working order and not adversely affected by the operation of another lamp, and these basic requirements affect all the lamps listed below. Headlamps must dip as a pair from a single switch. Their aim must be correctly adjusted and they should not be affected (even to the extent of flickering) when lightly tapped by hand. Each headlamp should match its partner in terms of size, colour and intensity of light, and can be white or yellow.

☐ 16. Side lights should show white light to the front and red light to the rear. Lenses should not be broken, cracked or incomplete.

☐ 17. Vehicles first used before 1 April 1986 do not have to have a hazard warning device, but if one is fitted, it must be tested, and it must operate with the ignition switch either on or

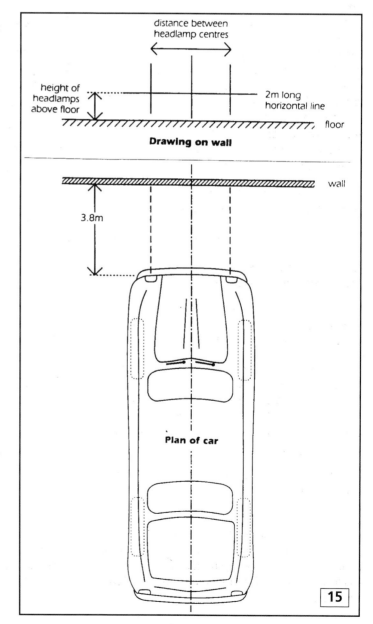

distance between headlamp centres

height of headlamps above floor

2m long horizontal line

floor

Drawing on wall

wall

3.8m

Plan of car

15

off. The lights should flash 60-120 times per minute, and indicators must operate independently of any other lights.

☐ 18. Check your stop lights. Pre-1971 cars need only one, but when two are fitted, both are tested, so you will not get away with one that works and one that doesn't! Stop lamps should produce a steady red light when the foot brake is applied.

☐ 19. There must be two red rear reflectors - always fitted by the manufacturers, of course! - which are clean, and securely and symmetrically fitted to the car.

☐ 20. Cars first used on or after 1 April 1980 must have one rear fog lamp fitted to the centre or offside of the car and, so far as fog lamps are concerned, the MoT tester is interested in this lamp on these cars only. It must comply with the basic requirements (listed under headlamps) and emit a steady red light. Its tell-tale lamp, inside the car, must work to inform the driver that it is switched on.

☐ 21. There must be a registration number plate at the front and rear of the car and both must be clean, secure, complete and unobscured. Letters and figures must be correctly formed and correctly spaced and not likely to be misread due to an uncovered securing bolt or whatever. The year letter counts as a figure. The space between letters and figures must be at least twice that between adjacent letters or figures.

☐ 22. Number plate lamps must be present, working, and not flickering when tapped by hand, just as for other lamps. Where more than one lamp or bulb was fitted as original equipment, all must be working.

The MoT tester will examine tyres and wheels while walking around the car and again when he is under the car.

☐ 23. Front tyres should match each other and rear tyres should match each other, both sets matching in terms of size, aspect ratio and type of structure. For example, you must never fit tyres of different sizes or types, such as cross-ply or radial, on the same 'axle' - both front wheels counting as 'on the same axle' in this context. Cross-ply or bias belted tyres should not be fitted on the rear axle, with radials on the front, neither should cross-ply tyres be fitted to the rear, with bias belted tyres on the front.

☐ 24. Failure of the test can be caused by a cut, lump, tear or bulge in a tyre, exposed ply or cord, a badly seated tyre, a re-cut tyre, a tyre fouling part of the vehicle, or a seriously damaged or misaligned valve stem which could cause sudden deflation of the tyre. To pass the test, the grooves of the tread pattern must be at least 1.6 mm deep throughout a continuous band comprising the central three-quarters of the breadth of tread, and round the entire outer circumference of the tyre.

All of the following photographs and information in the following 'tyres' section have been supplied with grateful thanks to Dunlop/SP Tyres.

☐ 24A. Modern cars have tread wear indicators built into the tread groves (usually about eight of them spread equidistantly around the circumference). These appear as continuous bars running across the tread when the original pattern depth has worn down to 1.6 mm. There will be a distinct reduction in wet grip well before the tread wear indicators start to show, and you should replace tyres before they get to this stage, even though this is the legal minimum in the UK.

☐ 24B. Lumps and bulges in the tyre wall usually arise from accidental damage or even because of faults in the tyre construction. You should run your hand all the way around the side wall of the tyre, with the car either jacked off the ground, or moving the car half a wheel's revolution, so that you can check

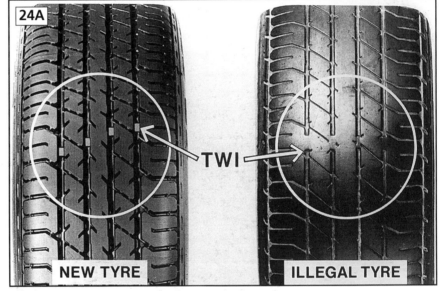

24A TWI NEW TYRE ILLEGAL TYRE

24B

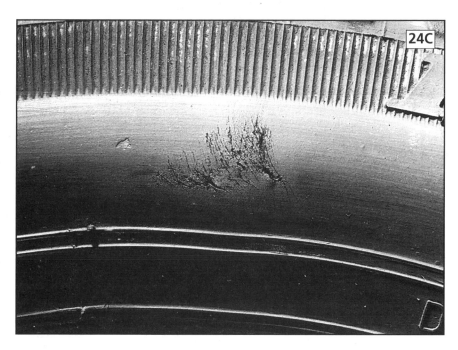

the part of the tyre that was previously resting on the ground. Since you can't easily check the insides of the tyres in day-to-day use, it is even more important that you spend time carefully checking the inside of each tyre - the MoT tester will certainly do so! Tyres with bulges in them must be scrapped and replaced with new, since they can fail suddenly, causing your car to lose control.

24C. Abrasion of the tyre side wall can take place either in conjunction with bulging, or by itself, and this invariably results from an impact, such as the tyre striking the edge of a kerb or a pothole in the road. Once again, the tyre may be at imminent risk or failure and you should take advice from a tyre specialist on whether the abrasion is just superficial, or whether the tyre will need replacement.

24D. All tyres will suffer progressively from cracking, albeit in most cases superficially, due to the effects of sunlight. If old age has caused the tyres on your car to degrade to this extent, replace them.

24E. If the outer edges of the tread are worn noticeably more than the centre, the tyres have been run under inflated which not only ruins tyres, but causes worse fuel consumption, dangerous handling and is, of course, illegal.

Over-inflation causes the centre part of the tyre to wear more quickly than the outer edges. This is also illegal but in addition, it causes the steering and grip to suffer and the tyre becomes more susceptible to concussion damage.

24F. Incorrect wheel alignment causes one side of the tyre to wear more severely than the other. If your car should ever hit a kerb or large pothole, it is worthwhile having the wheel alignment checked since this costs considerably less than new front tyres!

25. Road wheels must be secure and must not be badly damaged, distorted or cracked, or have badly distorted bead rims (perhaps due to "kerbing"), or loose or missing wheel nuts, studs or bolts.

26. Check the bodywork for any sharp edges or projections, caused by corrosion or damage, which could prove dangerous to other road users, including pedestrians.

☐ 27. Check that the fuel cap fastens securely and that its sealing washer is neither torn nor deteriorated, or its mounting flange damaged sufficiently to allow fuel to escape (for example, while the car is cornering).

UNDER THE BONNET

☐ 28. The car should have a Chassis Number or Vehicle Identification Number fitted to the bodywork. The modern VIN plate is required on all vehicles first used on or after 1 August 1980. This can be on a plate secured to the vehicle or, etched or stamped on the bodywork. Others have a more traditional 'chassis number' which the tester will need to refer to. See **Chapter 8, Facts and Figures** for information on where they should be located on your car!

☐ 29. Check the steering column clamp bolt for security by asking your assistant to turn the steering wheel from side to side while you watch what happens below.

More than 13 mm (approx. 0.5 in.) of free play, at the perimeter of the steering wheel, due to wear in the steering components, is sufficient grounds for a test failure. Note that the 13 mm criterion is based on a steering wheel of 380 mm (15 in.) diameter and will be less for smaller steering wheels. Also check for the presence and security of retaining and locking devices in the steering column assembly.

☐ 30. While peering under the bonnet check that hydraulic master cylinders and reservoirs are securely mounted and not severely corroded or otherwise damaged. Ensure that caps are present, that fluid levels are satisfactory and that there are no fluid leaks.

☐ 31. Also check that, if fitted, the servo is securely mounted and not damaged or corroded to an extent that would impair its operation. Vacuum pipes should be sound, that is, free from kinks, splits and excessive chafing and not collapsed internally.

☐ 32. Still under the bonnet have a thorough search for evidence of excessive corrosion, severe distortion or fracture in any load bearing panelling within 30 cm (12 in.) of important mounting points such as the master cylinder/servo mounting, subframe mountings etc.

UNDER THE CAR - FRONT END

SAFETY FIRST!
On some occasions there is no alternative but for your assistant to sit in the car whilst you go beneath. Therefore: 1) Place the car ramps as well as axle stands beneath the car's structure so that it cannot fall. 2) Don't allow your assistant to move vigorously or get in or out of the car while you are beneath it. If either of these are problematical, DON'T CARRY OUT THIS CHECK - leave it to your garage.

☐ 33. Have an assistant turn the steering wheel from side to side while you watch for movement in the steering rack mountings (make sure too that they are secure), and within the ball joints. While in this vicinity, visually examine the rack gaiters - no leaks should be evident, and the rubbers must not be split. The ball joint dust covers should also be in sound condition. Ensure that all split pins, locking nuts and so on are in place and correctly fastened, throughout the steering and suspension systems.

Rotate the wheels and check the condition of the driveshaft constant velocity joint boots and, where fitted, the inner rubber coupling. Check this carefully for swelling or deterioration of the rubber, and for soundness of the securing U-bolts.

☐ 34. Closely examine the suspension arm rubber bushes - these should not be severely squashed or breaking up. The rubber bushes at the front of the tie-bar also require close scrutiny. Next, employ a suitable lever (such as a long screwdriver) to test for excessive movement in each rubber bush.

☐ 35. Grasp each front wheel/tyre in turn at top and bottom, and attempt to 'rock' the wheel in and out. If more than just perceptible movement is evident at the rim, this could be due to wear in the upper and lower swivel pins, or in the front wheel bearings. Repeat the test while an assistant applies the foot brake. This will effectively lock the front hub assembly, so any movement remaining will be in the swivel pins.

☐ 36. Spin each front wheel in turn, listening for roughness in the bearings. There must be none!

☐ 37. Visually inspect the shock absorbers. They can leak and this will be apparent by signs of oil from the top shroud. Check also the rubber bushes at each end of the shock absorber. Although the rubber cone suspension can deteriorate and the lower knuckles wear, it is unlikely that it will ever be that bad to show up in the MoT. On cars fitted with hydrolastic suspension check for leaks.

☐ 38. With the wheels on the ground again, push down firmly a couple of times on each front wing of the car, then let go at the bottom of a stroke (rubber suspension cars only). The car should rise and then fall to approximately its original level. Continuing oscillations will earn your Mini a 'failure' ticket for worn front 'shockers'! Hydrolastic cars should be measured for equal left to right trim (ride) height.

UNDER THE CAR - REAR SUSPENSION

☐ 39. The rear shock absorbers (rubber suspension cars only) can suffer from leaks too - check carefully. Look for deterioration in the bushes at each end of the shock absorber. As with the front, check hydrolastic cars for leaks. While you are there, check the rear radius arms for excessive side to side movement indicating worn radius arm bearings.

☐ 40. A 'bounce' test can be carried out as for the front shock absorbers (rubber suspension cars only) as an approximate check on how efficient or otherwise the damping effect is! Once again, measure the right height on both sides, this time at the rear.

☐ 41. With the back of the car raised on axle stands (both rear wheels off the ground), rotate the rear wheels and check, as well as you can, for roughness in the bearings, just as you did at the front.

BRAKES

☐ 42. The MoT brake test is carried out on a special 'rolling road' set-up, which measures the efficiency in terms of percentage. For the foot brake, the examiner is looking for 50 per cent; the hand brake must measure 25 per cent. Frankly, without a rolling road of your own, there is little that you can do to verify whether or not your car will come up to the required figures. What you can do, though, is carry out an entire check of the brake system, which will also cover all other aspects the examiner will be checking, and be as sure as you can that the system is working efficiently.

☐ 43. The MoT examiner will not dismantle any part of the system, but you can do so. So, take off each front wheel in turn, and examine the front brake discs, if fitted (look for excessive grooving/crazing), the calliper pistons/dust seals (look for signs of fluid leakage and deterioration of the seals), and the brake pads - ideally, replace them if less than approximately 3 mm. (1/8th in.) friction material remains on each pad. At the front (if applicable) and rear, remove each brake drum and check the condition of the linings (renew if worn down to anywhere near the rivet heads), the brake drum (watch for cracking, ovality and serious scoring, etc.) and the wheel cylinders. Check the cylinder's dust covers to see if they contain brake fluid. If so, or if it is obvious that the cylinder(s) have been leaking, replace them or - ONLY if the cylinder bore is in perfect condition - fit a new seal kit.

SAFETY FIRST!
See Chapter 3, Service Intervals Step-by-Step *for important information before working on your car's brakes.*

☐ 44. Ensure that the front (if applicable) and rear brake adjusters are free to rotate (i.e. not seized!). If they are stuck fast, apply a little penetrating oil to the backs of the adjusters (but only from behind the backplate, not inside the brake drum where there would be some risk of getting oil onto the brake shoes), and gently 'work' the adjuster backwards and forwards with a brake adjuster spanner. Eventually the adjusters should free, and a little brake grease can be applied to the threads to keep them in this condition. With the rear brakes correctly adjusted, check hand brake action. The lever should rise three or four 'clicks' before the brake operates fully - if it goes further, the cable requires adjustment. Ensure too that the hand brake lever remains locked in the 'on' position when fully applied, even if the lever is knocked sideways. Especially important on Minis is to ensure that the handbrake releases fully. Check those handbrake cable swivel pivots (see Job 49 in **Chapter 3, Service Intervals Step-by Step**) they are prone to seizure thus preventing the cable from releasing fully and causing the rear brakes to bind even with the handbrake released.

☐ 45. As a very approximate check on brake operation, with the car securely supported with either both front or both rear wheels clear of the ground, get an assistant to apply the foot brake, then attempt to rotate each wheel in turn - they should not, of course, move! Repeat the test with the hand brake applied, but on the rear wheels only this time...

☐ 46. Closely check the state of ALL visible hydraulic pipework. If any section of the steel tubing shows signs of corrosion, replace it, for safety as well as to gain an MoT pass. Look too for leakage of fluid around pipe joints, and from the master cylinder. The fluid level in the master cylinder reservoir must also be at its correct level - if not, find out why and rectify the problem! At the front of the car, bend the flexible hydraulic pipes through 180 degrees (by hand) near each end of each pipe, checking for signs of cracking. If any is evident, or if the pipes have been chafing on the tyres, wheels, steering or suspension components, replace them with new items, re-routing them to avoid future problems.

☐ 47. Have an assistant press down hard on the brake pedal while you check all flexible pipes for bulges. As an additional check, firmly apply the foot brake and hold the pedal down for a few minutes. It should not slowly sink to the floor (if it does, you have a hydraulic system problem). Press and release the pedal a few times - it should not feel 'spongy' (due to the presence of air in the system). Now start the engine while the pedal is being held down. If all is well, as the vacuum servo (if fitted) starts to operate, the pedal should move a short distance towards the floor. Check the condition of the servo unit and its hoses - all MUST be sound. If there is the risk of any problems with the braking system's hydraulics, have a qualified mechanic check it over before using the car.

☐ 48. A test drive should reveal obvious faults (such as pulling to one side, due to a seized calliper piston, for example), but otherwise all will be revealed on the rollers at the MoT station...

BODYWORK STRUCTURE

A structurally deficient car is a dangerous vehicle, and rust can affect many important areas, including the rear subframe and subframe mountings, inner and outer sills and floor pans. Examine these areas carefully, since weakness here will bring MoT disappointment.

☐ 49. Essentially, fractures, cracks or serious corrosion in any load bearing panel or member (to the extent that the affected sections are weakened) need to be dealt with. In addition, failure will result from any deficiencies in the structural metalwork within 30 cm. (12 in.) of the seat belt mountings, and also the steering, subframe and suspension component attachment points. Repairs made to any structural areas must be carried out by 'continuous' seam welding, and the repair should restore the affected section to at least its original strength.

☐ 50. The MoT examiner will be looking for metal which gives way under squeezing pressure between finger and thumb, and will use his wicked little 'Corrosion Assessment Tool' (i.e. a plastic-headed hammer!), which in theory at least should be used for detecting rust by lightly tapping the surface. If scraping the surface of the metal shows weakness beneath, the car will fail.

☐ 51. Note that the security of doors and other openings must also be assessed, including the hinges, locks and catches. Corrosion damage or other weakness in the vicinity of these items can mean failure. It must be possible to open both doors from inside and outside the car.

EXTERIOR BODYWORK

☐ 52. Check for another area which can cause problems. Look out for surface rust, or accident damage, on the exterior bodywork, which leaves sharp/jagged edges and which may be liable to cause injury. Ideally, repairs should be carried out by welding in new metal, but for non-structural areas, riveting a plate over a hole, bridging the gap with glass fibre/body filler or even taping over the gap can be legally acceptable, at least as far as the MoT test is concerned.

FUEL SYSTEM

☐ 53. Another recent extension of the regulations brings the whole of the fuel system under scrutiny, from the tank to the engine. The system should be examined with and without the engine running, and there must be no leaks from any of the components. The tank must be securely mounted, and the filler cap must fit properly - 'temporary' caps are not permitted.

EMISSIONS

Oh dear! - even the thought of this aspect can cause headaches. In almost every case, a proper 'engine tune' will help to ensure that your car is running at optimum efficiency, and there should be no difficulty in passing the test, unless your engine, the distributor or the carburettor(s) really are well worn.

☐ 54. For cars first used before 1 August, 1975, the only test carried out is for 'visual smoke emission'. The engine must be fully warmed up, allowed to idle, then revved slightly. If smoke emitted is regarded by the examiner as being 'excessive', the car will fail. Often smoke emitted during this test is as a result of worn valve stem seals, allowing oil into the combustion chambers during tickover, to be blown out of the exhaust as 'blue smoke' when the engine is revved. In practice, attitudes vary widely between MoT stations on this aspect of the test.

☐ 55. For cars first used between 1 August, 1975 and 31 July, 1983, a 'smoke' test also applies. Again, the engine must be fully warmed up, and allowed to idle, before being revved to around 2,500 rpm for 20 seconds (to 'purge' the system). If dense blue or black smoke is emitted for more than five seconds, the car will fail. In addition, the exhaust gas is analysed. A maximum of 6 per cent carbon monoxide (CO), and 1,200 parts per million (ppm) hydrocarbons is allowable. The percentage of these gases are established using an exhaust gas analyser - home user versions are available for testing CO readings.

☐ 56. Normally, if the CO reading is within limits, the hydrocarbon emissions will be acceptable, but unfortunately, some cars fitted with twin S.U. carburettors (Minis included) give excessive hydrocarbon percentage readings when checked with the engine idling - EVEN WITH NEW CARBURETTORS! Therefore, many cars have been 'failing' the test and in some cases their owners persuaded to spend vast sums of money on replacement carburettors they didn't need, and which in any case had a marginal effect on the hydrocarbon levels in the exhaust gas.

Therefore, a little-known, but vitally important, exemption was introduced by the Vehicle Inspectorate Executive Agency, in the form of Special Notice SN 18/19, Section 2. Copies should have been circulated to all MoT Testing Stations, but an unofficial survey by members of a famous car club revealed that many examiners were apparently unaware of the exemption. Under this, it is acknowledged that some vehicles were unable to meet the specified hydrocarbon limit, even when new. These vehicles include early Minis, but not the fuel-injected 1.3 version of course! If such vehicles meet the CO requirements at normal idling speed, but fail the hydrocarbon test at the same speed, the hydrocarbon test should be repeated at an engine speed of 2,000 rpm, using the throttle, NOT cold start/cold running mechanisms to increase the engine speed. If the hydrocarbon reading is then 1,200 ppm or less, the car will pass. So, if you should have difficulties in this respect, politely show the examiner this book, and quote SN 18/19, Section 2!

CHAPTER 8 - FACTS AND FIGURES

This Chapter serves two main purposes. First, we aim to show you how to find the identification numbers on your car and then we show you which settings you will need to use in order to carry out servicing.

The "Data" sections of this chapter will also make essential reading when you come to carrying out the servicing on your car since you will then need to know things like tappet settings, spark plug gap, torque settings and a whole host of other adjustments and measurements that you will need to carry out in the course of maintaining your car.

1.1

1.2

SECTION 1 - IDENTIFICATION NUMBERS

1. MINI - ALL MODELS

BMC and British Leyland used to recommend that when parts were being purchased, the correct part numbers were referred to and, with the passage of time and the possibility of parts being interchanged, this becomes even more important. However, **the most important number of all is the car's chassis or VIN number** (1.1). On most models of MINI, this number can be located on a plate mounted on the bonnet locking platform.

The engine number (1.2) is stamped on a metal plate fixed to the right hand side of the cylinder block.

The commission number is stamped on a plate fixed to the bonnet locking platform.

The transmission housing number is stamped into the housing just below the starter motor.

The car body number is located on the radiator side of the bonnet locking platform.

SECTION 2 - WHAT THE NUMBERS MEAN

CHASSIS NUMBERS:

Translation of the BMC/BL codings is as follows:

   1st letter denotes make, i.e. A = Austin

   2nd letter denotes cubic capacity.

   3rd letter denotes type of bodywork, i.e. D = coupe, J = Convertible, S = 4 door saloon, 2S = 2 door saloon.

   4th prefix denotes Series, e.g. 1, 2 etc.

   5th prefix denotes differences from standard right hand drive, e.g. L = LH drive, D = De Luxe, S = Super or Super De Luxe.

Example of chassis Number: A/A2S7/12345

From 1st August 1980 Vehicle Identification Numbers replaced Chassis Numbers.

ENGINE NUMBER:

Translation of the BMC/BL codings is as follows:
First prefix group of digits:

   1st two digits denote engine capacity –
   e.g. 85 = 850 cc, 99 = 998 cc

   3rd digit denotes variation of engine type, A - Z

Second prefix group:

   The letter denotes gearbox type

   U = centrally positioned floor gearchange.

   O = overdrive.

   A = automatic.

Third prefix group of digits (in each case followed by the engine's individual serial number):

   H = High compression.

   L = Low compression.

   Example of Engine Number: 85H/U/H1234

SECTION 3 - MAINTENANCE INFORMATION AND SETTINGS

The following information will be required when carrying out certain service jobs. We have divided them into various sections of the car and have detailed the different models under each section.

ENGINE

Engine Data

Oil pressure (hot) (there may be slight variations between models - and between cars!):

FACTS AND FIGURES

Running | 60 p.s.i. - (1275 Cooper 'S' pressure can rise to 90 p.s.i.)

Idling | 15 p.s.i.

Mini 850 (all models) to 1983

Type	8MB
Bore	2.478 in. (62.94 mm)
Stroke	2.687 in. (68.26 mm)
Capacity	51.7 cu.in. (848 cc)
Compression ratio	8.3:1
Bhp	35 @ 5500 rpm

Mini 850 Automatic (as above, except -)

Type	8AH
Compression ratio	9:1
Bhp (DIN)	37 @ 5250 rpm

Mini 1000 (all models except Cooper) to 1989

Type	9WR, 99H
Bore	2.543 in. (64.588 mm)
Stroke	3.00 in. (76.2 mm)
Capacity	60.96 cu in (998 cc)
Compression ratio:	8.3:1 (1983-89, 10.6:1. 1989-on, 9.6:1)
Bhp* (DIN)	36 @ 4600 rpm

NB This figure fluctuated over the years. The figure given was that at launch.

Mini 1000 (with catalyst) 1989-on

Type	99HD81
Bore	2.543 in. (64.588 mm)
Stroke	3.00 in. (76.2 mm)
Capacity	60.96 cu.in. (998 cc)
Compression ratio	9.6:1
Bhp (DIN)	45 @ 5750 rpm

Mini Cooper (without injection) 1990-92

Type	12A2AF53
Bore	2.78 in. (70.61 mm)
Stroke	3.2 in. (81.28 mm)
Capacity	77.8 cu.in. (1275 cc)
Compression ratio	10.0:1
Bhp (DIN)	61 @ 5550 rpm

Mini Cooper (with injection) 1991-on

Type	12A2EF77
Bore	2.78 in. (70.61 mm)
Stroke	3.2 in. (81.28 mm)
Capacity	77.8 cu.in. (1275 cc)
Compression ratio	10.0:1
Bhp (DIN)	63 @ 5700 rpm

Mini 1.3i (with catalyst) 1991-on

Type	12A2DF75 (Auto: 12A2DF76)
Bore	2.78 in. (70.61 mm)
Stroke	3.2 in. (81.28 mm)
Capacity	77.8 cu.in. (1275 cc)
Compression ratio	9.4:1
Bhp (DIN)	50 @ 5000 rpm

Mini Cooper 997 1961-64

Type	9F
Bore	2.458 in. (62.43 mm)
Stroke	3.20 in. (81.28 mm)
Capacity	60.87 cu.in. (997 cc)
Compression ratio:	
High compression	9:1
Low compression	8.3:1
Bhp (DIN):	
High compression	55 @ 6000 rpm

Mini Cooper 998 1964-69

Type	9FA
Bore	2.543 in. (64.588 mm)
Stroke	3.00 in. (76.2 mm)
Capacity	60.96 cu.in. (998 cc)
Compression ratio:	
High compression	9:1
Low compression	7.8:1
Bhp (DIN):	
High compression	53.8 @ 5800 rpm
Low compression	50.2 @ 5900 rpm

Mini Cooper 'S' (all models) 1963-71

Type:	
970	9F
1071	10F
1275	12F
Bore (all models)	2.780 in. (70.6 mm)
Stroke:	
970 cc	2.4375 in. (61.91 mm)
1071 cc	2.687 in. (68.26 mm)
1275 cc	3.2 in. (81.33 mm)
Capacity:	
970 cc	59.1 cu.in. (970 cc)
1071 cc	63.35 cu.in. (1071 cc)
1275 cc	77.9 cu.in. (1275 cc)
Compression ratio:	
970 cc	10:1
1071 cc	9.0:1
1275 cc	9.75:1
Bhp (DIN):	
970 cc	64 @ 6500 rpm
1071 cc	67.5 @ 6500 rpm
1275 cc	76.1 @ 6000 rpm

Mini 1275 GT 1969-77

Type	12H
Bore	2.78 in. (70.61 mm)
Stroke	3.2 in. (81.28 mm)
Capacity	77.8 cu.in. (1275.86 cc)
Compression ratio:	
High compression	8.8:1
Low compression	8.3:1
Bhp (DIN)	57 @ 5500 rpm

Mini Clubman 1100

Bore	2.543 in. (64.588 mm)
Stroke	3.296 in. (83.73 mm)
Capacity	66.96 cu.in. (1098 cc)
Compression ratio	8.5:1
Bhp (DIN)	44.6 @ 5000 rpm

Compression pressure at cranking speed:

These are the manufacturer's "when new" figures. Expect yours to be different especially if the engine is worn (lower) or if the cylinder head has been skimmed (higher) but these figures are a good guide.

Mini 850 Mk I and II, Mini and Mini 1000 Mk II, Countryman and Traveller, Hornet/Elf Mk I, II and III, Van, Pick-up and Moke:
8.3:1 compression ratio   150 p.s.i. (10.56 kg/cm2)

Mini Clubman 1000:
8.3:1 compression ratio   150 p.s.i. (10.56 kg/cm2)

Mini 1275 GT:
8.8:1 compression ratio   180 p.s.i. (12.67 kg/cm2)

Mini Clubman 1100:
8.5:1 compression ratio   150 p.s.i. (10.56 kg/cm2)

Mini 1.3i:
9.4:1 compression ratio   190 p.s.i. (13.37 kg/cm2)

Mini Cooper 997 cc and 998 cc:
9.0:1 compression ratio   180 p.s.i. (12.67 kg/cm2)

Mini Cooper 'S' 1071 cc, 970 cc, 1275 cc and Mini Cooper 1.3i:
10.0:1 compression ratio   190 to 200 p.s.i.
                               (13.37 to 14.04 kg/cm2)

Firing order

All models	1, 3, 4, 2 (No. 1 cyl. nearest radiator)

Valve clearance (inlet and exhaust)

All models, except as below   0.012 in. (0.30 mm)

Mini 1000 1983-89, Type 99H engines
                0.012 to 0.014 in. (0.30 to 0.35 mm)

Mini 1000 (all models), 1989-on,
Type 99HE22, 99HE20 and 99HD81 engines
                0.011 to 0.013 in. (0.28 to 0.33 mm)

Mini Cooper (with catalyst), 1990-92, Type 12A2AF53 engines
                0.013 to 0.015 in. (0.33 to 0.38 mm)

Mini 1.3i, 1991-on (all models), Type 12A2D and 12A2E engines
                0.011 to 0.013 in. (0.28 to 0.33 mm)

IGNITION
Distributor

Contact breaker ignition	Lucas 23D4, 25D4, 45D4, 59D4 or Ducellier
Electronic ignition	Lucas 65DM4 or NJC 10034

Contact breaker points gap

All models	0.014 to 0.016 in. (0.35 to 0.40 mm)

Dwell angle

Lucas 23D4 and 25D4 distributor   60° ± 3°

Lucas 45D4 Distributor
    51° ± 5° (non-sliding contact breaker points)
    57° ± 5° (sliding contact breaker points)

Lucas 59D4 Distributor   54° ± 5°

Ducellier Distributor   57° ± 2°30'

Coil

All models except below	Lucas LA12
Mini Cooper and 'S'	Lucas HA12
1275 GT 1978 to 1990	Lucas 15C6
Mini 1000 1982 to 1983	AC Delco 9977230 or Ducellier 520035A
Mini 1000 1983 on	Unipart GCL 144
1275 cc 1990 on	Unipart GCL 143
Fuel injected models	1326 or ADU 8779

Spark plugs

We have quoted the recommended NGK spark plugs but other manufacturers equivalents can be used.

All models up to 1987   NGK-BP6ES
                             gap setting 0.25 in.(0.6 mm)

From 1987 onwards:
998 cc engines without catalytic converter
                             NGK-BP5ES or
                             NGK-BP4ES gap setting
                             0.025 in. (0.6 mm)

998 cc engines with catalytic converter
                             NGK-BPR4ES
                             gap setting 0.025 in.(0.6 mm)

From 1990 onwards:
1275 cc engines   NGK-BPR6ES
                             gap setting 0.35 in.(0.9 mm)

Ignition timing (static)

All 850 Saloon and Estates to 1972 and all 850 and 1000 Pick-ups and Vans to 1972   7° B.T.D.C

Mini Cooper 997 cc
    High compression   7° B.T.D.C.
    Low compression   5° B.T.D.C.

Mini Cooper 998 cc
    High compression   5° B.T.D.C.
    Low compression   5° B.T.D.C.

Cooper 'S' 970 cc   12° B.T.D.C.

Cooper 'S' 1071 cc   3° B.T.D.C.

Cooper 'S' 1275 cc   2° B.T.D.C.

Mini Clubman, Mini 1000 Saloons
and Estates up to 1972   5° B.T.D.C.

Mini 1000 Automatic and Clubman
Automatic 998 cc up to 1974   4° B.T.D.C.

1275 GT up to 1972   8° B.T.D.C.

Mini 850 Saloon and variants
1972 to 1974
    25D4 distributor   TDC
    45D4 distributor   9° B.T.D.C.

Mini 1000, Mini Clubman, Saloon
and variants 998 cc 1972 to 1974
    25D4 distributor   5° B.T.D.C
    45D4 distributor   10° B.T.D.C.

Mini 1275 GT 1972 to 1976   8° B.T.D.C.

Mini 850 Saloon and variants
    1974 to 1976   6° B.T.D.C.
Mini 1000, Clubman Saloon and Variants, manual and automatic
    1974 to 1976   4° B.T.D.C.

Mini Clubman 1100 1974 to 1976 9° B.T.D.C.

All models from 1976 onwards -
Stroboscopic timing only (see below)

Ignition timing (stroboscopic)

All 850 saloon and Estates to 1972 3° B.T.D.C. @ 600 rpm

All 850 and 1000 Pick-ups and Vans to 1972
                                       10° B.T.D.C. @ 600 rpm

Mini Cooper 997 cc
    High compression   9° B.T.D.C.@ 600 rpm
    Low compression   7° B.T.D.C.@ 600 rpm

Mini Cooper 998 cc   7° B.T.D.C.@ 600 rpm

Mini Cooper 'S' 970 cc   14° B.T.D.C. @ 600 rpm

Mini Cooper 'S' 1071 cc   5° B.T.D.C. @ 600 rpm

Mini Cooper 'S' 1275 cc   4° B.T.D.C. @ 600 rpm

Mini Clubman, Mini 1000 Saloons
and Estates up to 1972   8° B.T.D.C. @ 600 rpm

Mini 1000 Automatic and Clubman
Automatic 998 cc up to 1974   6° B.T.D.C. @ 600 rpm

1275 GT up to 1972   10° B.T.D.C. @ 600 rpm

Mini 850 Saloon and variants 1972 to 1974
    25D4 distributor   19° B.T.D.C. @ 1000 rpm
    45D4 distributor   14° B.T.D.C. @ 1000 rpm

Mini 1000, Mini Clubman, Saloon
and variants 998 cc 1972 to 1974
    25D4 distributor   11° B.T.D.C. @ 1000 rpm
    45D4 distributor   13° B.T.D.C. @ 1000 rpm

Mini 1275 GT 1972 to 1976   13° B.T.D.C. @ 1000 rpm

Mini 850 Saloon and variants
1974 to 1976   11° B.T.D.C. @ 1000 rpm

Mini 1000, Mini Clubman Saloon
and variants, manual and automatic
1974 to 1976   7° B.T.D.C. @ 1000 rpm

Mini Clubman 1100 1976 onwards 12° B.T.D.C. @ 1000 rpm

Mini 850, Saloon and variants 1976 onwards; Mini 1000, Clubman
Saloon and variants, manual and automatic
1976 to 1978   7° B.T.D.C. @ 1000 rpm

Mini 1275 GT 1976 onwards   13° B.T.D.C. @ 1000 rpm

Mini 1000, Mini Clubman Saloon and variants manual and
automatic
1978 onwards   8° B.T.D.C. @ 1000 rpm

Mini 1000 1983 to 1989   8° ± 2° B.T.D.C. @ 1500 rpm

Mini 1000 1989 onwards
    Low compression   8° ± 2° B.T.D.C. @ 1500 rpm
    High Compression   10° ± 2° B.T.D.C. @ 1500 rpm
Mini Cooper catalyst 1275 cc
1990 onwards   5° ± 1° B.T.D.C. @ 1500 rpm

Mini and Mini Cooper 1.3i Catalyst
1991 onwards   15° ± 1° B.T.D.C @ 850 rpm
Fuel injected models*   15° at idle
*Nominal value only, constantly varying under ECU control

ELECTRICAL EQUIPMENT
Battery
All models pre-1969   12 volt, positive earth
All models 1969 onwards   12 volt, negative earth

Battery capacity
Pre-1969   34 amp hour at 20 hour rate
1969 onwards   30 to 50 amp hour at 20 hour
                                       rate

Dynamo
Pre-1969 Minis only   Lucas C40 or C40/1

Voltage Regulator
Pre-1969 Minis only   Lucas RB 106/2

Alternator
1969 to 1982   Lucas 11AC or 16ACR
1982 to 1985   Lucas A115
1986 onwards   Lucas A127/45 or 127/55

Windscreen wiper motor

1959 to 1969

Early models	Lucas DR2
Later models	Lucas DR3A
1969 onwards	Lucas 14W

Starter motor

Pre-1969	Lucas M35G
1969 to 1986	Lucas M35G or M35J
1986 onwards	Lucas M79 (pre-engaged)

Fuses

Pre-1969 models:

A1 & A2 (35 amp), auxiliary units, interior light and horn protected by this fuse, the latter two will operate without the ignition switched on. Additional accessories which are required to operate independently of the ignition circuit should be connected to the 2 terminal.

A3 & A4 (35 amp), protects the auxiliary units which operate when the ignition is switched on. i.e. direction indicators windscreen wiper motor, heater blower and stop lights. Additional accessories which are required to operate only when the ignition is switched on should be connected to the A4 terminal.

Separate line fuses - Side and tail lights (8 amp), located adjacent to the wiring connectors on the engine bulkhead. Hazard Flasher (35 amp), located adjacent to the fuse block.

Post 1969 models:

1 & 2 (35 amp), Stop lights, reversing lights, direction indicators, heated rear window. These will only operate with the ignition switched on.

3 & 4 (25 amp), Horn, headlight flasher, brake failure circuit. These operate independently of the ignition switch.

5 & 6 (25 amp), Heater blower motor, windscreen wipers and washers, radio. These will operate with the ignition switch at I or II.

7 & 8 (15 amp), Side and tail lights, panel lights.

Separate Line fuses - Hazard warning, interior light (15 amp) on the engine compartment bulkhead. Radio, (the fuse rating should be as specified by the manufacturer) in the main feed line to the radio.

FUEL SYSTEM
Carburettor

Mini 850 Saloon and variants, Mini MK II 850 and 1000 cc Saloon and variants, Riley/Elf Mk I, II and III, Mini Clubman 1000 up to 1974, manual transmission - SU HS2

All above models in manual transmission and Mini Clubman 1100 1974 onwards - SU HS4

Mini Cooper - Twin SU HS2

Mini Cooper 'S' 1275, '69 on - Twin SU HS2

Mini Cooper 1990 onwards - SU HIF 44

1275 GT 1969 to 1992 - SU HS4, 1992 onwards - SU HIF 38

All automatic transmission models - SU HS4

Idle Speed

Model	Idle speed (Fast idle speed)
Mini 850 Mk I and II, Mini Clubman 1000, Mini 1000 Saloon and variants up to 1972	500 rpm (900 rpm)
Mini 850 Mk I and II, 1965 to 1969 and Mini 1000 1967 to 1969, Automatic	650 rpm (1050 rpm)
Mini 850 1972 to 1976	800 rpm (1200 rpm)
Mini 850 1976 onwards	750 rpm (1200 rpm)
Mini Clubman 1000, Mini 1000 Saloon and variants, manual 1972 to 1974	800 rpm (1200 rpm)
Mini Clubman 1000, Mini 1000 Saloon and variants, automatic 1969 to 1974	650 rpm (1050 rpm)
Mini Clubman 1000, Mini 1000 Saloon and variants, manual and automatic, 1974 onward	750 rpm (1150 rpm)
Mini Clubman 1100 1974 onwards	750 rpm (1150 rpm)
1275 GT 1969 to 1972	650 rpm (1050 rpm)
1972 to 1976	800 rpm (1200 rpm)
1976 to 1977	850 rpm (1300 rpm)
1978 onwards	750 rpm (1300 rpm)
Mini Cooper 997 cc 1961 to 1964, 998 cc 1964 to 1969	500 rpm (900 rpm)
1275 cc 1990 onwards	900 rpm (1200 rpm)
Mini Cooper 'S' 970 cc and 1071 cc 1963 to 1965, 1275 cc 1964 onwards	600 rpm (1000 rpm)

Fuel injection system

Modular Engine Management System (MEMS), ECU controlled single-point fuel injection system

Idle Speed

All fuel injected models   850 ± 25 rpm*

*For reference only, ECU controlled idle and fast idle speeds.

Fuel pump

Carburettor models	SU PD, SP, or AUF 201 electric type; SU AUF 700 or 800 mechanical type
Fuel injected models	Electric, immersed in fuel tank

COOLING SYSTEM
Pressure cap setting

All models up to 1969	7 p.s.i. (0.49 kg/cm²)
1969 to 1974	13 p.s.i. (0.91 kg/cm²)
1974 onwards	15 p.s.i. (10.5 kg/cm²)

CLUTCH
Fluid type
Hydraulic Fluid to SAE J1703, Castrol Universal Brake and Clutch Fluid, or similar.

BRAKING SYSTEM
Fluid type
As for Clutch fluid specification

SUSPENSION
Front trim height
Hydrolastic models (measured from wheel hub centre to wheel arch edge)   13.5 in.(343 mm) ± 0.37 in. (9.5 mm)

LUBRICATION SYSTEM
Oil pressure (when hot)
Mini 850, 1000 Mk I and II, Saloon and variants 1959 to 1969
    Idling - 15 to 25 p.s.i. (1.05 to 1.75 kg/cm^2).
    Normal motoring - 30 to 60 p.s.i. (2.1 to 4.2 kg/cm^2)

Mini 850, 1000, Clubman 1000, 1100, 1275 GT, and 1.3i Saloon and variants, 1969 onwards
    Idling - 15 p.s.i.(1.05 kg/cm^2).
    Normal motoring - 60 p.s.i. (4.22 kg/cm^2)

Mini Cooper 997, 998 and 1071 'S'
    Idling - 15 p.s.i.(1.05 kg/cm^2).
    Normal motoring - 70 p.s.i. (4.92 kg/cm^2)

Mini Cooper 'S' 970, 1275 and Mini Cooper from 1990 onwards
    Idling - 15 p.s.i. (1.05 kg/cm^2).
    Normal motoring - 60 p.s.i. (4.22 kg/cm^2)

CAPACITIES
Coolant capacity
Without heater	5.25 pints (2.98 litres)
With heater	6.25 pints (3.55 litres)

Engine/transmission oil capacity
All models 1959 to 1969:
Manual transmission	8.5 pints (4.84 litres)
Automatic transmission	9 pints (5 litres)

All models from 1969 onwards, manual and automatic transmission   9 pints (5 litres)

Steering rack capacity
All models 1959 to 1969	1/3 pint (0.2 litres)
All models 1969 onwards	1/6 pint (0.1 litres)

GENERAL DATA
TYRE PRESSURES (NORMAL DRIVING)
5.20 x 10 cross Ply	Front - 24 p.s.i.(1.68 kg/cm2)
	Rear - 22 p.s.i. (1.5 kg/cm2)
145 x 10 radial-ply	Front - 28 p.s.i.(1.96 kg/cm2)
	Rear - 26 p.s.i. (1.8 kg/cm2)
145/70SR x 12 radial ply	Front - 28 p.s.i.(1.96 kg/cm2)
	Rear - 28 p.s.i. (1.96 kg/cm2)

Mini 1275 GT with 155/65SF x 310 Denevo tyres
                Front - 26 p.s.i. (1.8 kg/cm2)
                Rear - 24 p.s.i. (1.7 kg/cm2)
165/70HR x 10 radial ply alloy option for Clubman 1100
                Front - 24 p.s.i. (1.7 kg/cm2)
                Rear - 26 p.s.i. (1.8 kg/cm2)

STEERING GEAR - TOE SETTING
(otherwise known as wheel alignment or tracking)
All models   Front - 1/16 in. (1.58mm) toe-out
                Rear - 1/8 in. (3.17mm) toe-in

TORQUE WRENCH SETTINGS
Only those settings relating to this book are shown here. If you wish to carry out further work, refer to torque wrench settings shown in the appropriate workshop manual.
Engine
    Tappet side cover screws - 2 lb. ft. (0.28 kg. m.)
    Rocker cover bolts - 4 lb. ft. (0.56 kg. m.)
    Manifold nuts - 15 lb. ft. (2.1. kg. m.)
    Oil drain plug - 25 lb. ft. (3.4 kg. m.)
    Oil filter retaining nut - 16 lb. ft. (2.2. kg. m.)
    Spark plugs - 18 lb. ft. (2.5 kg.m.)
Braking system
    Brake calliper bolts - 38 lb. ft. (5.2 kg. m.)
Suspension
    Track rod end to steering arm - 22 lb. ft. (3.0 kg. m.)
    Steering rack U-bolts - 11 lb. ft. (1.5 kg. m.)
    Steering column clamp pinch bolt - 12 lb. ft. (1.6 kg. m.)
    Roadwheel nuts - 45 lb. ft. (6.2 kg. m.)

REPLACEMENT BULBS
All models:
50/40 watts - Head lamp (bulb type)

60/45 watts - Head lamp (sealed beam type)

6 watts - Side lights, front, bayonet type

5 watts - Side lights, front, capless type

21/6 watts - Side lights and front direction indicators

21 watts - Front flashing direction indicator

21 watts - Rear flashing direction indicators

4 watts - Direction indicator repeaters

21/6 watts - Stop and tail lamps

6 watts - Number plate light (Saloon)

5 watts - Number plate light (Estate, Van and Pick-up)

1.5 watts - Brake pressure test/warning light

2.2 watts - Panel and warning lights

0.75 watts - Illuminated switches

6 watts - Interior light - festoon type

10 watts - Interior light - bayonet fitting

21 watts - Reverse lamp

21 watts - Rear foglamp

CHAPTER 9 - TOOLS AND EQUIPMENT

Basic maintenance on any Mini can be carried out using a fairly simple, relatively inexpensive tool kit. There is no need to spend a fortune all at once - most owners who do their own servicing acquire their implements over a long period of time. However, there are some items you simply cannot do without in order properly to carry out the work necessary to keep your Mini on the road. Therefore, in the following lists, we have concentrated on those items which are likely to be valuable aids to maintaining your car in a good state of tune, and to keep it running sweetly and safely and in addition we have featured some of the tools that are 'nice-to-have' rather than 'must have' because as your tool chest grows, there are some tools that help to make servicing just that bit easier and more thorough to carry out.

One vital point - always buy the best quality tools you can afford. 'Cheap and cheerful' items may look similar to more expensive implements, but experience shows that they often fail when the going gets tough, and some can even be dangerous. With proper care, good quality tools will last a lifetime, and can be regarded as an investment. The extra outlay is well worth it, in the long run.

The following lists are shown under headings indicating the type of use applicable to each group of tools and equipment.

LIFTING:

It is inevitable that you will need to raise the car from the ground in order to gain access to the underside of it.

SAFETY FIRST!
There are, of course, important safety implications when working underneath any vehicle. Sadly, many d-i-y enthusiasts have been killed or seriously injured when maintaining their automotive pride and joy, usually for the want of a few moments' thought. So - THINK SAFETY! In particular, NEVER venture beneath any vehicle supported only by a jack - of ANY type. A jack is ONLY intended to be a means of lifting a vehicle, NOT for holding it 'airborne' while being worked on.

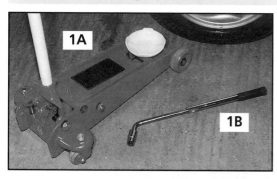

We strongly recommend that you invest in a good quality trolley jack, such as the Kamasa 2¼ ton unit shown here (1A) while alongside is an excellent 'nice-to-have' extendable wheel nut spanner from the same company (1B). This is also ideal for carrying in the car in case of punctures. If you've ever tried removing a wheel nut tightened by a garage gorilla, you know why this tool is so good!

Having raised the vehicle from the floor, always support it under either the front or rear subframes. Use only proper axle stands (2A), intended for the purpose, with solid wooden blocks on top, if necessary, to spread the load. These Kamasa stands are exceptionally strong and are very rapidly adjusted, using the built-in ratchet stops. Screw-type stands have an infinite amount of adjustments but are fiddly and time-consuming to use. *NEVER, NEVER* use bricks to support a car - they can crumble without warning, with horrifying results. Always chock all wheels not in the air, to prevent the car from rolling.

Frankly, if you don't need to remove the road wheels for a particular job, the use of car ramps (2B), which are generally more stable than axle stands - is preferable, in order to gain the necessary working height. However, even then there are dangers. Ensure that the car is 'square' to the ramps before attempting to drive up onto them, and preferably place the ramps on two long lengths of old carpet, extending towards the vehicle. The carpet should help prevent the ramps from sliding as the wheels mount them. If you have an assistant guiding you onto the ramps, be absolutely sure that he/she is well out of the way as you drive forwards. *NEVER* allow anyone to stand in front of the car, or immediately

Thanks are due to Kamasa Tools for their kind assistance with this chapter.
Almost all of the tools shown here and in Chapter 3 were kindly supplied by them.

TOOLS AND EQUIPMENT

beside it - the ramps could tip. Be very careful, too, not to 'overshoot' the ramps. When the car is safely positioned on the ramps, fully apply the handbrake, and firmly chock the pair of wheels still on the ground.

Whenever you are working underneath your Mini, preferably work with someone else, so that there are always two people around in case of an emergency. If this is not possible, and especially if you are working on the car at a location away from your house, make sure that someone knows exactly where you are and how long you intend to work on the vehicle, so that checks can be made if you are not home when expected.

In conclusion, here's a few more words on using and choosing jacks and supports.

JACKS: Manufacturer's jack - for emergency wheel changing ONLY - NOT to be used when working on the vehicle.

'Bottle' jack - screw or hydraulic types - can be used as a means of lifting the car, in conjunction with axle stands to hold it clear of the ground. Ensure that the jack you buy is low enough to pass beneath your Mini..

Trolley jack - extremely useful as it is so easily manoeuvrable. Again, use only for lifting the vehicle, in conjunction with axle stands to support it clear of the ground. Ensure that the lifting head of the jack will pass beneath the lowest points on the Mini. Aim for the highest quality jack you can afford. Cheap types seldom last long, and can be **VERY** dangerous (suddenly allowing a car to drop to ground level, without warning, for example).

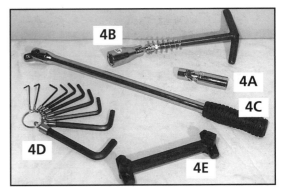

AXLE STANDS: Available in a range of sizes. Ensure that those you buy are sturdy, with the three legs reasonably widely spaced, and with a useful range of height adjustment.

CAR RAMPS: Available in several heights - high ones are easier for working beneath the car. The ultimate ramps are the 'wind-up' variety - easy to drive onto at their lowest height setting, then raised by means of screw threads to a convenient working height.

SPANNERS:

Inside Information: Most fasteners on the Mini have UNF (Unified National Fine) threads, compatible with AF (American Fine) or SAE threads. Some have UNC (Unified National Coarse) threads, and a very few use the BSF or BSW (British Standard Fine, and British Standard Whitworth - coarse) respectively. On early models, some BA (British Association) screws are also employed, as are BSP (British Standard Pipe) threads, in the fuel, lubrication and cooling systems. Metric threads were introduced on an increasing number of fasteners from the late 60's. Therefore, for most jobs, spanners in 'AF' sizes, measured across the flats of the spanner in fractions of an inch, and in metric sizes for later models, will be required, with some items requiring the use of implements designed for the other systems mentioned above.

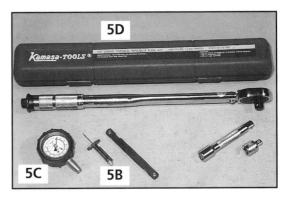

This Kamasa spanner set (3A) is very unusual in that it includes the more unusual types of spanner size in the same set. There are also 'stubby' ratchet handles available (3B) for that cramped engine bay!

Note - in every case, ring spanners provide a more positive grip on a nut/bolt head than open-ended types, which can spread and/or slip when used on tight fasteners. Similarly, 'impact' type socket spanners with hexagonal apertures give better grip on a tight fastener than the normal 12 point 'bi-hex' variety.

Open-ended spanners - set(s) covering the range ⅜ to ¹⁵⁄₁₆in AF.

Ring spanners - set(s) covering the range ⅜ to ¹⁵⁄₁₆in AF (alternatively, combination spanner set(s) (with one ring end, and one 'open' end of the same AF size, for each spanner) covering the same range.

Socket spanners - ⅜in and ½in square drive, covering the same range.

A long extension bar is a typical 'nice-to-have' tool. (4C)

Adjustable spanner - nine inch, to start off with. (11F)

Allen key set. (4D)

Spark plug spanner, with rubber 'plug grip' insert either for use with the ratchet set (4A) or the harder to use T-bar type. (4B)

Brake adjuster spanner.

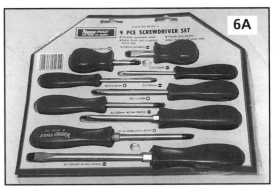

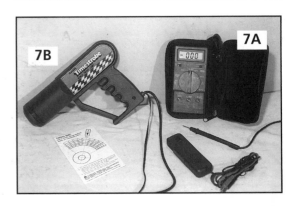

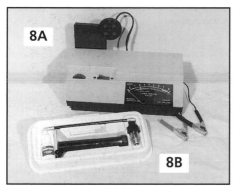

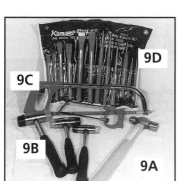

Torque wrench. For aluminium components, this is very nearly a 'must-have' item and for any serious mechanic, it becomes a 'must-have' once you have one. Prevents overtightening and shearing. (5D)

SCREWDRIVERS:

General-purpose set of cross-head variety and flat-bladed variety. (All available in various-sized sets.) (6A)

Impact driver (useful for releasing seized screws in brake drums, etc.). (12A)

'TUNING' AIDS:

Depending on how much of the servicing you want to carry out yourself, you'll need all of these - see **Chapter 3, Service Intervals Step-by-Step** for information on how to use them. The more expensive can be purchased gradually, as you save more money by doing your own servicing!

Compression gauge, preferably screw-in, rather than 'push-in' variety.

Set of feeler gauges.

'Automatic' valve clearance adjuster (can help to correctly set valve clearances when rockers have worn pads).

Spark plug adjuster tool. (Although many people lever the spark-plug electrode with a screwdriver, it's best gripped and bent with pliers if you don't have an adjuster.)

Dwell meter/multi-meter (preferably with built-in tachometer). (7A)

Xenon stroboscopic timing light (neon types can be used, but the orange light produced is less bright than the white light produced by the xenon lamps, so that the timing marks are correspondingly less easy to see). This is one of several from the highly regarded Gunson range. (7B)

Carburettor balancing/adjusting tool.

Simple CO meter. Gunson have now introduced an accurate exhaust gas analyser that is expensive but affordable. (8A)

Colortune. This enables you to see the spark - which changes colour as you adjust the carburettor and to set the carburation accordingly. (8B)

SUNDRY ITEMS:

Tool box - steel types are sturdiest..

Extension lead.

Small/medium ball pein hammer. This one is part of the huge Kamasa range. (9A).

Soft-faced hammer (available here, from Kamasa Tools, as a set). (9B)

Special, brass bristle wire brush for cleaning spark plugs. (10A)

12 volt test lamp (can be made using 12 volt bulb, bulb holder, two short lengths of cable and two small crocodile clips).

Copper-based anti-seize compound - useful during assembly of threaded components, including spark plugs, to make future dismantling easier!

Grease gun.

Oil can (with Castrol GTX multigrade oil, for general purpose lubrication).

Water dispellant 'electrical' aerosol spray.

Pair of pliers ('standard' jaw). (11A)

Pair of 'long-nosed' pliers. (11B)

Pair of 'side cutters'. (11C)

Kamasa also sell pliers in sets, as this shot indicates. (11D)

Self-grip wrench or - preferably - a set of three. (11E)

Junior hacksaw. (9C)

Oil filter removal tool.

Stud removing tools. A 'nice-to-have' when studs shear and all else fails. (12B)

Tyre pump.

Tyre tread depth gauge. (5B)

Tyre pressure gauge. (5C)

Drifts - a set is an extremely useful 'nice-to-have'. (9D)

Hub pullers, useful when you go beyond the straightforward servicing stage. (12C)

Electric drill. Not a servicing tool as such but a 'must-have' nevertheless. The Kamasa rechargeable drill (13A) is superb, enabling you to reach tight spots without trailing leads - and much safer out of doors. Recommended!

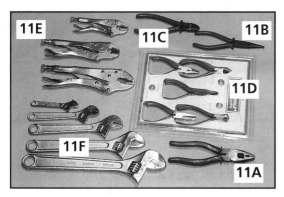

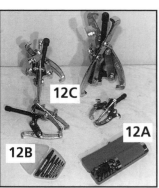

APPENDIX 1 – RECOMMENDED CASTROL LUBRICANTS
for Mini

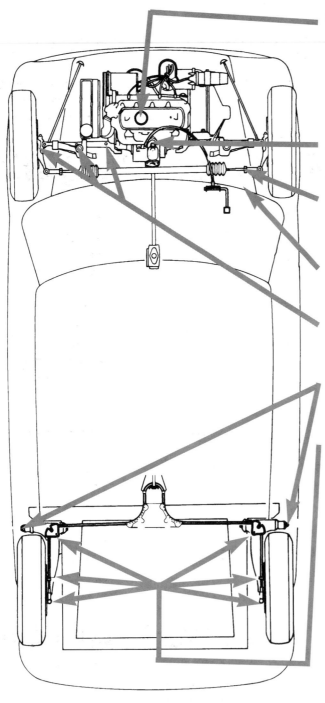

1 Engine/manual gearbox/automatic transmission
See Jobs 38 to 41
Castrol GTX

Overseas For territories with regular air temperatures below 5°C, there are various grades of Castrol lubricants available. Consult your local supplier.

2 Carburettor dash pots
See Job 30
Castrol GTX

3 Steering Rack
See Jobs 34
Early cars – Castrol EPX 80W/90
Later cars – Castrol Castrol CLS grease

4 Brake and Clutch Fluid
See Jobs 2, 3 and 140
Castrol Universal Brake & Clutch Fluid

5 Front Suspension
See Job 46
Castrol LM Grease (High Melting Point)

6 Rear suspension
See Job 48
Castrol LM Grease

7 Handbrake cable
See Job 49
Castrol LM Grease (High Melting Point)

8 Brake Mechanism - areas of metal-to-metal contact
See Jobs 45, 47 and 142
Proprietary brand of high melting point brake grease such as Castrol PH Grease – not conventional high point melting grease

9 General
Castrol Flick Easing Oil (aerosol)
Castrol Everyman Oil (in a can)

NB – Not every model will have all the grease points shown here. In general, the later the model, the fewer the grease nipples

Information issued by:
Castrol (UK) Limited,
Burmah Castrol House,
Pipers Way, Swindon SN3 1RE

APPENDIX 2
AMERICAN AND BRITISH TERMS

It was Mark Twain who described the British and the Americans as, "two nations divided by a common language". such cynicism has no place here but we do acknowledge that our common language evolves in different directions. We hope that this glossary of terms, commonly encountered when servicing your car, will be of assistance to American owners and, in some cases, English speaking owners in other parts of the world, too.

American	British
Antenna	Antenna
Axleshaft	Halfshaft
Back-up	Reverse
Carburetor	Carburettor
Cotter pin	Split pin
Damper	Shock absorber
DC Generator	Dynamo
Defog	Demist
Drive line	Transmission
Driveshaft	Propeller shaft
Fender	Wing or mudguard
Firewall	Bulkhead
First gear	Bottom gear
Float bowl	Float chamber
Freeway, turnpike	Motorway
Frozen	Seized
Gas tank	Petrol tank
Gas pedal	Accelerator or throttle pedal
Gasoline, Gas or Fuel	Petrol or fuel
Ground (electricity)	Earth
Hard top	Fast back
Header	Exhaust manifold
Headlight dimmer	Headlamp dipswitch
High gear	Top gear
Hood	Bonnet
Industrial Alcohol or Denatured Alcohol	Methylated spirit
Kerosene	Paraffin
Lash	Free-play
License plate	Number plate
Lug nut	Wheel nut
Mineral spirit	White spirit
Muffler	Silencer
Oil pan	Sump
Panel wagon/van	Van
Parking light	Side light
Parking brake	Hand brake
'Pinging'	'Pinking'
Quarter window	Quarterlight
Recap (tire)	Remould or retread
Rocker panel	Sill panel

American	British
Rotor or disk (brake)	Disc
Sedan	Saloon
Sheet metal	Bodywork
Shift lever	Gear lever
Side marker lights, side turn signal or position indicator	Side indicator lights
Soft-top	Hood
Spindle arm	Steering arm
Stabiliser or sway bar	Anti-roll bar
Throw-out bearing	Release or thrust bearing
Tie-rod (or connecting rod)	Track rod (or steering)
Tire	Tyre
Transmission	Drive line
Trouble shooting	Fault finding/diagnosis
Trunk	Boot
Turn signal	Indicator
Valve lifter	Tappet
Valve cover	Rocker cover
Valve lifter or tappet	Cam follower or tappet
Vise	Vice
Windshield	Windscreen
Wrench	Spanner

Useful conversions:

	Multiply by
US gallons to Litres	3.785
Litres to US gallons	0.2642
UK gallons to US gallons	1.20095
US gallons to UK gallons	0.832674

Fahrenheit to Celsius (Centigrade) -
Subtract 32, multiply by 0.5555

Celsius to Fahrenheit -
Multiply by 1.8, add 32

APPENDIX 3
SPECIALISTS AND SUPPLIERS

All of the products and specialists listed below have contributed in various ways to this book. All of the consumer products used are available through regular high street outlets.

A1 Mini & Metro Centre

82-92 Vallentin Road, Walthamstow, E17.
Tel: 081 520 1666

Autoline (Dinitrol)

Eagle House, Redstone Industrial Estate, Boston, Lincs, PE21 8EA. Tel: 0205 354500
Rust prevention treatment of various grades.

Automotive Chemicals Ltd

Bevis Green Works, Wallmersley, Bury, Lancs, BL9 8RE. Tel: 061 797 5899
Aerosol spray paint.

Automotive Products

Tachbrook Road, Leamington Spa, Warwicks, CV31 3ER. Tel: 0926 472251
Manufacturers of A P Lockheed 'original equipment' brakes.

Before 'n After Prestige

Tel: 0836 623857
Rustproofing services.

Castrol (UK) Ltd

Burmah House, Pipers Way, Swindon, Wiltshire, SN3 1RE. Tel: 0793 512712
One of the best quality and best known lubricant ranges, recommended by all the top manufacturers and used exclusively in this book. Contact their Customer Services Department on the above number for specific queries about specifying the correct lubricants to use.

Gunson Ltd

Pudding Mill Lane, Stratford, London, E15 2PJ Tel: 081 555 7421
Electrical and electronic engine tuning equipment.

Kamasa Tools

Saxon Industries, Lower Everland Road, Hungerford, Berkshire, RG17 0DX.
Huge range of hand and power tools, used throughout this book.

Mini Cooper Club

38 Arbour House, Arbour Square, London, E1 0PP.

Mini Cooper Register

7 Donemowe Drive, Sittingbourne, Kent, ME10 2RH. Tel: 0795 479397

Mini Owners' Club

15 Birchwood Road, Lichfield, Staffs, WS14 9UN Tel: 0543 257956
The largest club for Mini owners of all types. There are, however, too many different clubs to mention, covering all the various models and just about all corners of the globe. Mini World Magazine lists them regularly. See below.

Mini World Magazine

Link House Magazines Ltd, Dingwall Avenue, Croydon, CR9 2TA. Tel: 081 686 2599
The Mini specialist magazine although a number of other magazines are known to feature Minis more regularly than others: Cars & Car Conversions, for performance tuning; Practical Classics and Car Mechanics, (both from time to time) for DIY; Popular Classics for general classic car features.

NGK Spark Plugs (UK) Ltd

7-8-9 Garrick Industrial Centre, Hendon, London, NW9 6AQ. Tel: 081 202 2151
Top quality spark plugs as used in this book.

Partco.

See Yellow Pages for your local Partco centre (look under Motor Factors).
Just about all regular service items. Suppliers of almost every type of consumable and component used in automotive repair.

SP Tyres UK Ltd

Fort Dunlop, Birmingham, B24 9QT.
Tel: 021 384 4444
Manufacturers of Dunlop tyres in both modern and 'period' patterns.

W. David & Sons Ltd (Isopon)

Ridgemount House, 1 Totteridge Lane, Whetstone, London, N20 0EY. Tel: 081 445 0372
Manufacturers of Isopon filler and ancillaries - top quality products as used in this book.

Worcester Mintro Centre

Padmore Garage, Blockhouse Close, Worcester, WR1 2BU. Tel: 0905 22517
Impressively high standards of workmanship in a surprisingly large garage! Mini specialists.

APPENDIX 4 - SERVICE HISTORY

This Chapter helps you keep track of all the servicing carried out on your car and can even save you money! A car with a 'service history' is always worth more than one without. Although this book's main purpose is to give invaluable advice to anyone carrying out his or her own servicing, you could make full use of this section, even if you have a garage or mechanic carry out the work for you. It enables you to specify the jobs you want to have carried out to your car and, once again, it enables you to keep that all-important service history. And even if your car doesn't have a 'history' going back to when it was new, keeping this Chapter complete will add to your car's value when you come to sell it. Mind you, it obviously won't be enough to just to tick the boxes: keep all your receipts when you buy oil, filters and other consumables or parts. That way, you'll also be able to return any faulty parts if needs be.

IMPORTANT NOTE! The Service Jobs listed here are intended as a check list and a means of keeping a record of your car's service history. It is most important that you refer to *Chapter 3, Service Intervals, Step-by-Step* for full details of how to carry out each Job listed here and for essential SAFETY information, all of which will be essential when you come to carry out the work.

Before carrying out a service on your car, you will need to purchase the right parts. Please refer to *Chapter 2, Buying Spares* for information on how to buy the right parts at the right prices and Chapter 8, Facts and Figures for information on how to find your car's model type, 'identity numbers', and so on: information that you will need in order to buy the right parts, first time!

Wherever possible, the Jobs listed in this section have been placed in a logical order or placed into groups that will help you make progress on the car. We have tried to save you too much in the way of unnecessary movement by grouping Jobs around areas of the car and also - most important, this! - into groups of jobs that apply when the car is on the ground, when one front wheel is removed, when the front or rear of the car is off the ground, and so on. Therefore, at each Service Interval, you will see the work grouped into Jobs that need carrying out in the engine bay, around the car or under the car and another division into Bodywork and Interior Jobs, and Mechanical and Electrical Jobs.

You'll also see space at each Service Interval for you to write down the date, price and seller's name every time you buy consumables or accessories. And once again, do remember to keep your receipts! There's also space for you to date and sign the Service Record or for a garage's stamp to be applied.

As you move through the Service Intervals, you will notice that the work carried out at, say, 1,500 Miles or Every Month, whichever comes first, is repeated at each one of the following Service Intervals. The same applies to the 6,000 Miles or Six Months Interval: much of it is repeated at 12,000 Miles or Twelve Months. Every time a Job or set of Jobs is 'repeated' from an earlier Interval, we show it in a tinted area on the page. You can then see more clearly which jobs are unique to the level of Service Interval that you are on. And you may be surprised to find that all the major Intervals, right up to 36,000 Miles or Thirty Six Months contain Jobs that are unique to that Service Interval. That's why we have continued this Service History right up to the 3 Year Interval. There are sufficient Service History sheets for you to keep a record of your car's servicing for three years, and when that is full, you can purchase a set of continuation sheets from Porter Publishing at the address and telephone number shown at the end of this Chapter. If you keep your car and wish to continue your service record, you will be able to start the 3 year sequence all over again, in the knowledge that your car has been serviced as well as anyone could wish for!

500 MILES, WEEKLY OR BEFORE A LONG JOURNEY.

This list is shown, complete, only once. It would have been a bit much to have provided the list 52 times over for use once a week throughout the year! They are, however, included with every longer Service list from 3,000 miles/Three Months-on so that each of the 'weekly' Jobs is carried out as part of every Service.

500 mile Mechanical and Electrical - The Engine Bay

- [ ] Job 1. Engine oil level
- [ ] Job 2. Clutch fluid level
- [ ] Job 3. Brake fluid level
- [ ] Job 4. Battery electrolyte
- [ ] Job 5. Washer reservoir
- [ ] Job 6. Cooling system

500 mile Mechanical and Electrical - Around the Car

- [ ] Job 7. Check horns
- [ ] Job 8. Windscreen washers
- [ ] Job 9. Windscreen wipers
- [ ] Job 10. Tyre pressures
- [ ] Job 11. Check headlamps and front sidelamps
- [ ] Job 12. Check front indicators
- [ ] Job 13. Check rear sidelamps
- [ ] Job 14. Number plate lamps
- [ ] Job 15. Reversing lamps

Date serviced: ....

Carried out by: ....

Garage stamp or signature:

Parts/Accessories Purchased (Date, Parts, Source)..

....

....

....

....

1,500 MILES - OR EVERY MONTH, whichever comes first.

These Jobs are similar to the 500 Mile Jobs but don't need carrying out quite so regularly. Once again, these Jobs are not shown with a separate listing for each 1,500 miles/1 Month interval but they are included as part of every 3,000 miles/Three Month Service list and for every longer Service interval.

1,500 mile Mechanical and Electrical - Around the Car

- [ ] Job 16. Check tyres
- [ ] Job 17. Check spare tyre

1,500 mile Bodywork and Interior - Around the Car

- [ ] Job 18. Wash bodywork
- [ ] Job 19. Touch-up paintwork
- [ ] Job 20. Aerial/antenna
- [ ] Job 21. Valet interior
- [ ] Job 22. Improve visibility!

1,500 mile Bodywork - Under the Car

- [ ] Job 23. Clean mud traps

Date serviced: ....

Carried out by: ....

Garage stamp or signature:

Parts/Accessories Purchased (Date, Parts, Source)..

....

....

....

....

....

....

3,000 MILES - OR EVERY THREE MONTHS, whichever comes first.

All the Service Jobs in the tinted area have been carried forward from earlier service intervals and are to be repeated at this Service.

3,000 mile Mechanical and Electrical - The Engine Bay

First carry out all the Jobs listed under earlier Service Intervals.

- [ ] Job 2: Clutch fluid level
- [ ] Job 3. Brake fluid level
- [ ] Job 4. Battery electrolyte
- [ ] Job 5. Washer reservoir
- [ ] Job 6. Cooling system

- [ ] Job 24. Adjust spark plugs
- [ ] Job 25. Check HT circuit
- [ ] Job 26. The distributor
- [ ] Job 27. Generator belt
- [ ] Job 28. **OPTIONAL** SU carburettors
- [ ] Job 29. Check air filters
- [ ] Job 30. Top-up carburettor dash pots
- [ ] Job 31. **JAPANESE AND OTHER EXPORT CARS ONLY** Check drive belts
- [ ] Job 32. Pipes and hoses

3,000 mile Mechanical and Electrical - Around the Car

First carry out all the Jobs listed under earlier Service intervals.

- [ ] Job 7. Check horns
- [ ] Job 8. Windscreen washers
- [ ] Job 9. Windscreen wipers
- [ ] Job 10. Tyre pressures
- [ ] Job 11. Check headlamps and front sidelamps
- [ ] Job 12. Check front indicators
- [ ] Job 13. Check rear sidelamps
- [ ] Job 14. Number plate lamps

☐ Job 15. Reversing lamps

☐ Job 16. Check tyres

☐ Job 17. Check spare tyre

☐ Job 33. Handbrake travel

3,000 mile Mechanical and Electrical - Under the Car

☐ Job 34. Steering rack

☐ Job 35. Track rod ends

☐ Job 36. Constant velocity joint boot

☐ Job 37. Steering clamp bolt

Optional - Carry out Job 1

☐ Job 1. Engine oil level

or

☐ Job 38. Drain engine oil

☐ Job 39. Remove oil filter

☐ Job 40. New oil filter

☐ Job 41. Pour fresh oil

☐ Job 42. Check oil level

☐ Job 43. Check for oil leaks

☐ Job 44. Check front brake pads

☐ Job 45. Check front brake shoes

☐ Job 46. Lubricate front grease points

☐ Job 47. Check rear brakes

☐ Job 48. Lubricate rear suspension

☐ Job 49. Lubricate handbrake cable swivel and guide channels

3,000 mile Mechanical and Electrical - Road Test

☐ Job 50. Clean controls

☐ Job 51. Check instruments

☐ Job 52. Throttle pedal

☐ Job 53. Handbrake function

☐ Job 54. Brakes and steering

3,000 mile Bodywork and Interior - Around the Car

First carry out all the Jobs listed under earlier Service Intervals.

☐ Job 19. Touch-up paintwork

☐ Job 20. Aerial/antenna

☐ Job 21. Valet interior

☐ Job 22. Improve visibility

☐ Job 55. Wash and wax the bodywork

☐ Job 56. Wiper blades and arms

☐ Job 57. Check windscreen

☐ Job 58. Rear view mirrors

☐ Job 59. Check floors

☐ Job 60. Chrome trim and badges

3,000 mile Bodywork - Under the Car

First carry out all the Jobs listed under earlier Service Intervals.

☐ Job 23. Clean mud traps

☐ Job 61. Inspect underside

Date serviced: ....

Carried out by: ....

Garage stamp or signature:

Parts/Accessories Purchased (Date, Parts, Source) ....

....

....

....

....

....

....

....

....

6,000 MILES - OR EVERY SIX MONTHS, whichever comes first.

All the Service Jobs in the tinted area have been carried forward from earlier service intervals are to be repeated at this Service.

6,000 mile Mechanical and Electrical - The Engine Bay

First carry out all the Jobs listed under earlier Service Intervals.

☐ Job 2. Clutch fluid level

☐ Job 3. Brake fluid level

☐ Job 4. Battery electrode

☐ Job 5. Washer reservoir

☐ Job 25. Check HT circuit

☐ Job 27. Generator belt

☐ Job 29. Check air filters

☐ Job 30. Top-up carburettor dash pots

☐ Job 31. **JAPANESE AND OTHER EXPORT CARS ONLY**
Check drive belts

☐ Job 32. Pipes and hoses

☐ Job 62. Cooling system

☐ Job 63. Coolant check

☐ Job 64. Heater Valve

☐ Job 65. Check water pump

☐ Job 66. Accelerator controls

☐ Job 67. Dynamo bearing

☐ Job 68. **OPTIONAL**
Fit new spark plugs

☐ Job 69. Distributor advance

☐ Job 70. Renew cb points

☐ Job 71. Check ignition timing

☐ Job 72. Valve clearances

☐ Job 73. Rocker cover gasket

☐ Job 74. Fit fuel filter

☐ Job 75. Fuel connections

☐ Job 76. Set carburettors

☐ Job 77. **SPECIALIST SERVICE**
Exhaust emissions

☐ Job 78. Check clutch return stop

6,000 mile Mechanical and Electrical - Around the Car

First carry out all the Jobs listed under earlier Service Intervals.

- [ ] Job 7. Check horns
- [ ] Job 8. Windscreen washers
- [ ] Job 9. Windscreen wipers
- [ ] Job 10. Tyre pressures
- [ ] Job 11. Check headlamps and front sidelamps
- [ ] Job 12. Check front indicators
- [ ] Job 13. Check rear sidelamps
- [ ] Job 14. Number plate lamps
- [ ] Job 15. Reversing lamps
- [ ] Job 16. Check tyres
- [ ] Job 17. Check spare tyre
- [ ] Job 33. Handbrake travel

- [ ] Job 79. Adjust headlamps
- [ ] Job 80. **SPECIALIST SERVICE** Front wheel alignment
- [ ] Job 81. Rear ride height
- [ ] Job 82. Front ride height
- [ ] Job 83. Check wheel nuts

6,000 mile Mechanical and Electrical - Under the Car

Of all the Service intervals, this (like the 12,000 and 24,000 mile interval) is the one that involves most working under the car. For that reason, we have grouped areas of work together so that the work is in logical groups rather than strict numerical order.

FRONT OF CAR

First carry out all the Jobs listed under earlier Service Intervals.

- [ ] Job 34. Steering rack
- [ ] Job 35. Track rod ends
- [ ] Job 36. Constant velocity joint boot
- [ ] Job 37. Steering clamp bolt

Optional - Carry out Job 1

- [ ] Job 1. Engine oil level

or

- [ ] Job 38. Drain engine oil
- [ ] Job 39. Remove oil filter

- [ ] Job 40. New oil filter
- [ ] Job 41. Pour fresh oil
- [ ] Job 42. Check oil level
- [ ] Job 43. Check for oil leaks
- [ ] Job 44. Check front brake pads
- [ ] Job 45. Check front brake shoes
- [ ] Job 46. Lubricate front grease points

- [ ] Job 84. Front fuel lines
- [ ] Job 85. Front brake lines
- [ ] Job 86. Exhaust manifold
- [ ] Job 87. Front dampers or hydrolastic displacers
- [ ] Job 88. Driveshaft couplings
- [ ] Job 89. Engine stabilisers
- [ ] Job 90. Front subframe mounting rubbers
- [ ] Job 91. Clutch hydraulics

REAR OF CAR

- [ ] Job 47. Check rear brakes
- [ ] Job 48. Lubricate rear suspension
- [ ] Job 49. Lubricate handbrake cable swivel and guide channels

- [ ] Job 92. Check rear hub bearings
- [ ] Job 93. Rear brake lines
- [ ] Job 94. Rear fuel lines
- [ ] Job 95. Exhaust system
- [ ] Job 96. Rear dampers or hydrolastic displacers
- [ ] Job 97. Check rear sub-frame mounts

6,000 mile Mechanical and Electrical - Road Test

- [ ] Job 50. Clean controls
- [ ] Job 51. Check instruments
- [ ] Job 52. Throttle pedal
- [ ] Job 53. Handbrake function
- [ ] Job 54. Brakes and steering

6,000 mile Bodywork and Interior - Around the Car

First carry out all the jobs listed under earlier Service Intervals.

- [ ] Job 18. Wash bodywork
- [ ] Job 19. Touch-up paintwork
- [ ] Job 20. Aerial/antenna
- [ ] Job 21. Valet interior
- [ ] Job 22. Improve visibility!
- [ ] Job 55. Wash and wax the bodywork
- [ ] Job 56. Wiper blades and arm
- [ ] Job 57. Check windscreen
- [ ] Job 58. Rear view mirrors
- [ ] Job 59. Check floors
- [ ] Job 60. Chrome trim and badges

- [ ] Job 98. Bonnet release
- [ ] Job 99. Door locks
- [ ] Job 100. Boot lock
- [ ] Job 101. Check battery connections
- [ ] Job 102. Seats and seat belts

6,000 mile Bodywork - Under the Car

First carry out all the Jobs listed under earlier Service Intervals.

- [ ] Job 23. Clean mud traps
- [ ] Job 61. Inspect underside

- [ ] Job 103. Rustproof underbody

Be sure to carry out Job 104 after Job 103

- [ ] Job 104. Clean drain holes

Date serviced: ....

Carried out by: ....

Garage stamp or signature:

Parts/Accessories Purchased (Date, Parts, Source) ....

....

....

....

9,000 MILES - OR EVERY NINE MONTHS, whichever comes first.

All the Service Jobs at this Service Interval have been carried forward from earlier service intervals and are to be repeated at this Service.

9,000 mile Mechanical and Electrical - The Engine Bay

- [ ] Job 2. Clutch fluid level
- [ ] Job 3. Brake fluid level
- [ ] Job 4. Battery electrolyte
- [ ] Job 5. Washer reservoir
- [ ] Job 6. Cooling system
- [ ] Job 24. Adjust spark plugs
- [ ] Job 25. Check HT circuit
- [ ] Job 26. The distributor
- [ ] Job 27. Generator belt
- [ ] Job 28. **OPTIONAL** SU carburettors
- [ ] Job 29. Check air filters
- [ ] Job 30. Top-up carburettor dash pots
- [ ] Job 31. **JAPANESE AND OTHER EXPORT CARS ONLY** Check drive belts
- [ ] Job 32. Pipes and hoses

9,000 mile Mechanical and Electrical - Around the Car

- [ ] Job 7. Check horns
- [ ] Job 8. Windscreen washers
- [ ] Job 9. Windscreen wipers
- [ ] Job 10. Tyre pressures
- [ ] Job 11. Check headlamps and front sidelamps
- [ ] Job 12. Check front indicators
- [ ] Job 13. Check rear sidelamps
- [ ] Job 14. Number plate lamps
- [ ] Job 15. Reversing lamps
- [ ] Job 16. Check tyres
- [ ] Job 17. Check spare tyre
- [ ] Job 33. Handbrake travel

9,000 mile Mechanical and Electrical - Under the Car

- [ ] Job 34. Steering rack
- [ ] Job 35. Track rod ends
- [ ] Job 36. Constant velocity joint boot
- [ ] Job 37. Steering clamp bolt

Optional - Carry out Job 1

- [ ] Job 1. Engine oil level

or

- [ ] Job 38. Drain engine oil
- [ ] Job 39. Remove oil filter
- [ ] Job 40. New oil filter
- [ ] Job 41. Pour fresh oil
- [ ] Job 42. Check oil level
- [ ] Job 43. Check for oil leaks
- [ ] Job 44. Check front brake pads
- [ ] Job 45. Check front brake shoes
- [ ] Job 46. Lubricate front grease points
- [ ] Job 47. Check rear brakes
- [ ] Job 48. Lubricate rear suspension
- [ ] Job 49. Lubricate handbrake cable swivel and guide channels

9,000 mile Mechanical and Electrical - Road Test

- [ ] Job 50. Clean controls
- [ ] Job 51. Check instruments
- [ ] Job 52. Throttle pedal
- [ ] Job 53. Handbrake function
- [ ] Job 54. Brakes and steering

9,000 mile Bodywork and Interior - Around the Car

- [ ] Job 19. Touch-up paintwork
- [ ] Job 20. Aerial/antenna
- [ ] Job 21. Valet interior
- [ ] Job 22. Improve visibility
- [ ] Job 55. Wash and wax the bodywork
- [ ] Job 56. Wiper blades and arms
- [ ] Job 57. Check windscreen
- [ ] Job 58. Rear view mirrors

- [ ] Job 59. Check floors
- [ ] Job 60. Chrome trim and badges

9,000 mile Bodywork - Under the Car

- [ ] Job 23. Clean mud traps
- [ ] Job 61. Inspect underside

Date serviced: ....

Carried out by: ....

Garage stamp or signature:

Parts/Accessories Purchased (Date, Parts, Source) ....
....
....
....
....
....
....
....
....
....
....
....
....
....
....
....
....
....
....
....
....

SERVICE HISTORY

12,000 MILES - OR EVERY TWELVE MONTHS, whichever comes first.

All the Service Jobs in the tinted area have been carried forward from earlier service intervals and are to be repeated at this Service.

12,000 mile Mechanical and Electrical - Emission Control Equipment

- [ ] Job 105. Crankcase breather
- [ ] Job 106. Oil filler cap
- [ ] Job 107. **JAPANESE AND OTHER EXPORT CARS ONLY**
  Inspect air injection pipes and hoses
- [ ] Job 108. **JAPANESE AND OTHER EXPORT CARS ONLY**
  Renew fuel line filter
- [ ] Job 109. **JAPANESE AND OTHER EXPORT CARS ONLY**
  Renew charcoal adsorption canister
- [ ] Job 110. **JAPANESE AND OTHER EXPORT CARS ONLY**
  Check operation of gulp valve
- [ ] Job 111. **JAPANESE AND OTHER EXPORT CARS ONLY**
  Check operation of air diverter valve.
- [ ] Job 112. **JAPANESE AND OTHER EXPORT CARS ONLY**
  Test check valve
- [ ] Job 113. **JAPANESE AND OTHER EXPORT CARS ONLY**
  Air pump belt
- [ ] Job 114. **SPECIALIST SERVICE**
  Emission system

12,000 mile Mechanical and Electrical - The Engine Bay

First carry out all the Jobs listed under earlier Service Intervals.
- [ ] Job 2. Clutch fluid level
- [ ] Job 3. Brake fluid level
- [ ] Job 4. Battery electrode
- [ ] Job 5. Washer reservoir
- [ ] Job 25. Check HT circuit

- [ ] Job 27. Generator belt
- [ ] Job 29. Check air filters
- [ ] Job 30. Top-up carburettor dash pots
- [ ] Job 31. **JAPANESE AND OTHER EXPORT CARS ONLY**
  Check drive belts
- [ ] Job 32. Pipes and hoses
- [ ] Job 62. Cooling system
- [ ] Job 63. Coolant check
- [ ] Job 64. Heater Valve
- [ ] Job 65. Check water pump
- [ ] Job 66. Accelerator controls
- [ ] Job 67. Dynamo bearing
- [ ] Job 68. **OPTIONAL**
  Fit new spark plugs
- [ ] Job 69. Distributor advance
- [ ] Job 70. Renew cb points
- [ ] Job 71. Check ignition timing
- [ ] Job 72. Valve clearances
- [ ] Job 73. Rocker cover gasket
- [ ] Job 74. Fit fuel filter
- [ ] Job 75. Fuel connections
- [ ] Job 76. Set carburettors
- [ ] Job 77. **SPECIALIST SERVICE**
  Exhaust emissions
- [ ] Job 78. Check clutch return stop

- [ ] Job 115. Oil leaks
- [ ] Job 116. Clean radiator
- [ ] Job 117. **EARLY MODELS ONLY**
  Grease water pump
- [ ] Job 118. Remote brake servo filter
- [ ] Job 119. In-line brake servo filter
- [ ] Job 120. Check cylinder compressions

12,000 mile Mechanical and Electrical - Around the Car

First carry out all the Jobs listed under earlier Service Intervals.
- [ ] Job 7. Check horns
- [ ] Job 8. Windscreen washers
- [ ] Job 9. Windscreen wipers

- [ ] Job 10. Tyre pressures
- [ ] Job 11. Check headlamps and front sidelamps
- [ ] Job 12. Check front indicators
- [ ] Job 13. Check rear sidelamps
- [ ] Job 14. Number plate lamps
- [ ] Job 15. Reversing lamps
- [ ] Job 16. Check tyres
- [ ] Job 17. Check spare tyre
- [ ] Job 33. Handbrake travel
- [ ] Job 79. Adjust headlamps
- [ ] Job 80. **SPECIALIST SERVICE**
  Front wheel alignment
- [ ] Job 81. Rear ride height
- [ ] Job 82. Front ride height
- [ ] Job 83. Check wheel nuts

- [ ] Job 121. Test dampers
- [ ] Job 122. Alarm remote units

12,000 mile Mechanical and Electrical - Under the Car

Of all the Service intervals, this (like the 6,000 and 24,000 mile interval) is the one that involves most working under the car. For that reason, we have grouped areas of work together so that the work is in logical groups rather than strict numerical order.

FRONT OF CAR

First carry out all the Jobs listed under earlier Service Intervals.
- [ ] Job 34. Steering rack
- [ ] Job 35. Track rod ends
- [ ] Job 36. Constant velocity joint boot
- [ ] Job 37. Steering clamp bolt

Optional - Carry out Job 1
- [ ] Job 1. Engine oil level
or
- [ ] Job 38. Drain engine oil
- [ ] Job 39. Remove oil filter
- [ ] Job 40. New oil filter
- [ ] Job 41. Pour fresh oil
- [ ] Job 42. Check oil level
- [ ] Job 43. Check for oil leaks

- [ ] Job 44. Check front brake pads
- [ ] Job 45. Check front brake shoes
- [ ] Job 46. Lubricate front grease points
- [ ] Job 84. Front fuel lines
- [ ] Job 85. Front brake lines
- [ ] Job 86. Exhaust manifold
- [ ] Job 87. Front dampers or hydrolastic displacers
- [ ] Job 88. Driveshaft couplings
- [ ] Job 89. Engine stabilisers
- [ ] Job 90. Front subframe mounting rubbers
- [ ] Job 91. Clutch hydraulics

- [ ] Job 123. Wishbone bushes
- [ ] Job 124. Top and bottom swivel pins
- [ ] Job 125. Check front hub bearings
- [ ] Job 126. Steering rack mountings
- [ ] Job 127. Check free play
- [ ] Job 128. Check ball joints

REAR OF CAR

- [ ] Job 47. Check rear brakes
- [ ] Job 48. Lubricate rear suspension
- [ ] Job 49. Lubricate handbrake cable swivel and guide channels
- [ ] Job 92. Check rear hub bearings
- [ ] Job 93. Rear brake lines
- [ ] Job 94. Rear fuel lines
- [ ] Job 95. Exhaust system
- [ ] Job 96. Rear dampers or hydrolastic displacers
- [ ] Job 97. Check rear sub-frame mounts

- [ ] Job 129. Check rear radius arm bearing

12,000 mile Mechanical and Electrical - Road Test

- [ ] Job 50. Clean controls
- [ ] Job 51. Check instruments
- [ ] Job 52. Throttle pedal
- [ ] Job 53. Handbrake function
- [ ] Job 54. Brakes and steering

12,000 mile Bodywork and Interior - Around the Car

First carry out all the Jobs listed under earlier Service Intervals.

- [ ] Job 18. Wash bodywork
- [ ] Job 19. Touch-up paintwork
- [ ] Job 20. Aerial/antenna
- [ ] Job 21. Valet interior
- [ ] Job 22. Improve visibility!
- [ ] Job 55. Wash and wax the bodywork
- [ ] Job 56. Wiper blades and arm
- [ ] Job 57. Check windscreen
- [ ] Job 58. Rear view mirrors
- [ ] Job 59. Check floors
- [ ] Job 60. Chrome trim and badges
- [ ] Job 98. Bonnet release
- [ ] Job 99. Door locks
- [ ] Job 100. Boot lock
- [ ] Job 101. Check battery connections
- [ ] Job 102. Seats and seat belts

- [ ] Job 130. Seat runners
- [ ] Job 131. Toolkit and jack

12,000 mile Bodywork - Under the Car

First carry out all the Jobs listed under earlier Service Intervals.

- [ ] Job 23. Clean mud traps
- [ ] Job 61. Inspect underside

- [ ] Job 132. Top-up rustproofing

Be sure to carry out Job 104 after Job 132

- [ ] Job 104. Clean drain holes

Date serviced: ....

Carried out by: ....

Garage stamp or signature:

Parts/Accessories Purchased (Date, Parts, Source) ....
....
....
....
....
....
....
....
....
....
....
....
....
....
....
....
....
....
....
....
....
....
....
....
....
....
....
....
....

SERVICE HISTORY

15,000 MILES - OR EVERY FIFTEEN MONTHS, whichever comes first.

All the Service Jobs at this Service Interval have been carried forward from earlier service intervals and are to be repeated at this Service.

15,000 mile Mechanical and Electrical - The Engine Bay

- [ ] Job 2. Clutch fluid level
- [ ] Job 3. Brake fluid level
- [ ] Job 4. Battery electrolyte
- [ ] Job 5. Washer reservoir
- [ ] Job 6. Cooling system
- [ ] Job 24. Adjust spark plugs
- [ ] Job 25. Check HT circuit
- [ ] Job 26. The distributor
- [ ] Job 27. Generator belt
- [ ] Job 28. **OPTIONAL** SU carburettors
- [ ] Job 29. Check air filters
- [ ] Job 30. Top-up carburettor dash pots
- [ ] Job 31. **JAPANESE AND OTHER EXPORT CARS ONLY** Check drive belts
- [ ] Job 32. Pipes and hoses

15,000 mile Mechanical and Electrical - Around the Car

- [ ] Job 7. Check horns
- [ ] Job 8. Windscreen washers
- [ ] Job 9. Windscreen wipers
- [ ] Job 10. Tyre pressures
- [ ] Job 11. Check headlamps and front sidelamps
- [ ] Job 12. Check front indicators
- [ ] Job 13. Check rear sidelamps
- [ ] Job 14. Number plate lamps
- [ ] Job 15. Reversing lamps
- [ ] Job 16. Check tyres
- [ ] Job 17. Check spare tyre
- [ ] Job 33. Handbrake travel

15,000 mile Mechanical and Electrical - Under the Car

- [ ] Job 34. Steering rack
- [ ] Job 35. Track rod ends
- [ ] Job 36. Constant velocity joint boot
- [ ] Job 37. Steering clamp bolt

Optional - Carry out Job 1

- [ ] Job 1. Engine oil level

or

- [ ] Job 38. Drain engine oil
- [ ] Job 39. Remove oil filter
- [ ] Job 40. New oil filter
- [ ] Job 41. Pour fresh oil
- [ ] Job 42. Check oil level
- [ ] Job 43. Check for oil leaks
- [ ] Job 44. Check front brake pads
- [ ] Job 45. Check front brake shoes
- [ ] Job 46. Lubricate front grease points
- [ ] Job 47. Check rear brakes
- [ ] Job 48. Lubricate rear suspension
- [ ] Job 49. Lubricate handbrake cable swivel and guide channels

15,000 mile Mechanical and Electrical - Road Test

- [ ] Job 50. Clean controls
- [ ] Job 51. Check instruments
- [ ] Job 52. Throttle pedal
- [ ] Job 53. Handbrake function
- [ ] Job 54. Brakes and steering

15,000 mile Bodywork and Interior - Around the Car

- [ ] Job 19. Touch-up paintwork
- [ ] Job 20. Aerial/antenna
- [ ] Job 21. Valet interior
- [ ] Job 22. Improve visibility
- [ ] Job 55. Wash and wax the bodywork
- [ ] Job 56. Wiper blades and arms
- [ ] Job 57. Check windscreen
- [ ] Job 58. Rear view mirrors
- [ ] Job 59. Check floors

- [ ] Job 60. Chrome trim and badges

15,000 mile Bodywork - Under the Car

- [ ] Job 23. Clean mud traps
- [ ] Job 61. Inspect underside

Date serviced: ....

Carried out by: ....

Garage stamp or signature:

Parts/Accessories Purchased (Date, Parts, Source) ....
....
....
....
....
....
....
....
....
....
....
....
....
....
....
....
....
....
....
....

18,000 MILES - OR EVERY EIGHTEEN MONTHS, whichever comes first.

All the Service Jobs at this Service Interval have been carried forward from earlier service intervals and are to be repeated at this Service.

18,000 mile Mechanical and Electrical - The Engine Bay

- [ ] Job 2. Clutch fluid level
- [ ] Job 3. Brake fluid level
- [ ] Job 4. Battery electrode
- [ ] Job 5. Washer reservoir
- [ ] Job 25. Check HT circuit
- [ ] Job 27. Generator belt
- [ ] Job 29. Check air filters
- [ ] Job 30. Top-up carburettor dash pots
- [ ] Job 31. **JAPANESE AND OTHER EXPORT CARS ONLY**
  Check drive belts
- [ ] Job 32. Pipes and hoses
- [ ] Job 62. Cooling system
- [ ] Job 63. Coolant check
- [ ] Job 64. Heater Valve
- [ ] Job 65. Check water pump
- [ ] Job 66. Accelerator controls
- [ ] Job 67. Dynamo bearing
- [ ] Job 68. **OPTIONAL**
  Fit new spark plugs
- [ ] Job 69. Distributor advance
- [ ] Job 70. Renew cb points
- [ ] Job 71. Check ignition timing
- [ ] Job 72. Valve clearances
- [ ] Job 73. Rocker cover gasket
- [ ] Job 74. Fit fuel filter
- [ ] Job 75. Fuel connections
- [ ] Job 76. Set carburettors
- [ ] Job 77. SPECIALIST SERVICE
  Exhaust emissions
- [ ] Job 78. Check clutch return stop

18,000 mile Mechanical and Electrical - Around the Car

- [ ] Job 7. Check horns
- [ ] Job 8. Windscreen washers
- [ ] Job 9. Windscreen wipers
- [ ] Job 10. Tyre pressures
- [ ] Job 11. Check headlamps and front sidelamps
- [ ] Job 12. Check front indicators
- [ ] Job 13. Check rear sidelamps
- [ ] Job 14. Number plate lamps
- [ ] Job 15. Reversing lamps
- [ ] Job 16. Check tyres
- [ ] Job 17. Check spare tyre
- [ ] Job 33. Handbrake travel
- [ ] Job 79. Adjust headlamps
- [ ] Job 80. **SPECIALIST SERVICE**
  Front wheel alignment
- [ ] Job 81. Rear ride height
- [ ] Job 82. Front ride height
- [ ] Job 83. Check wheel nuts

18,000 mile Mechanical and Electrical - Under the Car

FRONT OF CAR

- [ ] Job 34. Steering rack
- [ ] Job 35. Track rod ends
- [ ] Job 36. Constant velocity joint boot
- [ ] Job 37. Steering clamp bolt

Optional - Carry out Job 1

- [ ] Job 1. Engine oil level

or

- [ ] Job 38. Drain engine oil
- [ ] Job 39. Remove oil filter
- [ ] Job 40. New oil filter
- [ ] Job 41. Pour fresh oil
- [ ] Job 42. Check oil level
- [ ] Job 43. Check for oil leaks
- [ ] Job 44. Check front brake pads
- [ ] Job 45. Check front brake shoes
- [ ] Job 46. Lubricate front grease points
- [ ] Job 84. Front fuel lines

- [ ] Job 85. Front brake lines
- [ ] Job 86. Exhaust manifold
- [ ] Job 87. Front dampers or hydrolastic displacers
- [ ] Job 88. Driveshaft couplings
- [ ] Job 89. Engine stabilisers
- [ ] Job 90. Front subframe mounting rubbers
- [ ] Job 91. Clutch hydraulics

REAR OF CAR

- [ ] Job 47. Check rear brakes
- [ ] Job 48. Lubricate rear suspension
- [ ] Job 49. Lubricate handbrake cable swivel and guide channels
- [ ] Job 92. Check rear hub bearings
- [ ] Job 93. Rear brake lines
- [ ] Job 94. Rear fuel lines
- [ ] Job 95. Exhaust system
- [ ] Job 96. Rear dampers or hydrolastic displacers
- [ ] Job 97. Check rear sub-frame mounts

18,000 mile Mechanical and Electrical - Road Test

- [ ] Job 50. Clean controls
- [ ] Job 51. Check instruments
- [ ] Job 52. Throttle pedal
- [ ] Job 53. Handbrake function
- [ ] Job 54. Brakes and steering

18,000 mile Bodywork and Interior - Around the Car

- [ ] Job 18. Wash bodywork
- [ ] Job 19. Touch-up paintwork
- [ ] Job 20. Aerial/antenna
- [ ] Job 21. Valet interior
- [ ] Job 22. Improve visibility!
- [ ] Job 55. Wash and wax the bodywork
- [ ] Job 56. Wiper blades and arm
- [ ] Job 57. Check windscreen
- [ ] Job 58. Rear view mirrors

SERVICE HISTORY

- [ ] Job 59. Check floors
- [ ] Job 60. Chrome trim and badges
- [ ] Job 98. Bonnet release
- [ ] Job 99. Door locks
- [ ] Job 100. Boot lock
- [ ] Job 101. Check battery connections
- [ ] Job 102. Seats and seat belts

18,000 mile Bodywork - Under the Car

- [ ] Job 23. Clean mud traps
- [ ] Job 61. Inspect underside
- [ ] Job 103. Rustproof underbody

Be sure to carry out Job 104 after Job 103

- [ ] Job 104. Clean drain holes

Date serviced: ....

Carried out by: ....

Garage stamp or signature:

Parts/Accessories Purchased (Date, Parts, Source) ....

....

....

....

....

....

....

....

....

....

....

....

....

....

....

....

....

21,000 MILES - OR EVERY TWENTY ONE MONTHS, whichever comes first.

All the Service Jobs at this Service Interval have been carried forward from earlier service intervals and are to be repeated at this Service.

21,000 mile Mechanical and Electrical - The Engine Bay

- [ ] Job 2. Clutch fluid level
- [ ] Job 3. Brake fluid level
- [ ] Job 4. Battery electrolyte
- [ ] Job 5. Washer reservoir
- [ ] Job 6. Cooling system
- [ ] Job 24. Adjust spark plugs
- [ ] Job 25. Check HT circuit
- [ ] Job 26. The distributor
- [ ] Job 27. Generator belt
- [ ] Job 28. **OPTIONAL** SU carburettors
- [ ] Job 29. Check air filters
- [ ] Job 30. Top-up carburettor dash pots
- [ ] Job 31. **JAPANESE AND OTHER EXPORT CARS ONLY** Check drive belts
- [ ] Job 32. Pipes and hoses

21,000 mile Mechanical and Electrical - Around the Car

- [ ] Job 7. Check horns
- [ ] Job 8. Windscreen washers
- [ ] Job 9. Windscreen wipers
- [ ] Job 10. Tyre pressures
- [ ] Job 11. Check headlamps and front sidelamps
- [ ] Job 12. Check front indicators
- [ ] Job 13. Check rear sidelamps
- [ ] Job 14. Number plate lamps
- [ ] Job 15. Reversing lamps
- [ ] Job 16. Check tyres
- [ ] Job 17. Check spare tyre
- [ ] Job 33. Handbrake travel

21,000 mile Mechanical and Electrical - Under the Car

- [ ] Job 34. Steering rack
- [ ] Job 35. Track rod ends
- [ ] Job 36. Constant velocity joint boot
- [ ] Job 37. Steering clamp bolt

Optional - Carry out Job 1

- [ ] Job 1. Engine oil level

or

- [ ] Job 38. Drain engine oil
- [ ] Job 39. Remove oil filter
- [ ] Job 40. New oil filter
- [ ] Job 41. Pour fresh oil
- [ ] Job 42. Check oil level
- [ ] Job 43. Check for oil leaks
- [ ] Job 44. Check front brake pads
- [ ] Job 45. Check front brake shoes
- [ ] Job 46. Lubricate front grease points
- [ ] Job 47. Check rear brakes
- [ ] Job 48. Lubricate rear suspension
- [ ] Job 49. Lubricate handbrake cable swivel and guide channels

21,000 mile Mechanical and Electrical - Road Test

- [ ] Job 50. Clean controls
- [ ] Job 51. Check instruments
- [ ] Job 52. Throttle pedal
- [ ] Job 53. Handbrake function
- [ ] Job 54. Brakes and steering

21,000 mile Bodywork and Interior - Around the Car

- [ ] Job 19. Touch-up paintwork
- [ ] Job 20. Aerial/antenna
- [ ] Job 21. Valet interior
- [ ] Job 22. Improve visibility
- [ ] Job 55. Wash and wax the bodywork
- [ ] Job 56. Wiper blades and arms
- [ ] Job 57. Check windscreen
- [ ] Job 58. Rear view mirrors
- [ ] Job 59. Check floors
- [ ] Job 60. Chrome trim and badges

21,000 mile Bodywork - Under the Car

- [ ] Job 23. Clean mud traps
- [ ] Job 61. Inspect underside

Date serviced: ....

Carried out by: ....

Garage stamp or signature:

Parts/Accessories Purchased (Date, Parts, Source) ....

....

....

....

....

....

....

....

....

....

....

....

....

....

....

....

....

....

....

....

....

....

....

....

....

....

....

24,000 MILES - OR EVERY TWENTY FOUR MONTHS, whichever comes first.

All the Service Jobs in the tinted area have been carried forward from earlier service intervals and are to be repeated at this Service.

24,000 mile Mechanical and Electrical - Emission Control Equipment

- [ ] Job 105. Crankcase breather
- [ ] Job 106. Oil filler cap
- [ ] Job 107. **JAPANESE AND OTHER EXPORT CARS ONLY** Inspect air injection pipes and hoses
- [ ] Job 108. **JAPANESE AND OTHER EXPORT CARS ONLY** Renew fuel line filter
- [ ] Job 109. **JAPANESE AND OTHER EXPORT CARS ONLY** Renew charcoal adsorption canister
- [ ] Job 110. **JAPANESE AND OTHER EXPORT CARS ONLY** Check operation of gulp valve
- [ ] Job 111. **JAPANESE AND OTHER EXPORT CARS ONLY** Check operation of air diverter valve.
- [ ] Job 112. **JAPANESE AND OTHER EXPORT CARS ONLY** Test check valve
- [ ] Job 113. **JAPANESE AND OTHER EXPORT CARS ONLY** Air pump belt
- [ ] Job 114. **SPECIALIST SERVICE** Emission system

24,000 mile Mechanical and Electrical - The Engine Bay

First carry out all the Jobs listed under earlier Service Intervals.

- [ ] Job 2. Clutch fluid level
- [ ] Job 3. Brake fluid level
- [ ] Job 4. Battery electrode
- [ ] Job 5. Washer reservoir

- [ ] Job 25. Check HT circuit
- [ ] Job 27. Generator belt
- [ ] Job 29. Check air filters
- [ ] Job 30. Top-up carburettor dash pots
- [ ] Job 31. **JAPANESE AND OTHER EXPORT CARS ONLY** Check drive belts
- [ ] Job 32. Pipes and hoses
- [ ] Job 62. Cooling system
- [ ] Job 63. Coolant check
- [ ] Job 64. Heater Valve
- [ ] Job 65. Check water pump
- [ ] Job 66. Accelerator controls
- [ ] Job 67. Dynamo bearing
- [ ] Job 68. **OPTIONAL** Fit new spark plugs
- [ ] Job 69. Distributor advance
- [ ] Job 70. Renew cb points
- [ ] Job 71. Check ignition timing
- [ ] Job 72. Valve clearances
- [ ] Job 73. Rocker cover gasket
- [ ] Job 74. Fit fuel filter
- [ ] Job 75. Fuel connections
- [ ] Job 76. Set carburettors
- [ ] Job 77. **SPECIALIST SERVICE** Exhaust emissions
- [ ] Job 78. Check clutch return stop
- [ ] Job 115. Oil leaks
- [ ] Job 116. Clean radiator
- [ ] Job 117. **EARLY MODELS ONLY** Grease water pump
- [ ] Job 118. Remote brake servo filter
- [ ] Job 119. In-line brake servo filter
- [ ] Job 120. Check cylinder compressions

- [ ] Job 133. Engine mountings
- [ ] Job 134. Refill cooling system
- [ ] Job 135. Radiator pressure cap
- [ ] Job 136. Drive belts

24,000 mile Mechanical and Electrical - Around the Car

Carry out all the Jobs listed under earlier Service Intervals.

- [ ] Job 7. Check horns
- [ ] Job 8. Windscreen washers
- [ ] Job 9. Windscreen wipers
- [ ] Job 10. Tyre pressures
- [ ] Job 11. Check headlamps and front sidelamps
- [ ] Job 12. Check front indicators
- [ ] Job 13. Check rear sidelamps
- [ ] Job 14. Number plate lamps
- [ ] Job 15. Reversing lamps
- [ ] Job 16. Check tyres
- [ ] Job 17. Check spare tyre
- [ ] Job 33. Handbrake travel
- [ ] Job 79. Adjust headlamps
- [ ] Job 80. **SPECIALIST SERVICE** Front wheel alignment
- [ ] Job 81. Rear ride height
- [ ] Job 82. Front ride height
- [ ] Job 83. Check wheel nuts
- [ ] Job 121. Test dampers
- [ ] Job 122. Alarm remote units

24,000 mile Mechanical and Electrical - Under the Car

Of all the Service intervals, this (like the 6,000 and 12,000 mile interval) is the one that involves most working under the car. For that reason, we have grouped areas of work together so that the work is in logical groups rather than strict numerical order.

FRONT OF CAR

First carry out all the Jobs listed under earlier Service Intervals.

- [ ] Job 34. Steering rack
- [ ] Job 35. Track rod ends
- [ ] Job 36. Constant velocity joint boot
- [ ] Job 37. Steering clamp bolt

Optional - Carry out Job 1

- [ ] Job 1. Engine oil level

or

- [ ] Job 38. Drain engine oil

- [ ] Job 39. Remove oil filter
- [ ] Job 40. New oil filter
- [ ] Job 41. Pour fresh oil
- [ ] Job 42. Check oil level
- [ ] Job 43. Check for oil leaks
- [ ] Job 44. Check front brake pads
- [ ] Job 45. Check front brake shoes
- [ ] Job 46. Lubricate front grease points
- [ ] Job 84. Front fuel lines
- [ ] Job 85. Front brake lines
- [ ] Job 86. Exhaust manifold
- [ ] Job 87. Front dampers or hydrolastic displacers
- [ ] Job 88. Driveshaft couplings
- [ ] Job 89. Engine stabilisers
- [ ] Job 90. Front subframe mounting rubbers
- [ ] Job 91. Clutch hydraulics
- [ ] Job 123. Wishbone bushes
- [ ] Job 124. Top and bottom swivel pins
- [ ] Job 125. Check front hub bearings
- [ ] Job 126. Steering rack mountings
- [ ] Job 127. Check free play
- [ ] Job 128. Check ball joints

- [ ] Job 137. Engine flushing oil
- [ ] Job 138. Check brake discs
- [ ] Job 139. Brake callipers
- [ ] Job 140. Renew brake fluid

REAR OF CAR

- [ ] Job 47. Check rear brakes
- [ ] Job 48. Lubricate rear suspension
- [ ] Job 49. Lubricate handbrake cable swivel and guide channels
- [ ] Job 92. Check rear hub bearings
- [ ] Job 93. Rear brake lines
- [ ] Job 94. Rear fuel lines
- [ ] Job 95. Exhaust system
- [ ] Job 96. Rear dampers or hydrolastic displacers

- [ ] Job 97. Check rear sub-frame mounts
- [ ] Job 129. Check rear radius arm bearing

- [ ] Job 141. Check brake drums
- [ ] Job 142. Brake back plates

24,000 mile Mechanical and Electrical - Road Test

- [ ] Job 50. Clean controls
- [ ] Job 51. Check instruments
- [ ] Job 52. Throttle pedal
- [ ] Job 53. Handbrake function
- [ ] Job 54. Brakes and steering

24,000 mile Bodywork and Interior - Around the Car

First carry out all the Jobs listed under earlier Service Intervals.

- [ ] Job 18. Wash bodywork
- [ ] Job 19. Touch-up paintwork
- [ ] Job 20. Aerial/antenna
- [ ] Job 21. Valet interior
- [ ] Job 22. Improve visibility!
- [ ] Job 55. Wash and wax the bodywork
- [ ] Job 56. Wiper blades and arm
- [ ] Job 57. Check windscreen
- [ ] Job 58. Rear view mirrors
- [ ] Job 59. Check floors
- [ ] Job 60. Chrome trim and badges
- [ ] Job 98. Bonnet release
- [ ] Job 99. Door locks
- [ ] Job 100. Boot lock
- [ ] Job 101. Check battery connections
- [ ] Job 102. Seats and seat belts
- [ ] Job 130. Seat runners
- [ ] Job 131. Toolkit and jack

- [ ] Job 143. Maintain window mechanism
- [ ] Job 144. Maintain door gear
- [ ] Job 145. Lamp seals

24,000 mile Bodywork - Under the Car

Carry out all the Jobs listed under earlier Service Intervals.

- [ ] Job 23. Clean mud traps
- [ ] Job 61. Inspect underside
- [ ] Job 132. Top-up rustproofing
Be sure to carry out Job 104 after Job 132
- [ ] Job 104. Clean drain holes

Date serviced: ....

Carried out by: ....

Garage Stamp (if applicable):

Parts/Accessories Purchased (Date, Parts, Source) ....

....

....

....

....

....

....

....

....

....

....

....

....

....

....

....

....

....

....

27,000 MILES - OR EVERY TWENTY SEVEN MONTHS, whichever comes first.

All the Service Jobs at this Service Interval have been carried forward from earlier service intervals and are to be repeated at this Service.

27,000 mile Mechanical and Electrical - The Engine Bay

- [ ] Job 2. Clutch fluid level
- [ ] Job 3. Brake fluid level
- [ ] Job 4. Battery electrolyte
- [ ] Job 5. Washer reservoir
- [ ] Job 6. Cooling system
- [ ] Job 24. Adjust spark plugs
- [ ] Job 25. Check HT circuit
- [ ] Job 26. The distributor
- [ ] Job 27. Generator belt
- [ ] Job 28. **OPTIONAL**
  SU carburettors
- [ ] Job 29. Check air filters
- [ ] Job 30. Top-up carburettor dash pots
- [ ] Job 31. **JAPANESE AND OTHER EXPORT CARS ONLY**
  Check drive belts
- [ ] Job 32. Pipes and hoses

27,000 mile Mechanical and Electrical - Around the Car

- [ ] Job 7. Check horns
- [ ] Job 8. Windscreen washers
- [ ] Job 9. Windscreen wipers
- [ ] Job 10. Tyre pressures
- [ ] Job 11. Check headlamps and front sidelamps
- [ ] Job 12. Check front indicators
- [ ] Job 13. Check rear sidelamps
- [ ] Job 14. Number plate lamps
- [ ] Job 15. Reversing lamps
- [ ] Job 16. Check tyres
- [ ] Job 17. Check spare tyre
- [ ] Job 33. Handbrake travel

27,000 mile Mechanical and Electrical - Under the Car

- [ ] Job 34. Steering rack
- [ ] Job 35. Track rod ends
- [ ] Job 36. Constant velocity joint boot
- [ ] Job 37. Steering clamp bolt

Optional - Carry out Job 1

- [ ] Job 1. Engine oil level

or

- [ ] Job 38. Drain engine oil
- [ ] Job 39. Remove oil filter
- [ ] Job 40. New oil filter
- [ ] Job 41. Pour fresh oil
- [ ] Job 42. Check oil level
- [ ] Job 43. Check for oil leaks
- [ ] Job 44. Check front brake pads
- [ ] Job 45. Check front brake shoes
- [ ] Job 46. Lubricate front grease points
- [ ] Job 47. Check rear brakes
- [ ] Job 48. Lubricate rear suspension
- [ ] Job 49. Lubricate handbrake cable swivel and guide channels

27,000 mile Mechanical and Electrical - Road Test

- [ ] Job 50. Clean controls
- [ ] Job 51. Check instruments
- [ ] Job 52. Throttle pedal
- [ ] Job 53. Handbrake function
- [ ] Job 54. Brakes and steering

27,000 mile Bodywork and Interior - Around the Car

- [ ] Job 19. Touch-up paintwork
- [ ] Job 20. Aerial/antenna
- [ ] Job 21. Valet interior
- [ ] Job 22. Improve visibility
- [ ] Job 55. Wash and wax the bodywork
- [ ] Job 56. Wiper blades and arms
- [ ] Job 57. Check windscreen
- [ ] Job 58. Rear view mirrors
- [ ] Job 59. Check floors
- [ ] Job 60. Chrome trim and badges

27,000 mile Bodywork - Under the Car

- [ ] Job 23. Clean mud traps
- [ ] Job 61. Inspect underside

Date serviced: ....

Carried out by: ....

Garage stamp or signature:

Parts/Accessories Purchased (Date, Parts, Source) ....

....
....
....
....
....
....
....
....
....
....
....
....
....
....
....
....
....
....
....
....
....

30,000 MILES - OR EVERY THIRTY MONTHS, whichever comes first.

All the Service Jobs at this Service Interval have been carried forward from earlier service intervals and are to be repeated at this Service.

30,000 mile Mechanical and Electrical - The Engine Bay

- [ ] Job 2. Clutch fluid level
- [ ] Job 3. Brake fluid level
- [ ] Job 4. Battery electrode
- [ ] Job 5. Washer reservoir
- [ ] Job 25. Check HT circuit
- [ ] Job 27. Generator belt
- [ ] Job 29. Check air filters
- [ ] Job 30. Top-up carburettor dash pots
- [ ] Job 31. **JAPANESE AND OTHER EXPORT CARS ONLY**
  Check drive belts
- [ ] Job 32. Pipes and hoses
- [ ] Job 62. Cooling system
- [ ] Job 63. Coolant check
- [ ] Job 64. Heater Valve
- [ ] Job 65. Check water pump
- [ ] Job 66. Accelerator controls
- [ ] Job 67. Dynamo bearing
- [ ] Job 68. **OPTIONAL**
  Fit new spark plugs
- [ ] Job 69. Distributor advance
- [ ] Job 70. Renew cb points
- [ ] Job 71. Check ignition timing
- [ ] Job 72. Valve clearances
- [ ] Job 73. Rocker cover gasket
- [ ] Job 74. Fit fuel filter
- [ ] Job 75. Fuel connections
- [ ] Job 76. Set carburettors
- [ ] Job 77. **SPECIALIST SERVICE**
  Exhaust emissions
- [ ] Job 78. Check clutch return stop

30,000 mile Mechanical and Electrical - Around the Car

- [ ] Job 7. Check horns
- [ ] Job 8. Windscreen washers
- [ ] Job 9. Windscreen wipers
- [ ] Job 10. Tyre pressures
- [ ] Job 11. Check headlamps and front sidelamps
- [ ] Job 12. Check front indicators
- [ ] Job 13. Check rear sidelamps
- [ ] Job 14. Number plate lamps
- [ ] Job 15. Reversing lamps
- [ ] Job 16. Check tyres
- [ ] Job 17. Check spare tyre
- [ ] Job 33. Handbrake travel
- [ ] Job 79. Adjust headlamps
- [ ] Job 80. **SPECIALIST SERVICE**
  Front wheel alignment
- [ ] Job 81. Rear ride height
- [ ] Job 82. Front ride height
- [ ] Job 83. Check wheel nuts

30,000 mile Mechanical and Electrical - Under the Car

FRONT OF CAR

- [ ] Job 34. Steering rack
- [ ] Job 35. Track rod ends
- [ ] Job 36. Constant velocity joint boot
- [ ] Job 37. Steering clamp bolt

Optional - Carry out Job 1

- [ ] Job 1. Engine oil level

or

- [ ] Job 38. Drain engine oil
- [ ] Job 39. Remove oil filter
- [ ] Job 40. New oil filter
- [ ] Job 41. Pour fresh oil
- [ ] Job 42. Check oil level
- [ ] Job 43. Check for oil leaks
- [ ] Job 44. Check front brake pads
- [ ] Job 45. Check front brake shoes
- [ ] Job 46. Lubricate front grease points
- [ ] Job 84. Front fuel lines

- [ ] Job 85. Front brake lines
- [ ] Job 86. Exhaust manifold
- [ ] Job 87. Front dampers or hydrolastic displacers
- [ ] Job 88. Driveshaft couplings
- [ ] Job 89. Engine stabilisers
- [ ] Job 90. Front subframe mounting rubbers
- [ ] Job 91. Clutch hydraulics

REAR OF CAR

- [ ] Job 47. Check rear brakes
- [ ] Job 48. Lubricate rear suspension
- [ ] Job 49. Lubricate handbrake cable swivel and guide channels
- [ ] Job 92. Check rear hub bearings
- [ ] Job 93. Rear brake lines
- [ ] Job 94. Rear fuel lines
- [ ] Job 95. Exhaust system
- [ ] Job 96. Rear dampers or hydrolastic displacers
- [ ] Job 97. Check rear sub-frame mounts

30,000 mile Mechanical and Electrical - Road Test

- [ ] Job 50. Clean controls
- [ ] Job 51. Check instruments
- [ ] Job 52. Throttle pedal
- [ ] Job 53. Handbrake function
- [ ] Job 54. Brakes and steering

30,000 mile Bodywork and Interior - Around the Car

- [ ] Job 18. Wash bodywork
- [ ] Job 19. Touch-up paintwork
- [ ] Job 20. Aerial/antenna
- [ ] Job 21. Valet interior
- [ ] Job 22. Improve visibility!
- [ ] Job 55. Wash and wax the bodywork
- [ ] Job 56. Wiper blades and arm
- [ ] Job 57. Check windscreen
- [ ] Job 58. Rear view mirrors

- [ ] Job 59. Check floors
- [ ] Job 60. Chrome trim and badges
- [ ] Job 98. Bonnet release
- [ ] Job 99. Door locks
- [ ] Job 100. Boot lock
- [ ] Job 101. Check battery connections
- [ ] Job 102. Seats and seat belts

30,000 mile Bodywork - Under the Car

- [ ] Job 23. Clean mud traps
- [ ] Job 61. Inspect underside
- [ ] Job 103. Rustproof underbody

Be sure to carry out Job 104 after Job 103

- [ ] Job 104. Clean drain holes

Date serviced: ....

Carried out by: ....

Garage stamp or signature:

Parts/Accessories Purchased (Date, Parts, Source) ....

....
....
....
....
....
....
....
....
....
....
....
....
....

33,000 MILES - OR EVERY THIRTY THREE MONTHS, whichever comes first.

All the Service Jobs at this Service Interval have been carried forward from earlier service intervals and are to be repeated at this Service.

33,000 mile Mechanical and Electrical - The Engine Bay

- [ ] Job 2. Clutch fluid level
- [ ] Job 3. Brake fluid level
- [ ] Job 4. Battery electrolyte
- [ ] Job 5. Washer reservoir
- [ ] Job 6. Cooling system
- [ ] Job 24. Adjust spark plugs
- [ ] Job 25. Check HT circuit
- [ ] Job 26. The distributor
- [ ] Job 27. Generator belt
- [ ] Job 28. OPTIONAL SU carburettors
- [ ] Job 29. Check air filters
- [ ] Job 30. Top-up carburettor dash pots
- [ ] Job 31. **JAPANESE AND OTHER EXPORT CARS ONLY** Check drive belts (bold)
- [ ] Job 32. Pipes and hoses

33,000 mile Mechanical and Electrical - Around the Car

- [ ] Job 7. Check horns
- [ ] Job 8. Windscreen washers
- [ ] Job 9. Windscreen wipers
- [ ] Job 10. Tyre pressures
- [ ] Job 11. Check headlamps and front sidelamps
- [ ] Job 12. Check front indicators
- [ ] Job 13. Check rear sidelamps
- [ ] Job 14. Number plate lamps
- [ ] Job 15. Reversing lamps
- [ ] Job 16. Check tyres
- [ ] Job 17. Check spare tyre
- [ ] Job 33. Handbrake travel

33,000 mile Mechanical and Electrical - Under the Car

- [ ] Job 34. Steering rack
- [ ] Job 35. Track rod ends
- [ ] Job 36. Constant velocity joint boot
- [ ] Job 37. Steering clamp bolt

Optional - Carry out Job 1

- [ ] Job 1. Engine oil level

or

- [ ] Job 38. Drain engine oil
- [ ] Job 39. Remove oil filter
- [ ] Job 40. New oil filter
- [ ] Job 41. Pour fresh oil
- [ ] Job 42. Check oil level
- [ ] Job 43. Check for oil leaks
- [ ] Job 44. Check front brake pads
- [ ] Job 45. Check front brake shoes
- [ ] Job 46. Lubricate front grease points
- [ ] Job 47. Check rear brakes
- [ ] Job 48. Lubricate rear suspension
- [ ] Job 49. Lubricate handbrake cable swivel and guide channels

33,000 mile Mechanical and Electrical - Road Test

- [ ] Job 50. Clean controls
- [ ] Job 51. Check instruments
- [ ] Job 52. Throttle pedal
- [ ] Job 53. Handbrake function
- [ ] Job 54. Brakes and steering

33,000 mile Bodywork and Interior - Around the Car

- [ ] Job 19. Touch-up paintwork
- [ ] Job 20. Aerial/antenna
- [ ] Job 21. Valet interior
- [ ] Job 22. Improve visibility
- [ ] Job 55. Wash and wax the bodywork
- [ ] Job 56. Wiper blades and arms
- [ ] Job 57. Check windscreen
- [ ] Job 58. Rear view mirrors
- [ ] Job 59. Check floors
- [ ] Job 60. Chrome trim and badges

33,000 mile Bodywork - Under the Car

- [ ] Job 23. Clean mud traps
- [ ] Job 61. Inspect underside

Date serviced: ....

Carried out by: ....

Garage Stamp (if applicable):

Parts/Accessories Purchased (Date, Parts, Source) ....

....

....

....

....

....

....

....

....

....

....

....

....

....

....

....

....

....

....

....

....

36,000 MILES - OR EVERY THIRTY SIX MONTHS, whichever comes first.

All the Service Jobs in the tinted area have been carried forward from earlier service intervals and are to be repeated at this Service.

36,000 mile Mechanical and Electrical - Emission Control Equipment

- [ ] Job 105. Crankcase breather
- [ ] Job 106. Oil filler cap
- [ ] Job 107. **JAPANESE AND OTHER EXPORT CARS ONLY** Inspect air injection pipes and hoses
- [ ] Job 108. **JAPANESE AND OTHER EXPORT CARS ONLY** Renew fuel line filter
- [ ] Job 109. **JAPANESE AND OTHER EXPORT CARS ONLY** Renew charcoal adsorption canister
- [ ] Job 110. **JAPANESE AND OTHER EXPORT CARS ONLY** Check operation of gulp valve
- [ ] Job 111. **JAPANESE AND OTHER EXPORT CARS ONLY** Check operation of air diverter valve.
- [ ] Job 112. **JAPANESE AND OTHER EXPORT CARS ONLY** Test check valve
- [ ] Job 113. **JAPANESE AND OTHER EXPORT CARS ONLY** Air pump belt
- [ ] Job 114. **SPECIALIST SERVICE** Emission system

36,000 mile Mechanical and Electrical - The Engine Bay

First carry out all the Jobs listed under earlier Service Intervals.

- [ ] Job 2. Clutch fluid level
- [ ] Job 3. Brake fluid level
- [ ] Job 4. Battery electrode
- [ ] Job 5. Washer reservoir

☐ Job 25. Check HT circuit

☐ Job 27. Generator belt

☐ Job 29. Check air filters

☐ Job 30. Top-up carburettor dash pots

☐ Job 31. **JAPANESE AND OTHER EXPORT CARS ONLY**
Check drive belts

☐ Job 32. Pipes and hoses

☐ Job 62. Cooling system

☐ Job 63. Coolant check

☐ Job 64. Heater Valve

☐ Job 65. Check water pump

☐ Job 66. Accelerator controls

☐ Job 67. Dynamo bearing

☐ Job 68. **OPTIONAL**
Fit new spark plugs

☐ Job 69. Distributor advance

☐ Job 70. Renew cb points

☐ Job 71. Check ignition timing

☐ Job 72. Valve clearances

☐ Job 73. Rocker cover gasket

☐ Job 74. Fit fuel filter

☐ Job 75. Fuel connections

☐ Job 76. Set carburettors

☐ Job 77. **SPECIALIST SERVICE**
Exhaust emissions

☐ Job 78. Check clutch return stop

☐ Job 115. Oil leaks

☐ Job 116. Clean radiator

☐ Job 117. **EARLY MODELS ONLY**
Grease water pump

☐ Job 118. Remote brake servo filter

☐ Job 119. In-line brake servo filter

☐ Job 120. Check cylinder compressions

☐ Job 146. Overhaul ignition

☐ Job 147. Clean float bowls

36,000 mile Mechanical and Electrical - Around the Car

Carry out all the Jobs listed under earlier Service Intervals.

☐ Job 7. Check horns

☐ Job 8. Windscreen washers

☐ Job 9. Windscreen wipers

☐ Job 10. Tyre pressures

☐ Job 11. Check headlamps and front sidelamps

☐ Job 12. Check front indicators

☐ Job 13. Check rear sidelamps

☐ Job 14. Number plate lamps

☐ Job 15. Reversing lamps

☐ Job 16. Check tyres

☐ Job 17. Check spare tyre

☐ Job 33. Handbrake travel

☐ Job 79. Adjust headlamps

☐ Job 80. **SPECIALIST SERVICE**
Front wheel alignment

☐ Job 81. Rear ride height

☐ Job 82. Front ride height

☐ Job 83. Check wheel nuts

☐ Job 121. Test dampers

☐ Job 122. Alarm remote units

36,000 mile Mechanical and Electrical - Under the Car

FRONT OF CAR

Carry out all the Jobs listed under earlier Service Intervals.

☐ Job 34. Steering rack

☐ Job 35. Track rod ends

☐ Job 36. Constant velocity joint boot

☐ Job 37. Steering clamp bolt

Optional - Carry out Job 1

☐ Job 1. Engine oil level

or

☐ Job 38. Drain engine oil

☐ Job 39. Remove oil filter

☐ Job 40. New oil filter

☐ Job 41. Pour fresh oil

☐ Job 42. Check oil level

☐ Job 43. Check for oil leaks

☐ Job 44. Check front brake pads

☐ Job 45. Check front brake shoes

☐ Job 46. Lubricate front grease points

☐ Job 84. Front fuel lines

☐ Job 85. Front brake lines

☐ Job 86. Exhaust manifold

☐ Job 87. Front dampers or hydrolastic displacers

☐ Job 88. Driveshaft couplings

☐ Job 89. Engine stabilisers

☐ Job 90. Front subframe mounting rubbers

☐ Job 91. Clutch hydraulics

☐ Job 123. Wishbone bushes

☐ Job 124. Top and bottom swivel pins

☐ Job 125. Check front hub bearings

☐ Job 126. Steering rack mountings

☐ Job 127. Check free play

☐ Job 128. Check ball joints

REAR OF CAR

☐ Job 47. Check rear brakes

☐ Job 48. Lubricate rear suspension

☐ Job 49. Lubricate handbrake cable swivel and guide channels

☐ Job 92. Check rear hub bearings

☐ Job 93. Rear brake lines

☐ Job 94. Rear fuel lines

☐ Job 95. Exhaust system

☐ Job 96. Rear dampers or hydrolastic displacers

☐ Job 97. Check rear sub-frame mounts

☐ Job 129. Check rear radius arm bearing

36,000 mile Mechanical and Electrical - Road Test

☐ Job 50. Clean controls

☐ Job 51. Check instruments

☐ Job 52. Throttle pedal

☐ Job 53. Handbrake function

☐ Job 54. Brakes and steering

36,000 mile Bodywork and Interior - Around the Car

Carry out all the Jobs listed under earlier Service Intervals.

- [ ] Job 18. Wash bodywork
- [ ] Job 19. Touch-up paintwork
- [ ] Job 20. Aerial/antenna
- [ ] Job 21. Valet interior
- [ ] Job 22. Improve visibility!
- [ ] Job 55. Wash and wax the bodywork
- [ ] Job 56. Wiper blades and arm
- [ ] Job 57. Check windscreen
- [ ] Job 58. Rear view mirrors
- [ ] Job 59. Check floors
- [ ] Job 60. Chrome trim and badges
- [ ] Job 98. Bonnet release
- [ ] Job 99. Door locks
- [ ] Job 100. Boot lock
- [ ] Job 101. Check battery connections
- [ ] Job 102. Seats and seat belts
- [ ] Job 130. Seat runners
- [ ] Job 131. Toolkit and jack

36,000 mile Bodywork - Under the Car

Carry out all the Jobs listed under earlier Service Intervals.

- [ ] Job 23. Clean mud traps.
- [ ] Job 61. Inspect underside
- [ ] Job 132. Top-up rustproofing

Be sure to carry out Job 104 after Job 132

- [ ] Job 104. Clean drain holes

YOU HAVE NOW COMPLETED ALL OF THE SERVICE JOBS LISTED IN THIS SERVICE GUIDE, 'THE LONGEST' INTERVAL BETWEEN ANY JOBS BEING 36,000 MILES OR THREE YEARS. WHEN YOU HAVE FILLED IN EACH OF THE SERVICE INTERVALS SHOWN HERE, YOU MAY PURCHASE CONTINUATION SHEETS TO ENABLE YOU TO CONTINUE AND COMPLETE YOUR SERVICE HISTORY FOR AS LONG AS YOU OWN THE CAR. PLEASE CONTACT

PORTER PUBLISHING

AT:

The Storehouse, Little Hereford Street, Bromyard, Hereford, HR7 4DE, England.

Tel: 0885 488800